D1381406

Racing with Death

Racing with Death

Douglas Mawson –
Antarctic Explorer

Beau Riffenburgh

BLOOMSBURY

First published in Great Britain 2008

Maps by Reginald Piggott

Photographs reproduced courtesy of the Mawson Collection, Australian
Polar Collection, Mawson Centre, South Australian Museum

Bloomsbury Publishing Plc
36 Soho Square
London W1D 3QY

. www.bloomsbury.com

Bloomsbury Publishing, London, New York and Berlin

A CIP catalogue record for this book is available from the British Library

Hardback ISBN 9780747580935
Trade Paperback ISBN 9780747596042
10 9 8 7 6 5 4 3 2 1

Typeset by Hewer Text UK Ltd, Edinburgh

Printed in Great Britain by Clays Ltd, St Ives plc

The paper this book is printed on is certified by the
© 1996 Forest Stewardship Council A.C. (FSC). It is
ancient-forest friendly. The printer holds FSC chain
of custody SGS-COC–2061

FSC
Mixed Sources
Product group from well-managed
forests and other controlled sources

Cert no. SGS-COC-2061
www.fsc.org
© 1996 Forest Stewardship Council

For my parents,
Angelyn and Ralph,
who have given lifelong guidance,
encouragement, support, and love

CONTENTS

III DISCOVERY

PREFACE

IN RECENT YEARS, the personalities and accomplishments of Robert Falcon Scott and Ernest Shackleton have dominated books, films, and research about the 'Heroic Age' of Antarctic exploration. The pair are justifiably remembered and celebrated as among the greatest of all British explorers and as dominating figures in the opening-up of the last continent. Yet there was once another man regarded throughout the English-speaking world as their equal amongst Antarctic legends. That man, Douglas Mawson, was a true giant of his time: admired throughout the world's scientific community, revered by the public, and generally considered the most renowned of Australian heroes.

Despite still being looked upon by some as 'the greatest figure in Antarctic science,' Mawson is now little known outside Australia. Indeed, his prominence has faltered even there. Not long ago, a school group in Adelaide – where Mawson lived – visited the South Australian Museum and were shown, along with other memorabilia, a classic photograph of Mawson aboard ship, surrounded by fellow expedition members. Taken in the far south, the picture shows men dressed for icy conditions – with hats, scarves, heavy sweaters, and coats – and Mawson's serious face is framed by a balaclava. It is the same image of him once used as the basis for the Australian $100 note – surely a statement

of the honour in which he was held. But when asked what
they knew of this man, the pupils – perhaps confusing him
with the helmeted bushranger Ned Kelly – could only
answer, 'Was he a bank robber?'

There is an even greater dearth of knowledge about the
three major expeditions on which much of Mawson's fame
was based – the British Antarctic Expedition of 1907–09,
the Australasian Antarctic Expedition of 1911–14, and the
British, Australian, New Zealand Antarctic Research Expedition of 1929–31. On the first of these, Mawson was
effectively the leader for one of the longest and most difficult
sledging journeys in history, on which his party became the
first ever to reach the region of the South Magnetic Pole.
The second venture – which Mawson conceived, developed,
and led – was responsible for the exploration of more
territory than any other Antarctic effort, and included a
scientific investigation of the far south on a scale never before
attempted. It consisted of three land bases, thirty-two
members of the shore party, seven major sledging journeys,
and a full oceanographic programme. Yet what was intended
as a scientific exercise devoid of adventure also proved to
be a tale of death, determination, and raw courage that the
late Sir Edmund Hillary described as 'the greatest story of
lone survival in Polar exploration.' Mawson's final expedition
not only continued aspects of his earlier scientific studies
but was the basis for Australian claims to the Antarctic –
and that led to more than two and a quarter million square
miles being incorporated into what is now known as the
Australian Antarctic Territory.

This book is the story of those epic ventures and of
Mawson's career as it related to the Antarctic. Because even
when Mawson was not in the far south, he seemed to be
planning his next journey there, raising the required funds
for such massive undertakings, working up his scientific
results, or being involved in major governmental, scientific,
or policy decisions about the Antarctic. Eventually, he became

recognised as perhaps the world's most eminent authority on Antarctica.

Today, scientists, adventurers, and even tourists travel almost at will through the Antarctic continent. It is a part of the planet that David Attenborough, Sir Ranulph Fiennes, and others have, each in his own way, made familiar to much of the Western world. This book, however, goes back to a time when people knew far less about this region, and when it was almost unimaginably remote. As much as anybody in history, it was Douglas Mawson who opened up these hostile lands to scientific and geographical experts, to governments, and to the public. It is only fitting, therefore, that he, and his remarkable efforts, be re-introduced to a generation that has been deprived of his great story.

ACKNOWLEDGEMENTS

THIS BOOK BENEFITED inestimably from the generosity and kindness of numerous individuals and organisations. My heartfelt thanks must go first to Mark Pharaoh of the South Australian Museum's Mawson Centre, the world's largest archival source for materials about Mawson and his expeditions. For a period of several years, Mark gave unstintingly of his time: guiding me through the collections of unpublished documents, ferreting out rare materials, photo-copying, counselling, helping me gain permissions, and commenting on the manuscript. It is fair to say that without his consideration and contributions this book would never have been finished.

I am deeply indebted to the kindness of the Mawson family, and most particularly that of Gareth Thomas, one of Douglas Mawson's grandsons. His good graces – including allowing me to see previously closed documents and helping me with the use of copyrighted books and images – have been invaluable to this project. I am also most grateful to Nancy Flannery, whose advice and encouragement were of enormous value.

My sincere appreciation is extended to Jennifer Broomhead and Martin Beckett of the State Library of New South Wales, Herbert Dartnall, Ingrid Davis, Sara Fisher of A.M. Heath, Ian Flannery, Stephen Haddelsey, Desmond J. Lugg, Allan

Mornement, Jenya Osborne, Graeme Powell of the National Library of Australia, Bill Swainson and Emily Sweet of Bloomsbury, Rosanne Walker of the Basser Library, and Clive Wilson-Roberts of the Mawson Centre.

During my research, I made extensive use of the Library and Archives of the Scott Polar Research Institute, University of Cambridge, and I would like to thank Professor Julian Dowdeswell, Naomi Boneham, Judy Heath, Heather Lane, Lucy Martin, and Shirley Sawtell for their friendly help. For additional access to documents, I thank the Basser Library of the Australian Academy of Science; the British Newspaper Library; the Cambridge University Library; the Mawson Centre; the Mitchell Library, State Library of New South Wales; the National Library of Australia; and the National Archives, Kew.

I am grateful to the following for permission to use copyrighted or privately held material: John Ainsworth, for the writings of George F. Ainsworth; Philip Ayres, for quotations from his book *Mawson: a Life*; the Basser Library, for the correspondence of Frank Stillwell; Rosanna Bickerton, for the writings of Frank Bickerton; Louise Crossley, for quotations from her book *Trial by Ice*; Nancy Flannery, for quotations from her book *This Everlasting Silence*; Anne M. Fright, for the correspondence of her uncle, Frank Wild; Winfried Hoerr, for quotations from his mother's book *Clipped Wings, or Memories of My Childhood and Youth*; Clive Lincoln, for the diary of Bertram Lincoln; the Mawson Centre, Science Centre, South Australian Museum, for the diaries, reports, publications, and correspondence of Douglas Mawson, Robert Bage, John King Davis, William Heinemann, Sidney Jeffryes, Harvey Johnston, Bertram Lincoln, Cecil Madigan, Archibald McLean, Xavier Mertz, A. Grenville Price, Kathleen Scott, R.G. Simmers, Eric Webb, and others involved in Mawson's expeditions, as well as for the photographs used in this book; Alasdair McGregor, for quotations from his book *Frank Hurley: a Photographer's*

Life; the Mitchell Library, State Library of New South Wales, for the diaries of Walter Hannam, Charles Laseron, and Archibald McLean; Toni Mooy-Hurley, for the writings of Frank Hurley; Allan Mornement, for the diaries and correspondence of B.E.S. Ninnis; the National Library of Australia, for the diary of Cedric Hackworth and the correspondence of S.E. Jones; Jenya Osborne and Ingrid Davis, for the writings of John King Davis; Judith Richter, for the writings of Charles Laseron; Ann Savours, for quotations from her book *The Voyages of the Discovery*; the Scott Polar Research Institute, for the diaries or papers of Frank Bickerton, J.W.S. Marr, Eric Marshall, James Martin, Douglas Mawson, B.E.S. Ninnis, Raymond Priestley, Ernest Shackleton, Eric Webb, and Frank Wild; and Gareth Thomas, for quotations or illustrations from *The Home of the Blizzard, Mawson of the Antarctic*, and other unpublished documents. If I have overlooked anybody, or failed to trace the correct copyright holders, I hope they will forgive me.

Finally, I would like to record my special thanks to my wife, Elizabeth Cruwys, for her encouragement, enthusiasm, and patience, as well as her insightful assessments and editorial recommendations.

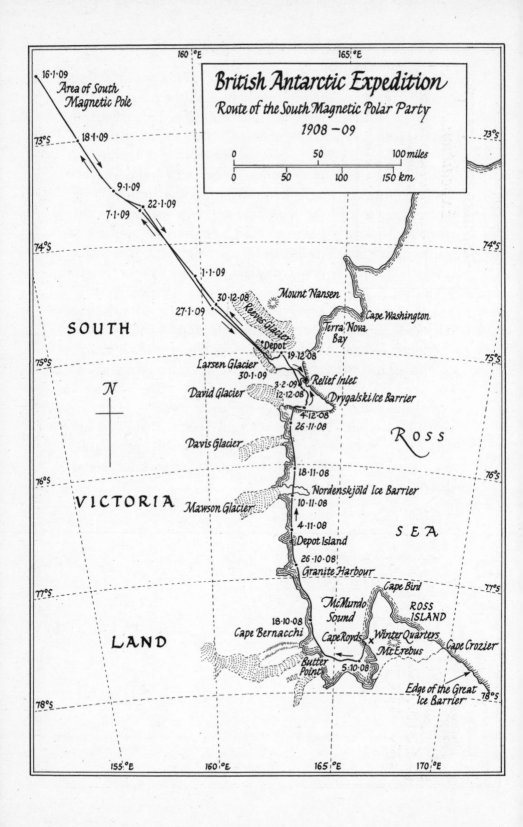

British Antarctic Expedition

Route of the South Magnetic Polar Party

1908 – 09

0		50		100 miles

0	50	100	150 km

160 °E

165 °E

73°S

73°S

16·1·09
Area of South
Magnetic Pole

18·1·09

9·1·09

22·1·09

7·1·09

74°S

74°S

1·1·09

30·12·08

Mount Nansen

27·1·09

Cape Washington

SOUTH

Reeves Glacier

*Terra Nova
Bay*

Depot

19·12·08

75°S

75°S

Larsen Glacier

Relief Inlet

30·1·09

3·2·09

David Glacier

12·12·08

Drygalski Ice Barrier

4·12·08

26·11·08

R O S S

Davis Glacier

18·11·08

76°S

76°S

Nordenskjöld Ice Barrier

VICTORIA

10·11·08

Mawson Glacier

4·11·08

S E A

Depot Island

26·10·08

Granite Harbour

Cape Bird

77°S

77°S

*McMurdo
Sound*

ROSS
ISLAND

18·10·08

Cape Bernacchi

Winter Quarters

LAND

Cape Royds

×

Mt Erebus

Cape Crozier

*Butter
Point*

5·10·08

*Edge of the Great
Ice Barrier*

78°S

78°S

155 °E

160 °E

165 °E

170 °E

N

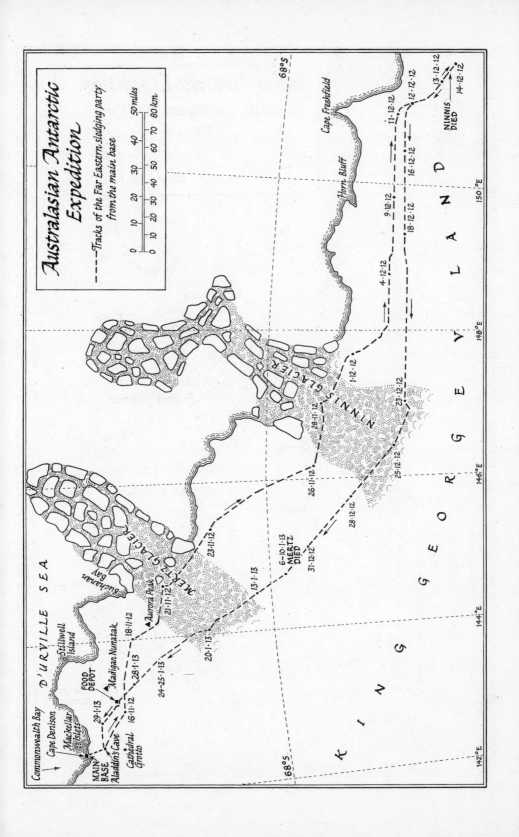

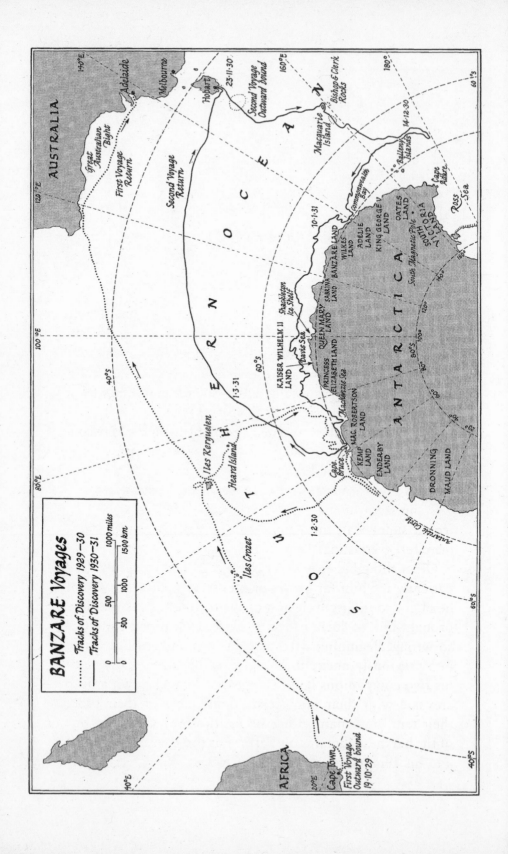

BANZARE Voyages

········· Tracks of Discovery 1929–30
———— Tracks of Discovery 1930–31

0   500   1000 miles
0   500   1000   1500 km

AUSTRALIA

Great Australian Bight

First Voyage Return

Second Voyage Return

Adelaide

Melbourne

Hobart

25·11·30

Second Voyage Outward bound

Macquarie Island

Bishop & Clerk Rocks

14·12·30

Balleny Islands

Cape Adare

Ross Sea

O C E A N

Commonwealth Bay

10·1·31

OATES LAND

King George V Land

ADELIE LAND

WILKES LAND

SABRINA LAND

QUEEN MARY LAND

Shackleton Ice Shelf

Davis Sea

KAISER WILHELM II LAND

1·3·31

60°S

PRINCESS ELIZABETH LAND

MAC. ROBERTSON LAND

Mackenzie Sea

KEMP LAND

ENDERBY LAND

Cape Bruce

A N T A R C T I C A

South Magnetic Pole

SOUTH VICTORIA LAND

DRONNING MAUD LAND

Murdule Creek

S O U T H E R N

Îles Kerguelen

Heard Island

Îles Crozet

1·2·30

Cape Town

First Voyage Outward bound 19·10·29

AFRICA

20°E

40°E

80°E

100°E

120°E

140°E

160°E

180°

40°S

60°S

60°S

40°S

PROLOGUE

HE HUNG LIMPLY in space, a thin Alpine rope slowly spinning him round over a black, bottomless chasm. He was mentally exhausted, physically drained, and virtually frozen from the snow and ice that had seeped inside his clothing. And he was totally alone, some eighty miles from the closest living person.

It would only take a moment, thought Douglas Mawson, the leader of the grandly named Australasian Antarctic Expedition, and then he would never again feel the pain, the anguish, the torment of recent weeks. All he needed to do was slip from his harness, and he could be free at last; he would simply fall through the air and thence into a deep, merciful, everlasting sleep.

Other thoughts crowded his mind: of his fiancée waiting patiently for him far away, of the 'secrets of eternity' that he might soon discover, and of the terrible events that had brought him to such a forlorn place. Everything had gone so wrong, beginning with that day a month before when, in a previously unexplored region of the Antarctic, one of his two companions had disappeared forever down a deep crevasse with their best sledge dogs, most of their food, their tent, and many other necessities for existing in one of the harshest climates on Earth. For three weeks, Mawson and his remaining colleague, the Swiss ski expert Xavier

Mertz, had engaged in a frantic, resolute race against time, desperately trying to cover the 300 miles back to their coastal base. They were soon wracked by exposure, dehydration, and starvation. Even eating the remaining dogs – which became too weak to pull the sledge – did not provide them with enough sustenance, and they were soon confronted by a mysterious condition that saw their skin slough off, their sores not heal, and their will-power overwhelmed by lethargy. Finally, the ailing Mertz rejected the option of continuing, and Mawson was forced to play nursemaid – until Mertz's death had ended *his* suffering.

But that placed Mawson in an even more appalling situation. There was inadequate food, even for one, the sledge was too heavy for a single man to haul, and the weather daily threatened to trap him in his tent at a time when lack of action could prove fatal. Moreover, he was unable to move without pain, writing about his condition: 'My whole body is apparently rotting from want of proper nourishment – frost-bitten fingertips festering, mucous membrane of nose gone, saliva glands of mouth refusing duty, skin coming off whole body.'

But Mawson was made of stern stuff, even by the demanding standards of the Antarctic explorers of the time, and after cutting the sledge in two with a small knife, he struggled on for more than a week. He had no choice but to keep moving, and one morning as he blundered blindly along in a weak light that made it difficult to see, he was suddenly pulled up with a jerk, and found himself dangling fourteen feet down a crevasse. The sledge continued to slide towards the gaping hole. 'So this is the end,' he said to himself, expecting it to crash through the ice and carry him to the depths below. But it did not happen. Miraculously, the sledge ground to a halt near the edge.

His prospects were daunting, nevertheless. The crevasse was six feet wide, and he could not reach either side. Above him, he could see that the rope had sawed into an overhanging lid of ice, which would make it difficult to draw himself onto the surface, should he even get that far. The more he looked, the farther it seemed, particularly in his weakened condition. In addition, his fingers and hands were frost-damaged, and, being gloveless, were fast losing sensation. His torso was also numb since, due to the exertion of pulling the sledge, he had taken off much of his clothing and left the rest pulled open – so it had filled with snow and ice when he crashed through the covering of the crevasse.

But, he thought, Providence had given him a last chance, and so, with a superhuman effort, he reached along the rope and drew himself up, and then again, and again, each time expecting the change in position to pull the sledge over the edge, but finally reaching a knot in the rope, which gave him just enough of a hold to rest. After some time, he repeated the process, the small knots holding out the promise of success, and of life. Finally, seemingly after an age, he reached the overhanging snow lid and managed to crawl out on its surface, almost to safety, when it suddenly burst into pieces, propelling him back down again.

Now truly chilled, with his strength almost gone, he swung back and forth, convinced that his life would soon be over. Above, the surface might have been miles away, while below, the black depths beckoned, promising to end his misery and toil. Undoing his harness was easy enough, and would allow him to end this torture. Mawson's hands were slowly drawn to the harness, and to eternity.

I
NIMROD

I

TRESPASSERS IN A WORLD OF ICE

IT WAS NOT the first time Mawson had found himself
down a crevasse, wondering if each moment would be his
last. Virtually no one who travelled on the great ice shelves
or the Polar Plateau that covers most of the Antarctic continent avoided unexpected plunges into those treacherous,
often hidden, fissures in the glacier ice. But most of the time
the falls entailed only going part way through the snow
covering, or dropping a few feet due to being tied closely to
a sledge. Mawson's worst previous encounter had been four
years before, when he had plummeted, unroped, eighteen
feet onto a small ledge just at the moment when, after months
of desperate struggles, he thought he had been rescued from
his travails.

That had been as a member of the British Antarctic
Expedition (BAE), which had first introduced him to the
wonders and dangers of the far south, and concurrently helped
set the course of his later years. For afterwards, whether as
explorer, scientist, imperial expansionist, or government
adviser, Mawson's was truly a life given to the Antarctic.

Despite the career that Mawson would carve out, his
initial involvement in the far south was pure happenstance.
It was, in fact, due in great part to a combination of his
close relationship with one of his former professors and the

capricious nature of a young British explorer. Yet Mawson's appointment proved to be one of those seemingly random events recorded throughout the history of exploration that benefit not only the man and the mission, but the entire scientific and geographical community.

Even from an early age, there were sparks that indicated Mawson might become a man to make such contributions. Born on the outskirts of Shipley, in Yorkshire, in 1882, he was named for the town of Douglas on the Isle of Man, whence his mother originated, and where she met her future husband. When Douglas was two years old, and his brother William four, their parents followed the dream of a new and prosperous life and moved to New South Wales. There, in a suburb of Sydney, Mawson eventually entered the renowned Fort Street Model Public School, where he was first introduced to geology and where, according to legend, the headmaster stated at Speech Night that 'if there be a corner of this planet of ours still unexplored, Douglas Mawson will be the organiser and leader of an expedition to unveil its secrets.'

Shortly thereafter, at the age of only sixteen, Mawson entered the University of Sydney, where he excelled in geology and mineralogy and fell under the spell of the celebrated Professor T.W. Edgeworth David, known widely and affectionately as 'the Prof.' Mawson engaged in fieldwork under David while completing his Bachelor of Engineering degree and then, with the support of David, was appointed junior demonstrator in the Department of Chemistry, although still only nineteen. He also began working towards a BSc in geology, receiving it in 1904 after conducting several geological surveys, including the first systematic examination of the New Hebrides (now known as Vanuatu), where he investigated areas so difficult to reach they had never before been visited by Europeans.

After graduation, Mawson became a lecturer in mineralogy and petrology at the University of Adelaide, where he came to know Walter Howchin, a remarkable combination of clergyman and geologist, who had proven that South Australia had experienced two great glaciations – including one in the Precambrian era, considerably earlier than had previously been known. The research and support of Howchin and David encouraged Mawson's interest in ice ages. Meanwhile, Mawson proceeded towards his doctorate with fieldwork between the Flinders Ranges and the remote town of Broken Hill, New South Wales. In September 1907, he was at Broken Hill when he heard the astounding news that David was going to, of all places, the Antarctic, accompanying an expedition led by the bold and charismatic Ernest Shackleton.

Shackleton had first come to public attention several years earlier after serving as one of Robert Falcon Scott's two companions (along with Edward Wilson) on the most publicised part of Scott's *Discovery* Expedition. In the summer of 1902–03, from their base at Hut Point on Ross Island, next to McMurdo Sound off the Ross Sea, the three men had made a record sledge journey. Pushing into the heart of the Great Ice Barrier (now known as the Ross Ice Shelf), a vast, floating mass of ice larger than Spain, they sledged farther south than anybody had ever reached before: 82°17′S. They then overcame scurvy and inadequate food supplies to struggle back to base. Although Scott and most of his party thereafter remained in the Antarctic for a second year, Scott invalided Shackleton back home, very much against the wishes of the junior officer.

While Scott became a national hero upon his eventual return to England, Shackleton felt stigmatised by having been sent home early. As time passed, he dreamed more and more of leading an expedition to the South Pole, an achievement that would not only erase any taint of weakness, but would, he hoped, bring him fame and fortune. In early 1907 he received the backing of the Scottish industrialist William Beardmore, allowing him to move ahead with what, despite the name British Antarctic Expedition, was very much a private affair. In the whirlwind of the next six months, he raised funds, purchased and refitted the former sealing ship *Nimrod*, obtained supplies required for spending two years in the Antarctic, and put together a shore party and ship's crew.

Nimrod sailed for Lyttelton, New Zealand – the expedition's launching pad for the Antarctic – in August 1907, and Shackleton followed two months later, stopping *en route* in Australia, where he was scheduled to give two public lectures. These speaking engagements had been planned in order to raise some much-needed capital for the expedition's coffers. But even Shackleton, sunny optimist that he was, could not have foreseen how significant these proposed lectures would prove, not only for the BAE, but for the history of Antarctic science and for Australian involvement in the far south. The key to all of this was a slight, dignified, exceedingly formal yet totally delightful academic, whose scholarly mind was equalled only by his political astuteness: Professor David.

Shackleton made little pretence that science would play much of a role on his expedition; his interest was attaining the South Pole. However, he was thoroughly taken with David – who, according to Shackleton, could 'charm a bird off a bough.' He was also aware of David's powerful political connections, so he invited the Prof to accompany the expedition to the Antarctic to train the youngsters Raymond Priestley and Sir Philip Brocklehurst in geological field techniques before returning north on *Nimrod*. David accepted with alacrity, and subsequently wrote to the Prime Minister of Australia asking for financial aid for the expedition. Such was the esteem in which David was held that the Australian government awarded Shackleton £5,000, which, together with £1,000 from New Zealand, allowed improvements to be made to *Nimrod*, more supplies to be purchased, and more shore staff to be hired.

Mawson knew little of these developments, other than that David was heading south with the prospect of obtaining vast amounts of geological and glaciological data. But that news so excited him, and the concept proved so appealing, that when RMS *India*, with Shackleton aboard, docked at Adelaide on its way to Melbourne, Mawson sought out the explorer and asked if he, too, could book passage to the Antarctic. 'My idea was to see a continental ice-cap in being and become acquainted with glaciation and its geological repercussions,' Mawson later wrote. 'This especially interested me for in glaciological studies in South Australia I was face to face with a great accumulation of glacial sediments of Pre-Cambrian age, the greatest thing of the kind recorded anywhere in the world. So I desired to see an ice age in being.'

Mawson's enthusiasm clearly impressed Shackleton, as did the fact that the Australian was six feet, three inches tall, physically powerful, and had a superb intellect. But at that point Shackleton did not yet have the money to take another scientist. However, when the government awarded Shackleton the £5,000, he was in obvious debt to David, and the Prof wanted his protégé included. Mawson received a telegram appointing him physicist for the duration of the expedition.

'This was rather a surprise for I had not suggested spending a year in Antarctica,' Mawson wrote. 'Nor were my interests in Physics as I was a geologist.' Nevertheless, he accepted – Mawson was heading to the Antarctic.

On 1 January 1908, a crowd of 50,000 – stunning both in its size and in that people had travelled from all over New Zealand – descended upon Lyttelton to bid farewell to Shackleton's party, as it departed for the Antarctic. But the explorers' thrills at brass bands, cheering crowds, bobbing flotillas of pleasure steamers, and salutes from ships of the Royal Navy's Australian fleet quickly gave way to the sea-sickness and fright brought by a fierce gale that caught them soon out of port and then raged for ten days. Conditions were made even worse by *Nimrod* being so overcrowded with personnel, equipment, supplies, sledge dogs, and ten ponies Shackleton planned on using as his main mode of transport, that she had only three feet six inches of freeboard. Moreover, the ship did not have enough space for the necessary coal, so Shackleton had arranged for her to be towed south by the steamer *Koonya*, and the tons of chain connecting the two vessels forced the bow of *Nimrod* down into the sea, allowing raging masses of green water constantly to sweep her decks and swamp her holds.

Nowhere did the battering and buffeting seem worse than in the recently refurbished aft hold, where most of the shore party were crammed, along with their luggage and many of the scientific instruments. A sodden, unventilated little room entered by a ladder through a hole two feet by two feet, it earned the curious name 'Oyster Alley,' and was, according to geologist Raymond Priestley, 'a place that under ordinary circumstances I wouldn't put ten dogs in, much less 15 of the shore-party. It . . . is more like my idea of Hell than anything I have ever imagined.' Mawson concurred, calling it simply 'an awful hole.'

Not that Mawson spent much time there early in the voyage. His severe sea-sickness drove him to seek a place where he might not feel so wretched, although not before his uncon-cealed misery led the arrogant chief surgeon, Eric Marshall, to dismiss him as a total waste of space. 'Mawson is useless & objectionable, lacking in guts & manners,' Marshall wrote during the tempest, noting that he simply lay 'in a sleeping bag . . . vomiting when he rolled to starboard, whilst the cook handed up food from the galley beneath him.' Without the slightest compunction, the physician succinctly concluded: 'Could leave him behind without a regret.'

Others proved more sympathetic. One of these was John King Davis, the first mate, who later recalled:

[A]s daylight came, I noticed a man lying prostrate in one of the lifeboats ... 'What are you doing there, why don't you get below?' I shouted. All I could get from him in response to my queries was 'Can't you stop this b— boat rocking?' He had been lying there sea-sick and wet through without food or drink since the gale began. After some delay in obtaining them I persuaded him to try and eat some tinned pears and was relieved to see him 'wolf them down' quickly. All he said was 'Thanks' and I left him, feeling that I had done my good deed for the day.

That evening ... he was still lying in the lifeboat ... he asked if I could get him some more pears. Obtaining some, and noting that he looked much better, I persuaded him to get up and come down into the galley and dry off, while I made some hot cocoa. This warmed him and, after a while, he became quite talkative. He was the physicist of the expedition, a young Australian from Adelaide University, only two years older than myself.

It was to prove the start of a lifelong friendship, one of numerous lengthy associations Mawson derived from the expedition. Others included Priestley, assistant geologist Sir Philip Brocklehurst, second mate Æneas Mackintosh, Frank Wild, who had been placed in charge of provisions, and Shackleton himself. Another relationship given an unexpected chance to develop further was that with Mawson's mentor, Professor David. In mid-January, shortly before *Nimrod* was cut loose by *Koonya* near the Antarctic Circle, David and Shackleton announced that the Prof would stay in the Antarctic rather than travel straight home, as had originally been planned. It was a decision of incalculable significance for the expedition, because it secured instant scientific credibility for what had previously been a rather haphazardly organised effort.

Some ten days later, the scientific programme received another major boost. Shackleton had planned to establish his base on the Great Ice Barrier or farther east at King Edward VII Land. However, thick ice prevented *Nimrod* from reaching the latter and although Shackleton considered landing at what he named the Bay of Whales, he decided that the vast sections of ice that calved off in that region of the Barrier made attempting to winter there unreasonably dangerous. So instead, with David urging him to take advantage of the greater opportunities for geological and biological studies at McMurdo Sound – and others also advocating that destination – he headed towards Scott's old base, which happened to be near the start of the only known route towards the South Pole. However, halted again by heavy sea ice in his efforts to reach Scott's Hut Point, Shackleton landed instead at Cape Royds, a rocky promontory that is an extension of the great active volcano Mount Erebus as it tumbles down to the sound some eighteen miles north of Hut Point.

Throughout February, the men worked beyond exhaustion, unloading the ship, building a hut, and establishing the base. No aspect of the process was more agonisingly difficult than transporting the eighteen tons of coal that the shore party would need to get through the winter. With the ship often a full mile from the landing area, David, Mawson, Leo Cotton (one of David's current students), Davis, and several others laboured incessantly, covered by half-frozen slush that was a mixture of coal dust and sea spray, rowing and poling back and forth, often at stretches of more than twelve consecutive hours.

'First about 20 strong canvas bags ... would be let down into the boat (about 24 bags go to the ton),' wrote the Prof, continuing:

> we would pull for about half a mile across a nearly ice free sea; then we would reach the belt of dense floe ice ... Davis had to choose, and choose quickly, from moment to moment down which opening to force our boat ... so narrow that

they were barely wide enough for the boat itself; indeed, we frequently had to force the floes apart in order to make room for the boat, so that the blades of the oars had nothing on which to catch but the soft snow or an occasional lump of ice frozen down onto the top of the ice floe . . . After much meandering and skilful steering, but not without a few slight scrunches, Davis piloted us at last safely to the landing place.

By night, the men moving the coal were totally oblivious to the outside world. Davis, according to Shackleton, 'had gone sound asleep with his spoon in his mouth,' while Cotton 'had fallen asleep on the platform of the engine-room steps.' Mawson was out like a light in a little room within the engine department. 'His long legs, protruding through the doorway, had found a resting-place on the cross-head of the engine, and his dreams were mingled with a curious rhythmical motion which was fully accounted for when he woke up, for the ship having got under way, the up-and-down motion of the piston had moved his limbs with every stroke.'

On 22 February, Shackleton felt preparations had progressed to the point where he could send *Nimrod* back north. Unfortunately, in the preceding days, a fierce blizzard had broken up the ice that had kept them from reaching Hut Point and had blown it out of McMurdo Sound. Since any southward movement on land was out of the question due to the impassable glaciers, ice falls, and cliffs of Mount Erebus, Shackleton could not reach the Great Ice Barrier until McMurdo again froze over as far north as Cape Royds. He and his party were cut off.

The week after *Nimrod* left, life for the party of fifteen consisted of little more than finishing the hut, building stables for the ponies, and setting to work with picks, axes, and crowbars to chip hundreds of boxes of stores out of the concrete-like ice that had covered them during the blizzard. However, Shackleton knew that, deprived for the time being of the opportunity to work towards the journey south, the men might become frustrated by the lack of meaningful activity.

Therefore, Shackleton, David, Marshall, and Jameson Adams, the expedition's second-in-command, discussed the possibility of making the first ascent of Mount Erebus. First seen sixty-seven years before on a Royal Navy expedition under James Clark Ross, the active volcano had been named after one of Ross' ships (in turn named for the part of the underworld in Greek mythology through which the dead passed before reaching Hades). Then, four years previously, three of Scott's men – two of whom, Frank Wild and Ernest Joyce, were now with Shackleton – had climbed its flanks to some 3,000 feet above sea level, although this was only a fraction of its then-undetermined height.

On 4 March, in his typically impulsive fashion, Shackleton announced that not only would the peak be climbed, but the effort would commence the following morning. The summit party would consist of David, Mawson, and Scottish surgeon Alistair Mackay, supported by Marshall, Brocklehurst, and Adams. None of the men had significant mountaineering experience, but Shackleton was a great believer in resourcefulness and improvisation, so that evening the base exploded in frenetic preparations, the men trying to overcome a lack of proper equipment by such innovations as poking nails through strips of leather to serve as crampons for the bottom of the climbers' finnesko, the soft Laplander boots of reindeer fur that were commonly worn by Antarctic explorers.

The next morning, not long after the final pieces of equipment were completed in the early hours, the novice mountaineers left; the summit group was provisioned for eleven days and the support party for six. After hauling for about a mile, they had to carry their 600-pound sledge over a glacial moraine, and for the rest of the day they pushed and dragged it up steep patches of slick, blue ice, their progress hindered by a series of sastrugi – hard, wind-blown ridges in the snow – which they had to struggle over or around. By evening they had travelled seven miles and ascended approximately 2,750 feet. The next day, sastrugi in greater numbers and size made the sledge flip over frequently, forcing the men to stop to right it and re-stow their supplies. Facing a steeper gradient throughout the day, they doubled their elevation but managed only three miles before camping near the base of the volcano's main cone.

On 7 March, Adams announced that the support party would continue to the top with the summit group. However, the grade soon proved such that they had to depot the sledge and much of their provisions. Without any rucksacks to carry the equipment, each man had to manage as best he could with more than forty pounds, the total including tents, sleeping bags, and rations for three days. Left behind, however, were the tent poles, without which they could only lay the tents over their sleeping bags. That night, while camped next to a rocky arête at 8,750 feet, the temperature crashed to −34°F (−37°C) and a blizzard descended, the snow so thick and the roar of the wind so loud that the two groups could neither see nor hear each other, despite being only ten yards apart.

When the blizzard finally subsided early in the morning of 9 March, they had been confined to their sleeping bags for thirty-two hours with nothing to drink and only a biscuit and a piece of chocolate to eat. Brocklehurst's feet had felt progressively colder since he had left the sleeping bag to answer a call of nature, and then been forced to spend an extended period outside after a mitten was carried away in a fierce gust and he, dashing after it, had been swept by the wind down a ravine. By the time he was finally helped back inside by Adams, a great deal of fine snow had crept into the three-man sleeping bag, and Brocklehurst was unable to warm up again.

Despite these trials, David was determined to climb on, so the entire party slogged towards the summit of the lower, main crater. The angle of ascent was steeper than ever, and more than once potentially dangerous slides were only arrested by the men frantically using their ice axes. When they reached the summit of the main crater, Marshall examined Brockle-hurst's feet, discovering that six toes, including the two big ones, were severely frostbitten. Brocklehurst had declined to change from ski boots to finnesko and the crease across his boots, which were too large, had cut off his circulation.

The next morning the party was greeted with a stunningly beautiful vista, with the shadow of Erebus projecting obliquely on a rolling sea of cumulus clouds. Leaving Brock-lehurst in his sleeping bag, the others roped together and headed towards the summit of the higher, active crater. After four hours of painfully slow progress, they reached its edge. For a while it was all they could do to watch and listen in amazement. Although the Barrier was obscured by clouds, in front of them was a massive abyss estimated at half a mile across and 900 feet deep. And within it was a huge mass of steam that soared aloft 1,000 feet. 'After a continuous loud hissing sound, lasting for some minutes,' wrote David, 'there would come from below a big dull boom, and immediately afterwards a great globular mass of steam would rush upwards to swell the volume of the snow-white cloud which ever sways over the crater.'

But there was little time to enjoy these marvels. They were already feeling the effects of the high altitude, exacerbated by high latitude – where the air is thinner. So while Mawson took photographs, Marshall used a hypsometer – which measures the temperature at which distilled water boils – to determine their elevation. Since the temperature at which water boils drops as height above sea level increases, such measure-ments in theory allow a determination of altitude. In this case, Marshall figured that the summit was 13,500 feet, but his conclusion was inaccurate, overestimating the 12,448-foot Mount Erebus by approximately a thousand feet.

As the party started its descent, David and Mawson

collected samples for later geological analysis and took levels for constructing a geological section. When they reached their earlier camp, they ate a hurried lunch and then continued their retreat with Brocklehurst. Reaching an ice slope, they hurled their loads before them, sat, and slid down. Despite the inherent dangers in such a manoeuvre, they reached the bottom of the slope safely, and, encouraged with that success, repeated the wild process again and again down the seemingly endless succession of snow slopes towards the foot of the main cone. This reckless manner of travel allowed them to make excellent progress, despite frequently having to stop their slides part way down and retrieve equipment that had not gone all the way to the bottom. That night they reached the depot, from where, rising at 3 a.m., they returned quickly to their first camp. Fearing a building south-easterly would turn into a blizzard, they cached the sledge and raced back to the base, arriving, in the words of Marshall, 'nearly dead.'

In the period following the ascent of Mount Erebus, the men prepared in as many ways as possible for the cold and darkness of the approaching winter. Mawson in particular played a key role in the expedition's scientific studies. Not only did he work with David and Priestley on building comprehensive geological collections, he also carried out structural analyses of ice and snow; kept meteorological logs, most notably wind-speed readings and magnetic measurements; studied atmospheric electricity; and recorded auroral observations. Early on, he had a small physics laboratory off the hut's porch, but everything there soon became covered with ice crystals, making it unusable, and it was turned into a storage room.

With the demise of his lab, the part of the hut in which Mawson could most often be found was the photographic darkroom. Although Marshall was officially the expedition's photographer, it was Mawson and David who fitted out the darkroom with all of the necessary equipment for working with both glass-plate negatives and film. And it was Mawson and Brocklehurst who carried out by far the most developing and printing.

The rest of the hut's interior comprised a private room for Shackleton, a series of cubicles around the edges – each sleeping two men and with its own name and distinctive features – and a central communal section that served as the dining room or, when the table was hauled above head level by ropes, a work area. David and Mawson shared a cubicle known as the 'Pawn Shop' or 'The Old Curiosity Shop' due to the 'picturesque confusion' of the jumble of specimens and instruments – cameras, spectroscopes, thermometers, microscopes, electrometers, callipers, hammers, and more – that it held. David, according to Shackleton, 'made a pile of glittering tins and coloured wrappers at one end of his bunk, and the heap looked like the nest of the Australian bower bird.'

Another cubicle was shared by Wild, Joyce, and a printing press, which was a key component for the production of the first book ever produced in the Antarctic. Entitled *Aurora Australis*, it featured ten articles by expedition members, including 'Bathybia' by Mawson, a rare work of fiction dealing with a party that reached the South Pole, only to find the region dominated by giant mushroom-shaped fungi and equally large insects. Wild and Joyce not only printed the book but also did much of the work in preparing the sledges and other equipment for the upcoming journeys.

By early August, even though the sun had not yet appeared above the horizon, everyone seemed anxious to escape the confines of the hut and begin those sledging trips. For Mackay in particular, the long, dark winter had proved a little too stressful. On 3 August, William Roberts, the cook, put his foot on Mackay's locker to lace up his boot, and the Scotsman, always tightly wound, exploded. 'Aroused by expostulations of Bobs whom Mac had gripped by the throat in a more than friendly manner,' Marshall recorded disinterestedly. Roberts was only saved from a throttling by the good graces of Mawson, who walked over to Mackay and 'choked him off and turned him back to bed.'

It was apparent that not just Mackay, but all of them, had been indoors too long, and that they needed to focus on the real work of the expedition. So, despite the darkness and the frigid temperatures, Shackleton decided it was time they 'received a good baptism of frost.' For during the winter he had determined that they would bag not one Pole, but two.

2

THE OTHER POLE

Throughout august and much of September, Shackleton had different groups of men drag supplies to Hut Point, not only effectively making Scott's old base an advance station for his attempt on the South Pole, but introducing the newcomers to the unpleasant realities of man-hauling. Even before the winter it had become apparent that man-hauling – described as the hardest work ever done by free men – would be used for most of the upcoming journeys. It had quickly been shown that the motor-car Shackleton brought south to much publicity would not function where there was even a slight amount of snow – something of a drawback in Antarctica – and therefore was unusable except occasionally on hard sea ice in McMurdo Sound. More importantly, six of the ten Manchurian ponies that sailed south on *Nimrod* had died either aboard ship or within the first months at Cape Royds. Left with only four ponies, Shackleton allocated all of them to his assault on the geographic South Pole. Everyone else would man-haul.

Two big questions during the winter, however, were *who* would be in the field and *where*. After juggling his options, Shackleton decided to take Adams, Marshall, and Wild south with him. He sent Priestley, Brocklehurst, and Bertram Armytage – the third Australian to join after that government's grant – to Dry Valley across McMurdo Sound to conduct geological investigations. And he assigned David, Mawson, and Mackay to the Northern Party, with a goal of the South Magnetic Pole, estimated to be some 400 to 500 miles north-northwest, high on the little-known Polar Plateau. The key objectives, according to Shackleton's orders, were:

(1) To take magnetic observations at every suitable point with a view of determining the dip and the position of the Magnetic Pole. If time permits . . . you will try and reach the Magnetic Pole.

(2) To make a general geological survey of the coast of Victoria Land . . .

(3) I particularly wish . . . Mawson to spend at least one fort-night at Dry Valley to prospect for minerals of economic value on your return . . . I consider that the *thorough* investigation of Dry Valley is of supreme importance.

The plan thus was simple: head west across McMurdo Sound, travel north along the Victoria Land coast, find a passage through the mountains to the Polar Plateau and then the Magnetic Pole, and return in time to find valuable minerals that would instantly pay off all the debts of the expedition. Shackleton made it sound easy – but it would not be.

David – the leader of the Northern Party – had hoped to leave by 1 October, but thick weather prevented their depar-ture until the fifth. Even then, uncertain ice conditions forced David, Mawson, and Mackay to go well south before turning west and crossing the sea ice via two already established depots towards Butter Point – named by Scott's party for a tin of butter left there – where they would make their first landing on the Antarctic continent.

When the three men took on the 200 pounds of supplies that had been left at the second depot, the difficulties facing them suddenly became horribly apparent. The combined weight of their two sledges now approached half a ton, and, with Mackay recently having broken a bone in his wrist, they were not able to pull both at the same time. They were forced to relay: hauling one sledge – nicknamed the 'Christmas Tree' sledge because so many things remembered at the last moment had been tied on it willy-nilly – for up to a mile, then returning for the 'Plum Duff' sledge on which they kept most of their provisions. This required them to travel three miles for every one gained, and restricted real progress to about four miles per day, although actually travelling twelve.

There were other problems, too. The partially thawed sea ice formed a sticky surface under the sledge runners, and made their work agony. The constant strain quickly led to short tempers, and Mawson soon tired of his mentor's eccentricities. 'Prof . . . comes in late for [three-man sleeping] bag and sits on everybody. God only knows what he does,' he groused in his diary on only the fourth day out. 'He is so covered with clothes that he can hardly walk and hardly get into bag – that is to say, hardly leaves any room for us as he very nicely made us take side places.'

It was eight days before they finally reached Butter Point, where, concerned about their poor speed, they depoted a large amount of food and equipment to lighten their load. But even rigging sails on the sledges made from the floorcloth of the tent did not help their progress greatly, and they continued to make only about four miles per day. They did buck up temporarily on the morning of 17 October when they reached Cape Bernacchi, a low, rocky promontory dominated by pure white crystalline marble. Here, with a flag that motor-car driver Bernard Day had made out of a jumble of fabrics, they took possession of Victoria Land for the British Empire.

Almost a week later, they were still crawling at a snail's pace over slowly decaying sea ice while the Sound gradually broke up to their one side and the mountains loomed over them on their other. Frustrated, Mawson proposed that they forsake the Magnetic Pole altogether and concentrate on 'what I had understood was to be the work of the expedition provided the Mag Pole were not reasonably obtainable ... the coast geographic and magnetic survey with detailed geological reconnaissances at picked spots, the whole allowing us to return to Dry Valley.' But David was adamant that they proceed, countering that, if need be, the Magnetic Pole would be reached on half-rations. For the time being, they continued their march, the ultimate decision postponed.

Unable to see an end to it, Mawson became more and more irritable, particularly with David's over-the-top Victorian politeness, which masked his roundabout efforts to gain information. 'Have just found out he thinks I have lost my burberry helmet,' Mawson wrote with annoyance in late October, continuing:

> 2 hours ago he remarked: 'Do you find that helmet warm enough today without your burberry helmet?' I answered in the affirmative, saying had had it almost as cold in Adelaide. Long silence for 2 hours. Now he says: 'I suppose you have your burberry in the bag.' I said: 'Yes, evidently you think I have lost it.' He said: 'Well, I have lately been wondering whether you had lost it or not.' That is the way of the Prof. He will take all day putting roundabout questions to one in order to get a simple Yes or No answer. This worries one almost to distraction.

The Prof's measured, methodical activity was equally frustrating to Mawson. 'He is full of great words and deadly slow action,' Mawson noted irritably. 'The more we bustle to get a move on the more he dawdles, especially tying strings to one another and all over the sledges, which all have to come off again in unpacking ... I cannot see how it is at all possible for us to reach the Magnetic Pole in one season under such conditions.'

Finally the situation came to a head, as it could no longer be denied that it was impossible to reach the Magnetic Pole *and* return to Dry Valley. David and Mackay were in agreement that all else should be sacrificed to reach the Pole, so Mawson dealt with the situation practically, suggesting they preserve a full ration of sledging food for the inland journey by going on half-rations until they left the coast. Until then, their diet could be supplemented by seal meat, and upon their return to the coast they could again live on seal while waiting for *Nimrod* – if the three men did not return to Butter Point, the ship had orders to search for them along the shores of Victoria Land. Mawson's ideas carried the day, so they built a cairn on the edge of a sheer cliff, where they felt it could not be missed by the ship, and within it they left a note indicating where and when they could be collected. Shortly thereafter, Mackay was able to construct a cooker that burned blubber, permitting them to conserve their paraffin as well for the passage inland.

So they continued, relaying through a two-day blizzard despite not being able to see more than a few yards, and then trekking over the previously uncrossed Nordenskjöld Ice Barrier. That part of the journey concluded with them being forced to lower their sledges hand-over-hand down the forty-foot cliffs that formed the Barrier's north terminus. But their progress remained painfully slow, and in late November their distances decreased further still. Mawson and Mackay attributed this to David's physical limitations, a fact not surprising if true, as he celebrated his fifty-first birthday on the journey. 'The Prof is certainly a fine example of a man for his age,' Mawson wrote, 'but he . . . does not pull as much as a younger man . . . seeing he travels with thumbs tucked in his braces . . . one concludes he lays his weight on harness rather than pulling. Several times when we have been struggling heavily . . . he has continued to recite poetry or tell yarns.'

However, things were to get much worse. Ahead lay the vast Drygalski Ice Barrier, the surface of which was 'formed

of jagged surfaces of ice very heavily crevassed, and projecting
in the form of immense séracs separated from one another
by deep undulations or chasms.' At one point, three hours'
hard labour gained only half a mile, and it took ten days of
cruel hauling to cross an area that looked as though a stormy
sea had suddenly been frozen solid. Then, shortly before
they reached the coast on the north side – taking two full
days to go the last four miles – disaster almost struck. They
halted to allow Mackay to reconnoitre ahead and, taking
advantage of the break, Mawson disappeared into the tent
to change photographic plates, while David decided to make
some sketches. 'I had scarcely gone more than six yards from
the tent, when the lid of a crevasse suddenly collapsed under
me,' David wrote. 'I only saved myself from going right
down by throwing my arms out and staying myself on the
snow lid on either side.'

Mawson was the Prof's only chance of rescue, but he did
not immediately go to his mentor's aid, as he later explained:

I was busy changing photographic plates in the only place
where it could be done – inside the sleeping bag ... Soon
after I had done up the bag, having got safely inside, I heard
a voice from outside – a gentle voice – calling: 'Mawson,
Mawson.'

'Hallo!' said I.

'Oh, you're in the bag changing plates, are you?' said the
Professor.

'Yes, Professor.'

There was silence for some time. Then I heard the Professor
calling in a louder tone: 'Mawson!'

I answered again. Well, the Professor heard by the sound
I was still in the bag. So he said: – 'Oh, still changing plates
are you?'

'Yes.'

More silence for some time. After a minute, in a rather
loud and anxious tone: 'Mawson!'

I thought there was something up, but could not tell what he was after. I was getting rather tired, and called out: 'Hallo. What is it? What can I do?'

'Well, Mawson, I am in a rather dangerous position. I am really hanging on by my fingers to the edge of a crevasse, and I don't think I can hold on much longer. I shall have to trouble you to come and assist me.'

I came out rather quicker than I can say. There was the Professor, just his head showing, and hanging onto the edge of a dangerous crevasse.

Mawson soon had David out of the crevasse, and the older man calmly began his sketching.

The Drygalski Ice Barrier proved to be the last major hurdle on the coast, and on 16 December they depoted one sledge and the material they did not need for the ascent to the Plateau near where they hoped to meet *Nimrod*. They then began winding their way up a series of glaciers towards the inland heights. For the first time in more than two months they were not relaying, and their daily mileage immediately improved, but within days they found themselves in a labyrinth of pressure ridges and crevasses, including a massive barranca – a shallow, icy, heavily crevassed ravine – more than 120 yards wide. When crossing one ice bridge, Mawson dropped clear through, only stopped eight feet below the surface when the rope connecting him to the sledge yanked him back. Mackay and David hastily hauled him up, but not before he 'secured some ice crystals from the side of the crevasse, and threw them up for examination.'

They continued up a series of glaciers, and then, leaving the crevasses behind, began to move more quickly across hard névé – the compacted snow that is in a stage of transition between soft, loose snow and glacier ice. Their distances increased to ten or eleven miles day, despite a continual ascent that took them to 6,500 feet above sea level. However, they found they could not stop thinking about eating. 'We are now almost mad on discussing foods,' Mawson wrote, 'all varieties having a great attraction for us. We dote on what sprees we shall have on return – mostly run to sweet foods and farinaceous compounds.' On 12 January, they planned two dinners to be arranged by David when they returned to Sydney, one for Mackay, the other for Mawson. That night, each of them carefully listed in his diary both entire meals, the nine-course Scots banquet and the 'Yorkshire Empire Dinner.'

On 15 January, Mawson's readings finally showed them to be nearing the Magnetic Pole, although precise measurement was impossible as 'the polar centre executes a daily round of wanderings about its mean position.' Mawson determined that if they waited where they were for twenty-four hours, the Pole would likely come to them, but rather than do this, they decided to push on thirteen miles to where he calculated the mean position to lie. The next day, they continued until lunch, after which, leaving behind all gear other than a flag and a camera, they trudged the final five miles to Mawson's 'mean position' at 72°15'S, 155°16'E. There, at a height of 7,260 feet, they hoisted the flag made by Day, claimed the area for the British Empire, and gave three cheers. David pulled a string attached to the camera to snap a picture of them. This done, there was no reason to linger, so they did an immediate about-turn. Their major task now was to reach the coast in time for the ship to collect them.

Only a week before, 1,114 statute miles farther south, Shackleton, Wild, Marshall, and Adams had held a similar ceremony. Their journey had begun on 29 October, when they left Cape Royds, each leading a pony hauling a sledge. Unfortunately, the beasts soon proved unequal to the challenge of the Great Ice Barrier, and within a month three had been shot to be put out of their misery. Nevertheless, the men passed Scott's record for the farthest south, and in early December, confronted by the Transantarctic Mountains, began an ascent of what they called the Great Glacier (later named the Beardmore Glacier). Within days, the last pony was lost down a black, bottomless pit. Wild was pulled in after it, and was only saved because the crossbar attaching the pony to him and the sledge snapped. For the next three weeks they struggled up the massive river of ice, eventually reaching the Plateau at some 10,000 feet. Despite suffering from inadequate nutrition, altitude sickness, temperatures dropping to −20°F (−29°C), powerful winds blowing in their faces, and difficult sledging surfaces, they carried on. But it soon became apparent that they could not reach the Pole and return alive, so on 9 January they made a final push before stopping at 88°23'S, only 97 geographic miles (112 statute miles) from the Pole. There, after their own proclamation and photograph, they turned for home. The dash back was a tale of desperation, as more than once they ran out of food and reached the next depot with 'the cupboard empty.' But somehow they continued, Shackleton and Wild finally leaving Adams to care for the ailing Marshall and going on towards Hut Point in a frantic effort to catch the ship before she left.

Wild's quiet efficiency throughout the entire expedition could not have helped but impress Mawson, and his remarkable sledging efforts with the Southern Party clearly marked him as a master of that incredibly demanding task. These were points Mawson would remember. Similarly, Wild must have gained respect for Mawson when he heard the story of the Northern Party.

When Mawson, David, and Mackay turned their backs on the Magnetic Pole, they were racing against time. They were 250 miles from the coast and had only fifteen days to reach it to meet *Nimrod*. They had to average better than sixteen miles per day, far more than they had previously travelled. Despite the Professor showing his age and Mawson injuring his leg, they forced themselves to slog that distance each day, even if it meant pulling longer hours, and for eight of the next nine days they reached their target. As if to add to their woes, they found themselves short of tea. They resolved this 'emergency' by stopping at their previous outward camps and retrieving the used tea leaves, which they boiled again.

On 28 January, they woke to a strong wind, so they raised the tent's floorcloth as a sail and proceeded to race twenty miles. 'Occasionally, in an extra strong puff of wind, the sledge took charge,' David wrote. 'On one of these occasions it suddenly charged into me from behind, knocked my legs from under me, and nearly juggernauted me. I was quickly rescued from this undignified position under the sledge runners.' The next day another twenty-mile performance meant they could almost smell the coast.

But on 30 January they made a critical mistake, descending what they named the Larsen Glacier straight towards the Drygalski Ice Barrier, rather than retracing their earlier, more circuitous route. It proved to be the most hideously difficult ice they ever faced, with drops of forty-five degrees, and, near the bottom, a chaotic nightmare of sérac ice and hidden 'hell holes.' One after another, they fell into crevasses, and at one point they were confronted by such an enormous pressure ridge that they were forced to unload the sledge and manhandle each individual item over it.

They exhaustedly worked through the terrible conditions, but in the process, knowing that even then the ship might be taking a last look for them, both David and Mackay started mentally coming apart at the seams. '[The Prof] is apparently half demented [judging] by his actions – the strain has been too great,' Mawson recorded. 'He says himself that had he known the magnitude he would not have undertaken it.'

In the following days things became even worse: while David struggled on frostbitten feet, Mackay kicked him viciously to 'encourage' him to pull harder. The Professor was, according to Mawson, 'now certainly partially demented,' and the darker side of Mackay's personality seemed to be coming to the fore, conditions not helped by, at one point, being forced, with back-breaking effort, to haul the sledge back up a high face from which they had already lowered it into a barranca. Nevertheless, on the night of 3 February, they reached the coast, where hundreds of seals and penguins were at least a guarantee against starvation or scurvy.

The question now was: would *Nimrod* find them? Little did the weary men know that on that very morning, the ship, now under the command of Captain Frederick Evans, had passed by while they slept. Following Shackleton's vague orders, Evans had made his way up the coast, but, despite the ship's officers using telescopes to view the shoreline, they had not noticed the cairn the three men had built. Then, as they steamed north of the Drygalski in the early hours, a sudden squall made it impossible for Davis, still the first mate, to see clearly, even from the look-out barrel on the main topmast. He was disturbed by the lack of clarity, but, as all he could make out was a group of tabular icebergs, the ship continued on her way. Later that day, they reached Cape Washington, the northern limit of the search. Evans was anxious about the supply of coal, and decided to head straight back to Cape Royds, leaving the Northern Party to its fate.

Davis, however, expressed his concerns that the icebergs he had seen through the swirling snow might have masked an inlet. With his mind foremost on his coal, Evans was annoyed with Davis' request to retrace their route, but grudgingly acceded to it. When they reached the area, the air was clear, and behind the icebergs – no longer hidden – was indeed a small inlet.

David, Mawson, and Mackay were sitting in their tent, debating whether they should attempt to make their way down the coast towards Cape Royds – hundreds of perilous miles away – or wait there for *Nimrod*, when a loud boom reverberated through the air. 'In a second,' wrote Mawson, 'I had overturned the cooker and was through the door where the bow of the *Nimrod* was just appearing round a corner in the inlet.'

'At the sight of the three of us running frantically,' recalled David, who was the last out of the tent, 'hearty ringing cheers burst forth from all on board. How those cheers stirred every fibre of one's being . . . In a moment, as dramatic as it was heavenly, we seemed to have passed from death into life.'

And immediately back again, as Mawson suddenly dropped down a crevasse. David and Mackay dashed over to find him, with incredible good fortune, only eighteen feet down, flat on his back on a thin ledge. The two dropped one end of a sledge harness down to Mawson, but were too weak to pull him up – and were worried that they might send masses of snow or ice crashing down on him. So as *Nimrod* reached the ice edge, Mackay raced towards her, screeching: 'Mawson has fallen down a crevasse, and we got to the Magnetic Pole.'

Davis, already responsible for the rescue, again became Mawson's saviour. He quickly led a party from the ship and had the crevasse bridged with a piece of timber. Then he was lowered to the ledge, where he took off the rope and tied it around Mawson, who was hauled to safety; Davis was then brought out as well. It was only after their reunion that those aboard *Nimrod* learned that the Prof and his companions had not actually reached what became known as Relief Inlet until *after* the ship had passed. When Davis saw the icebergs, they were still camped several miles away. So, Davis wrote:

had the weather been clear we might perhaps have sighted the flag they were flying above their tent. But had we missed it, under those circumstances, we should certainly have

steamed straight for Cape Royds. Therefore, in some strange
and providential way, my mistake in not taking the ship
closer inshore to examine the tabular bergs ... had made
their rescue certain and assured!

Now all that remained was to collect the Southern Party,
but that was to cause every bit as much anxiety as finding
the Northern Party had done. After a sledge team gathered
the specimens from the depot established before David and
company marched inland, and collected a set of instruments
they had left eight miles inland, Nimrod sailed south. She
easily reached Cape Royds, but then they were forced to
wait for weeks, watching the weather deteriorate while hopes
for an appearance by Shackleton slowly dissipated. Mawson,
who had been selected by Shackleton to head a relief effort
if the Southern Party did not arrive, began to make plans
for another winter.

But on 1 March, when Nimrod approached Hut Point to
drop off the wintering party – the real purpose of which,
according to Evans, was to look for the bodies – to the everlasting delight of all on board, they saw two men on shore
waving a flag. They were Shackleton and Wild, who had left
Marshall in the care of Adams thirty-three miles back and
marched on for help. Within a brief period of time, Mawson
and several others joined Shackleton in going back out onto
the Barrier and bringing his two companions back safely. And
then Shackleton ordered all steam towards the north – and
home.

Shackleton's story of nearly reaching the South Pole immediately made him an international hero. His triumphal progress
took him from New Zealand to Australia and on to Britain.
But no adulation he received was greater than that accorded
to David and Mawson by their countrymen. Australians had
longed for – and now found – their own heroes.

David's return to Sydney was marked by a magnificent

welcome, as he was met by a large crowd at the docks and then feted by students and scholars at the university's Great Hall. He received a second, official reception at the Sydney Town Hall. In one of his speeches, in typical, modest fashion, David tried to deflect the adulation he was receiving to Mawson, likening him to Fridtjof Nansen, the Norwegian then considered the greatest of polar explorers. 'Just as Shackleton was the general leader,' David said, 'so, in all sincerity and without the pride that apes humility, I say that Mawson was the real leader and was the soul of our expedition to the magnetic pole. We have in him an Australian Nansen, of infinite resource, splendid physique, astonishing indifference to frost.'

With this endorsement, it is not surprising that Mawson's return was celebrated equally as ecstatically. Starting in Sydney, it reached a crescendo when he arrived in Adelaide, where he was met at the railway station by a host of students and other admirers. Legend has it that he was taken from his carriage and borne on the throng's shoulders to a hand-drawn vehicle, on which he was pulled along North Terrace to the university, where an even larger crowd awaited him.

Although he soon resumed his normal, hectic academic schedule – including conducting the research that he wrote up for his doctoral thesis – Mawson's thoughts began to stray from Adelaide. Some undoubtedly revolved around Paquita Delprat, a dark-haired beauty with intense black eyes, whom he had met at a dinner party in Broken Hill. But others gravitated far to the south, where, during long, agonising days of pulling a sledge across perpetual ice and endless snow-fields, an idea had been born, which months later still captivated him. 'I suddenly found myself eager,' he wrote, 'for more than a glimpse of the great span of Antarctic coast lying nearest to Australia.'

II
AURORA

3

AUSTRALASIAN ANTARCTIC EXPEDITION

IT IS NOT surprising that a man with Mawson's broad
scientific curiosity should have been fascinated by the great
arc of the Antarctic coast south of Australia. For one thing,
the two continents lie in remarkably close proximity to each
other; Mawson himself noted that Hobart is actually closer
to Antarctica than it is to Perth. For another, virtually nothing
was known about the area west of Cape Adare at the northern
tip of Victoria Land. Three great national expeditions had
attempted to explore this coastline in the early 1840s, but
their findings had long been contentious. The French under
Jules-Sébastien-César Dumont d'Urville had made one
landing on a rocky inlet and taken possession of what they
named Terre Adélie, but they had been unable to determine
conclusively if the massive ice cliffs they saw were floating
on the sea or standing above solid ground. Charles Wilkes,
while commanding the United States Exploring Expedition,
had claimed several sightings of land during his 1,500-mile
survey, but many of his distances were vastly underestimated
and the coastal features he recorded – ice *and* land – were
sometimes wildly misplaced on his charts. Thus, when James
Clark Ross, on a Royal Navy expedition, sailed over where
land had been charted by Wilkes, it cast grave doubts on

all the American's alleged coastlines. Thereafter, no significant efforts had been made in the vicinity for more than six
decades.

However, any thoughts Mawson might have had about
exploring the region remained unspoken until the end of
1909, when his notion of participating in – or leading –
another expedition was actively rekindled. Having been
granted leave from his teaching duties for the first half of
1910, in December Mawson sailed for England, with letters
of introduction from David to many of the world's most
prominent geologists. During a stop in Fremantle, he heard
that David had been asked to suggest a geologist for Scott's
upcoming expedition, so he immediately cabled Scott, telling
him that he hoped to meet about Antarctic matters.

Arriving in London in mid-January, Mawson quickly fell
in with John King Davis, who, after captaining *Nimrod* on
her voyage back to England, had continued to work for
Shackleton, who was then away in Germany. Within several
days, Mawson visited Scott, who erroneously thought the
Australian would be desperate for a position on the upcoming
British expedition. Instead, Mawson expounded the value of
scientific research in the area west of Cape Adare and offered
to join Scott's expedition if he could be landed with his own
independent party there. Scott was nonplussed and tried to
convince Mawson to join the main thrust of his expedition
to McMurdo Sound, guaranteeing him a handsome salary
and a position as one of three members of the final polar
party.

But Scott had misjudged Mawson, who had no interest
whatsoever in the South Pole, and hoped only to conduct
serious scientific research. Besides, Mawson had already
participated in the longest man-hauling journey ever accomplished without support parties, so it is unlikely he would
have wished to serve under a man who had achieved considerably less during his own efforts. Nevertheless, he returned
for a second meeting, hoping to persuade Scott and his chief

of science, Edward Wilson, of the benefits of his independent scientific programme.

Scott, however, remained inflexible, because, he revealed, his plans already included a second party scheduled to go to King Edward VII Land, east of the Great Ice Barrier. Mawson therefore declined the offer of a post, saying he would go on his own. Scott became defensive and 'stated that it had always been his intention to do what he could around the north coast but could promise nothing,' Mawson wrote. 'In fact he had now set his mind on picking the plums out of the north coast by a boat reconnaissance on the return of the ship. I said finally that as I could not be landed on the north coast I would go in no other capacity than as Chief Scientist and that as Wilson had been appointed to that position I would not dream of making the suggestion nor indeed would I henceforth accept a post on the expedition.'

Yet Scott maintained hope and invited Mawson to dinner, where he and his wife Kathleen tried unsuccessfully to convince him to join up. Scott 'stated finally that he would keep my name on his staff until his arrival in Australia,' Mawson wrote, 'should I then have finally decided not to go with him I, in conjunction with Prof David, was to select an Australian geologist to take my place. I told him that there was no hope of my joining.'

Instead, Mawson turned for help in launching his own expedition to Shackleton, who, upon his return from the Continent, provided encouragement by stating that he could obtain financial support for Mawson's plan. More than encouragement, in fact, as one morning Shackleton startled Mawson by stating, 'I have decided to go to the coast west of Cape Adare and you are to be Chief Scientist. I hope you will agree to this. I can get the money, and that would be your trouble were you taking it yourself.'

Mawson was 'rather taken aback' that Shackleton was commandeering his expedition, but, being more interested

in conducting the science than in who was in command, he
'decided to fall in with him for he said that he could lay his
hands on about £70,000.' So together, they moved ahead on
two fronts: Shackleton seeking funding and Mawson developing a plan for the most encompassing scientific programme
yet launched in the Antarctic. He envisioned three bases, with
men wintering on different sections of the coast as well as the
use of a ship for a survey of all accessible coasts in the areas
Mawson – using names proposed in the 1830s and 1840s –
referred to as Adelie Land, Clarie Land, and Sabrina Land.

The greatest financial hopes of the two men centred on
Gerald Lysaght, a steel industrialist who had contributed to
the BAE. After spending five hours with Mawson, Lysaght
promised them £10,000. But that was still far short of what
would be needed, so Mawson found himself drawn into one
of Shackleton's many unsuccessful schemes to find wealth.
In the spring, accompanied by Davis and Æneas Mackintosh,
the former second mate of *Nimrod*, Mawson went to
Hungary to assess the economic potential of undeveloped
gold mines Shackleton was hoping to buy. However, although
they appeared to have great possible value, it turned out
that the owner had no serious intention of selling, and the
effort eventually came to nothing.

When Mawson returned to London in April 1910, he had
not had significant contact with Shackleton since the latter
had sailed for New York to begin a lecture tour. But he was
inordinately puzzled by Shackleton's mixed messages about
the expedition. Was Shackleton truly falling in with a purely
scientific programme? Was he throwing his hat in a race for
the South Pole? Was he doing none of these, because his
wife Emily did not want him to leave? All had been speculated
upon in the press. Mawson decided the only way to find
out was to force an answer from Shackleton, so he sailed
to New York and then made his way to Omaha, Nebraska,
in the American heartland, where Shackleton's tour had
temporarily floundered.

The two explorers spent four days together, by the end of which Mawson believed Shackleton 'had many get-rich-quick schemes in view and I felt that the chances of his going to Antarctica were lessening.' Mawson therefore took steps to protect both his own financial position and the expedition. On 16 May, he drew up a document in which Shackleton guaranteed to pay him £400 for his unpaid BAE salary and his work in Hungary, as well as assigning him shares in any exploitation of the mines. But more importantly, it gave Mawson assurances for the Antarctic plan:

> I intend to proceed with arrangements for an antarctic expedition to commence in the latter half of 1911, and shall appoint D Mawson as director of the scientific work with power to make all necessary arrangements . . . In the event of my not accompanying the expedition as commander, D Mawson will be in charge and I shall still use my influence with my supporters in regard to raising the necessary funds.

With Shackleton bound by such a document, Mawson immediately began promoting the expedition when he reached Australia, giving public lectures, seeking more funding, and, since he firmly believed Shackleton would not end up participating, emphasising his own role as head of an Australian expedition. However, as months passed, Mawson did not receive any confirmation one way or the other from Shackleton. Instead, he discovered Shackleton had spoken at the Royal Geographical Society (RGS) and had released plans to the press about his 'forthcoming' expedition – Mawson's exact plans. It was all both frustrating and baffling, as Mawson noted: 'I understood that he had abandoned the idea of going himself, so that these notices were very confusing.'

Such uncertainty also hurt Mawson's fund-raising. He had not initially made any appeals for financial backing in

Australia, as he had told Scott: 'on purpose so that you may never regard me as a usurper of funds which might otherwise have gone towards your enterprise. After you have got away, I shall endeavour to raise the money necessary.' But even after Scott's departure, Shackleton's silence made it difficult for Mawson to ask for funds – since he did not know if the expedition was his or Shackleton's – so on 1 December, in desperation, he cabled Shackleton requesting an immediate response. In return, Shackleton sent the cable Mawson was most hoping for: 'that he could not go but would support me.'

Receiving Shackleton's message allowed Mawson to move ahead not only on the expedition front but on the personal one. Throughout the winter and spring of 1910 he had regularly visited the Adelaide and Brighton (South Australia) homes of G.D. Delprat, the general manager of the large mining company Broken Hill Proprietary. Early on, the pretext had been a friendship with Delprat's son Willy, but after a while it had become evident that the real draw was Willy's youngest sister, Paquita, a nineteen-year-old beauty Mawson had first met in Broken Hill the previous August. Within a week of Shackleton's message, Mawson proposed to Paquita and was accepted with alacrity. Although Paquita was not keen on her new fiancé disappearing for an extended time to the Antarctic, she became one his staunchest supporters.

Forward movement on Mawson's expedition began on 11 January 1911 in the Geology Department at the University of Sydney, when he launched a drive to gain scholarly, scientific, and governmental approval and patronage for the 'Australasian Antarctic Expedition, 1911.' Speaking to the Australasian Association for the Advancement of Science (AAAS), he explained how multiple bases spread along the Antarctic coast would engage in meteorological, magnetic, geological, and geographical work to open up the mysteries of what he called 'the Australian Quadrant' of the Antarctic. In addition, he claimed other benefits would accrue: a ship-based oceanographic programme, the expansion of Australian whaling and sealing, the establishment of meteorological stations for weather forecasting, and the verification of Australia as a key component of the British Empire.

Within days, with the backing of David Orme Masson, professor of chemistry at the University of Melbourne and president of the AAAS, Mawson was voted £1,000, one-third of the Association's liquid assets. In addition, a special committee for the expedition was organised to arrange the details of the scientific work and officially to appoint expedition members. With Professor David as chairman, and Masson as another key member, Mawson had powerful scholarly and political backing, as was immediately shown when, within days, he met with Australian Prime Minister Andrew Fisher, who proved most positive.

With the support of the scientific community and the Prime Minister in hand, Mawson quickly turned to financial targets, and by the middle of January he had received pledges of £1,000 each from Robert Barr Smith, a renowned philanthropist with connections to the University of Adelaide; Sir Hugh Dixson and his nephew Hugh Denison, tobacco manufacturers; and Samuel Hordern, a wealthy retail merchant 'selling everything from a needle to an anchor.'

An earlier pledge from Roderick Murchison of the Melbourne Club meant that Mawson could now count on £6,000, but he was worried about Lysaght's promised £10,000. So he decided he should 'make all haste for Europe to collect other money (especially Lysaght's) and to appeal to wealthy Australians in London at [George V's] Coronation.'

Mawson left for London on 26 January 1911 hoping not only to raise funds, but to purchase a ship and other materials necessary for such an expedition. Before doing any of that, however, he decided to hire his first expedition member, someone who could serve as second-in-command of the expedition and master of the vessel, as well as taking charge of any ship-related issues. There was no doubt in his mind who this man should be: John King Davis.

Davis, meanwhile, had finally given up on Shackleton leading an expedition and had sailed for Montreal, where he understood he could obtain a position with the Canadian Northern Railway. Once there, he was sent on to Toronto, but proving unsuccessful there, he was considering continuing to Calgary to seek his fortune when, 'my problem was solved by a cablegram from Dr Mawson in London, asking me to go with him to the Antarctic ... I cabled an acceptance [although] I knew nothing whatever about the expedition.'

While Davis was *en route* back to London, Mawson – still with no ship, virtually no funding, and little public interest – gained the first two members of his shore party. One was Wild, designated to be in charge of one of the bases. The other was Belgrave Edward Sutton Ninnis, a young lieutenant in the Royal Fusiliers, whose father had been a surgeon on the British Arctic Expedition of 1875–76. After unsuccessful attempts to gain a place on Scott's expedition, the younger Ninnis had been hired by Shackleton instead and then passed on as a *fait accompli* to Mawson.

Shackleton also was the key figure in Mawson's greatest disappointment. For months Mawson had not been given a straight answer by Shackleton about the status of Lysaght's £10,000. Finally, after reaching Britain, Mawson wrote directly to Lysaght himself, receiving back terrible news from Lysaght's wife: 'My husband is ill in a nursing home ... I am afraid he would not in any case have been able to support your expedition, as all that he could afford – indeed more – he did for Sir Ernest Shackleton this time last year. Sir Ernest can, & will no doubt, tell you what this was.'

He did not have to. Mawson knew instantly that the donation had vanished into the nothingness of one or another of Shackleton's many quixotic business ventures. Although Mawson had to continue dealing with Shackleton, he never forgave him, writing more than two decades later to the author of the first Shackleton biography: 'He certainly had a very fertile and poetic mind. But when it comes to the normal side of things S and I part brass rags, as they say in the navy; that is why I have not rushed into print to heap eulogies upon him.'

Nor was Shackleton the only British explorer by whom Mawson felt betrayed. When Scott's ship *Terra Nova* returned to Lyttelton from the Antarctic, the British newspapers and public were outraged to find that Roald Amundsen had set up at the Bay of Whales on the Great Ice Barrier, stealing a march, the press bristled, on Scott. But to Mawson, Scott's behaviour was equally shocking. Scott's secondary party, unable to reach King Edward VII Land, had established a base instead at Cape Adare. Not only had Mawson first suggested that idea to Scott, but in October Scott asked him for his plans, which Mawson had graciously provided. The situation was even more galling because, four years before, Scott had demanded a thoroughly unreasonable promise from Shackleton to stay away from McMurdo Sound, to which Scott insisted he had prescriptive rights. When Shackleton landed at Cape Royds, Scott was livid. Yet now he recognised no such rights for Mawson. 'I do wish Captain Scott had been franker with me,' Mawson wrote to Kathleen Scott. 'Had Captain Scott truly desired to settle an Eastern party at K.E. VII Land this year it seems to me that the men he has had pluck enough to do it.' Yet the situation and his fuming letter were unexpectedly to benefit Mawson. Three days later, he rather suspiciously lunched with Kathleen Scott, who not only eased his resentment, but would prove, in the months and years ahead, to be an exceedingly valuable friend.

Mawson's attention now turned to two things. First, a presentation at the RGS, which he hoped, along with its accompanying publicity, would expand his base of potential donors. And second, the purchase of a ship, since his first choice, Scott's old *Discovery*, would not be sold or lent by its current owners, the Hudson's Bay Company. On 10 April, he addressed the RGS, modifying his previous proposal by eliminating Cape Adare from the programme, but maintaining his concept of multiple bases. Following the lecture, Leonard Darwin, in the presidential chair, announced that the Society would grant £500 to the AAE.

The next day Mawson travelled to Paris to meet the famed French explorer Jean-Baptiste Charcot, whose ship *Pourquoi Pas?* had caught his fancy after he and Davis had enquired about a number of other vessels. These included *Scotia*, which had been used for the Scottish National Antarctic Expedition, the sealer *Viking*, and *Nimrod*. He returned desperate for *Pourquoi Pas?*, particularly as he thought he could buy her relatively inexpensively. 'She is splendid . . . fitted out for Polar scientific work – with laboratories and communications quarters. For that price she is a gift . . . I want her <u>very badly</u>, and shall certainly never get the chance of anything like again if this is lost.' Unfortunately, in the ensuing weeks, negotiations fell through, as the French government designated the vessel a marine research laboratory.

Mawson and Davis now focused on a ship from the Newfoundland sealing fleet that had been recommended to Davis by the famed Arctic navigator Bob Bartlett. Her name was *Aurora*, and she was already old – having been built in Dundee in 1876 – but she was still sound and strong, being constructed of stout oak planks sheathed with greenheart, lined with fir, and then armoured with steel plates. She was 165 feet long, had a beam of 30 feet, a draught of 18, and was registered at 386 tons. After a lengthy dance with Bowerings, her owners, Mawson and Davis were pleasantly surprised when Bowerings sold *Aurora* to them for £6,000, less than half of their original demand. 'I think,' wrote Davis, 'we two must have been the happiest young men alive.'

Unfortunately, Mawson and Davis could not actually afford her. But such hiccups did not unduly influence

Mawson, who continued to spend as if he were simply putting it all on a credit card. With help from Shackleton, Wild, and Alfred Reid – who served the expedition as an England-based manager – Mawson ordered polar equipment and other supplies from around Europe. Woollens came from Jaeger of London, as did blankets and ski boots. For wear outside the Jaeger clothing, Mawson selected Burberry gabardine. And the necessary furs – wolfskin mittens, finnesko, and reindeer-skin sleeping bags – were produced, as they had been for Shackleton, by W.C. Møller of Drammen, Norway. Mawson also followed Shackleton's lead by having sledges and skis produced in Norway at Hagen & Co., although he ordered additional ones in Australia.

There was also one item Mawson purchased despite it not having any Antarctic precedent: an aeroplane. Although untested in the far south, its potential was vast: it could be used for reconnaissance, search and rescue, and transport, and it would generate the same kind of publicity as Shackleton's motor-car had done. Moreover, Kathleen Scott was something of an expert on aeroplanes, and had connections at Vickers, the London-based manufacturer. She recommended a monoplane that Vickers had just imported from France, one 'infinitely more stable, heavier and more solid and will carry more weight. Its cost is £1000, but I think it could be worked to get it for £700 or even less.' Mawson was quickly convinced, and ordered a Vickers REP D-type with a five-cylinder engine, 60 HP, a cruising speed of 48 knots, and a price tag of £955 4s. 8d. He then hired pilot Hugh Watkins, also recommended by Kathleen, to fly it. Frank Bickerton – who had trained in engineering with study in aeronautics and was a close friend of Mackintosh – became its engineer, thus adding not only the aeroplane but two salaries to Mawson's growing financial mess.

Even before this, Mawson had added another staff member from – for an Australasian expedition – a most unexpected place: Basle, Switzerland. Xavier Mertz was a 28-year-old

Swiss lawyer who had worked as a carpenter, plumber, and locksmith. He was also an experienced mountaineer – having climbed Mount Blanc – and in 1908 had won the Swiss ski-jumping championship. In a letter of application, he expressed the hope that 'you intend making use of skys as ... they have proved so good for the purpose & knowing that I am as good as any one on skys.' The offer of a potential ski instructor was too important to refuse, and Mawson added another cost to his growing list of debts.

Fortunately, he did not have long to worry about the mounting bills. In early May, Shackleton lived up to the promise he had made in Omaha and approached Lord North-cliffe, owner of, amongst other newspapers, the *Daily Mail*, the *Daily Mirror*, and *The Times*. Shackleton's charm again worked its magic, and Northcliffe agreed that an appeal for funding for the AAE could appear free in the *Daily Mail*. On 8 May, under Shackleton's name, an appeal was made for Britain to come to the aid of the Australasian enterprise by raising £12,000 for Mawson.

Money poured in – within the week Mawson had received enough to purchase *Aurora* and begin paying his debts. More than 140 cash donations totalling an estimated £9,843 were made. The appeal also led to donations of equipment and supplies by companies such as Jaeger, Burberry, Colman's, Colonial Sugar, Cadbury Brothers, Glaxo, Bovril, Heinz, Horlick's, and Nestlé. In addition, Messrs Mackie of Glasgow provided two cases of White Horse whisky, which went under the heading of 'medical comforts,' and British American Tobacco made such a generous donation of cigars, cigarettes, and tobacco that the *Daily Mail* predicted the members of the expedition would be able to 'smoke to their hearts' content without coming to the end of their stock.'

Having done all he could in limited time, Mawson departed for Australia to return to teaching, attempt to obtain government grants, and oversee the multitude of expedition tasks there. In London, Davis was left in charge, but most of his attention was given to the refitting of *Aurora*, while other tasks were taken over by Wild, Reid, or Brocklehurst, who oversaw the expedition's finances.

The ship, it turned out, was in desperate need of repair, and Davis ordered that she receive a new foremast, have the rig altered from schooner to barquentine, have portions of the topgallant mast renewed, and have the main engines, windlass, and winches overhauled. The deck below the topgallant forecastle was fitted as crew quarters, the accommodation aft was enlarged to house twenty-five men, two scientific laboratories were constructed on deck, and a Lucas sounding machine was installed. There were also numerous supplies to purchase, including anchors and sails. Davis also hired a crew, which was not easy, as several of the men he wanted were unavailable.

Yet all these difficulties seemed as nothing when, only five days before scheduled departure, a Board of Trade official performed an unscheduled inspection of *Aurora* and demanded that four additional hold ventilators be installed, a load-line survey be carried out, and a Plimsoll mark cut into the side of the ship. A dock strike had been threatened for weeks, and Davis believed that a delay for these alterations could stop their departure entirely, scuppering the expedition. Moreover, the Plimsoll line would mean the 500 tons of coal that Mawson and Davis hoped would be donated in Cardiff would not be able to taken on, as it would leave the ship too low in the water. But his appeals to higher authorities were ignored, and the date for departure passed with no permission to sail. 'The Board of Trade . . . have tried to wreck the expedition by condemning everything,' he wrote to Mawson. '[B]ut we will beat them all yet. I have got the bit between my teeth now and can only say damn them we will win.'

Davis' way of winning consisted of, shortly after midnight on 28 July, boarding the crew, forty-eight Greenland dogs, and Ninnis and Mertz, who were assigned to look after the dogs, and sailing without permission. Fortunately for him, and for the expedition, by the time *Aurora* reached Cardiff the decision-makers at the Board of Trade had more or less come to their senses, and the ship was allowed to coal and sail for Australia without major difficulties. Three months to the day after departure, *Aurora* docked at the Queen's Wharf shed in Hobart, after dropping off Ninnis, Mertz, and the dogs at the local quarantine station.

Mawson and his new expedition secretary, Conrad Eitel, had arrived in Hobart two days previously. Only a handful of the thirty-one members of the shore party were already there – most were either being trained in different scientific techniques or overseeing the collection of materials in different parts of Australia. Selecting his staff from the hundreds of applicants had been a major task in the short three months Mawson had been back in Australia, but it had been only one of many jobs in a process so overwhelming that he commented shortly before leaving Adelaide: 'I feel I would never have the energy to get up another expedition. I am prepared to go on exploring for the rest of time, but it is the organization from which one shrinks.'

That effort had started virtually immediately upon his return to Adelaide. He had given himself a few days to visit Paquita, and then dashed off to Melbourne and Sydney to meet with several AAAS committees and to search for funding from governments and individuals as well as donations of equipment and instruments from businesses and museums.

It took only three weeks before Mawson was rewarded with his first governmental success. A deputation led by Sir Samuel Way, the Chancellor of the University of Adelaide, asked the Premier of South Australia for £5,000, which was quickly granted along with £500 worth of South Australian produce. Almost immediately thereafter, a grant of £2,000 was endorsed by the British government. Hoping success would breed success, Mawson made a strong push with the governments of both New South Wales and the Commonwealth of Australia. With key support from Professor David, Mawson ultimately was promised £7,000 by New South Wales, £6,000 by Victoria, £5,000 by the Commonwealth, and £500 from Tasmania, although Western Australia, Queensland, and New Zealand claimed lack of sufficient funds to contribute anything. Unfortunately, individual donations did not amount to as much as hoped, although David gave a series of lectures that allowed him to contribute £100. Eventually, Mawson 'had to sell shares, etc, and put all the money into it that I could lay hands on.'

Meanwhile, one of Mawson's gimmicks to solicit financing went horribly wrong. The aeroplane, shipped on the P&O steamer *Macedonia*, arrived in Adelaide at the end of September, and Watkins, Bickerton, and Wild immediately started prepping it for a fund-raising display at the Cheltenham Racecourse. Although a test flight the day before the event revealed certain problems, they seemed to be resolved, and several hours before the crowd was due to arrive Watkins and Wild took off for a last test. However, according to Watkins, the plane 'got into a fierce tremor, and then into an air pocket, and was brought down about 100 ft, got straight, and dropped into another, almost a vacuum. That finished it. We hit the ground with an awful crash, both wings damaged, one cylinder broken, and the Nose bent up, the tail in half.' It was a miracle that Wild and Watkins were not killed, the former later recalling that:

to my surprise I found I was still alive, lying on my back, my legs mixed up in the body of the machine & a fearful weight on my chest, unable to move. I could not see Watkins, but . . . I heard him say 'Poor old bus, she's done.' It seemed at least an hour before anyone came, but in reality it was only about two minutes before Bickerton's white face appeared; poor old chap, I believe his shock was as bad or worse than ours, racing across that course wondering what sort of a mess he was going to find.

It was a mess Mawson's men could not put back together again. So he decided to scrap the notion of flying, leave the wings behind, and take the engine and body south as a motor sledge. He then placed Bickerton in charge of what became known as the air-tractor, and dismissed Watkins, whom he believed was responsible for the accident.

The aeroplane was only one example of Mawson's fascination with the possibilities created by new technology. Another was wireless telegraphy. Mawson knew that wireless did not have the power to transmit from Antarctica to Australia, but when H.A. Hunt, director of the Commonwealth Meteorological Bureau, presented a potential solution, Mawson immediately recognised it. Hunt believed that wireless equipment at Macquarie Island, 930 miles south-southeast of Tasmania, could be used to transmit atmospheric and climatic data to Australia, which would help Australian weather forecasting and give valuable guidance to shipping. Mawson realised that such a station could concurrently serve as a wireless relay from Antarctica. Moreover, establishing a base would allow the first significant compilation of scientific information and the preparation of the first reliable map of Macquarie. Mawson jumped at the idea of accomplishing all of this, and immediately planned for a station on Macquarie Island, which would give him a total of four.

As if manning three Antarctic bases were not enough, Mawson now had to find five men for Macquarie. He offered the position as its leader to George Ainsworth of the Weather Bureau in Melbourne. Hunt approved the selection, and, much to Mawson's delight, Ainsworth was allowed to join the expedition while still being paid by the government. Also assigned to Macquarie were geologist and cartographer Leslie Russell Blake, the New Zealand biologist Harold Hamilton, and two wireless experts, Arthur Sawyer and Charles Sandell.

Meanwhile, there would also be twenty-six men to serve at the three Antarctic mainland locations. Mawson himself was to command the Main Base, which would have eleven other men; Wild would oversee the Central Base, with five others; and the Western Base, with a total of eight, was eventually placed under the command of 31-year-old Herbert Dyce Murphy – the scion of a wealthy Queensland sheep-farming family who had spent a year at Oxford – after Mawson's earlier choices did not come to fruition.

No other position was more significant in Mawson's scheme than that of chief magnetician. Amongst the expedition's most important objectives were establishing a magnetic observatory and making a field survey of terrestrial magnetism from north of the South Magnetic Pole, thereby extending the information that Mawson and David had compiled. Mawson was unable to hire the men he really wanted for this job, so he settled instead for Eric Webb, a 21-year-old graduate in civil engineering from Canterbury University College, Christchurch.

The member of the shore party that Mawson most actively recruited was Cecil Madigan, who had received a BSc in mining engineering at the University of Adelaide in 1910 and then was selected as the South Australian Rhodes Scholar for 1911. Madigan departed for Oxford, but Mawson appealed to Sir Samuel Way, the Chancellor of the University of Adelaide, for aid. Thus, when Madigan arrived in Oxford, he was encouraged by Lord Milner, former High Commissioner of South Africa and a trustee for the Rhodes Trust, to go back to Australia and join Mawson's expedition. With Milner's backing, Madigan deferred his entry to Oxford, and accepted the job as the Main Base's meteorologist.

Throughout November, these and the other members of the shore party reached Hobart, where they were met by Mawson, shown where to drop off their luggage, and immediately directed to Queen's Wharf. There, under the command of Wild, more than 5,200 boxes, crates, and packages were opened, checked, repacked, and sorted. Cases were packed to weigh between fifty and seventy pounds, and each was marked with a coloured band: black for those materials going to Macquarie Island, red for Main Base, blue for Wild's base, and yellow for Murphy's.

'The exertion of it was just what was wanted to make us fit,' Mawson wrote. 'It also gave the opportunity of personally gauging certain qualities of the men, which are not usually evoked by a university curriculum.'

The largest influx of men and *matériel* arrived on 23 November from Sydney: biologists John Hunter and Charles Laseron, surgeons Archie McLean and Sydney Evan Jones, geologist Andy Watson, photographer Frank Hurley, Walter Hannam, in charge of the wireless programme, and Blake, Sawyer, and Sandell of the Macquarie Island party. With them came one of the huts, as well as 'sledges and skis ... cases of bacon, tobacco, biscuits, hams and ... all that was necessary for the collection and preservation of zoological specimens at four bases. There were dredges and sieves, skinning knives and forceps, collecting jars and boxes, stocks of alcohol, formalin, arsenical soap.'

In the week before departure, the men each worked all day every day, building a powerful camaraderie and a strong dedication to the expedition. Simultaneously, with little time remaining, they were not hesitant to play when they could. 'Bickerton, Kennedy, Moyes and I go out for strawberries and cream,' Ninnis recorded a few days before the ship sailed.

In nearly every fruiterer's shop here there is a kind of little back parlour where you can sit and gorge this delicious pottage ... behind the curtains dividing it from the shop, we see Hurley, Hodgeman and Jones with two girls. In a moment of frivolity I suggest that we shall each stroll into the shop as if separately, look into the back parlour, say 'Oh sorry' or the like, and then come out again. This we do, first of all the four of us singly, and then in a body, by which time the shop people are convulsed with laughter, after which we desist from our senseless sport.

By 1 December, the hard work had paid off, and everything was ready for departure. The crew and shore party had been dined, prayed for, honoured, and taken to the hearts of the locals in almost every way imaginable, and that last night the Premier of Tasmania hosted a farewell event. There were mixed emotions and mounting tensions, as the shore party thought about abandoning civilisation for more than a year. Little did they know, although it must have been on the minds of some, that a few of them would never return.

4

THE ONLY AVAILABLE PLACE

WITHIN HOURS OF the departure of *Aurora*, Mawson, Wild, or Davis might have been forgiven for thinking they had been transported back in time, to when *Nimrod* sailed four years previously. The wind freshened, the seas became rough and confused, and then, according to Wild: 'We had the usual luck of Antarctic exploring ships & ran into a gale.' In the following days, the increasingly violent intensity of the hurricane and the mountainous seas forced Davis to heave to, facing *Aurora* into the wind, where she wallowed helplessly. Battered by the waves smashing over the ship, the men on deck could only hold on for their lives and hope that the sea would not carry away either them or the items lashed on the overcrowded decks, while those incapacitated by sea-sickness below must have felt the best way to measure the sheets of water pouring through the ship was with a tide-gauge. 'It seemed as if no power on earth could save the loss of at least part of the deck cargo,' Mawson wrote. 'Would it be the indispensable huts amidships, or would a sea break on the benzine aft and flood us with inflammable liquid and gas?'

It was all a far cry from the gay departure from what some of the younger members of the expedition had begun to look upon as the land of strawberries and cream. At 4 p.m.

on 2 December, 'the seamen threw away their last coins,' according to Mertz. 'This is a seaman's tradition. At sea only empty pockets should bring luck.' As *Aurora* pulled away from the wharf and glided through the harbour, Mawson and fourteen members of his team waved to the thousands of well-wishers at the Hobart docks.

Among those waving back were half of the shore party, scheduled to leave five days later. More than two months before, when the plans materialised for a base at Macquarie Island, Mawson realised that he needed 'an auxiliary vessel to transport our deck cargo, and the whole of the Macquarie Island equipment, and extra coal for the "Aurora", to Macquarie ... In this way we shall eliminate much risk of losing deck cargo, and we shall arrive in Antarctica with a much more abundant supply of coal.' Mawson had lobbied for Royal Navy assistance, but having been turned down flat, he chartered a small (120 gross tons) steam-packet named *Toroa*, which normally did not go farther afield than Melbourne. Carrying sixteen members of the shore party, cargo, coal, and some fifty-five sheep, she would be packed to the gills, although no more so than the main expedition ship.

When *Aurora* sailed, there looked to be not an iota more of space aboard her. The poop deck was monopolised by segments of the magnetic observatory, additional sledges, and 4,000 gallons of benzine and 1,300 gallons of kerosene – for the air-tractor, motor-launch, and wireless plants. In addition, 'On the main deck the cargo was brought up flush with the top of the bulwarks, and consisted of the wireless masts, two huts, a large motor-launch, cases of dog biscuits and many other sundries,' wrote Mawson, continuing:

Butter to the extent of a couple of tons was accommodated chiefly on the roof of the main deckhouse, where it was out of the way of the dogs. The roof of the chart-house, which formed an extension of the bridge proper, did not escape, for the railing offered facilities for lashing sledges; besides, there was room for tide-gauges, meteorological screens, and cases of fresh eggs and apples. Somebody happened to think of space unoccupied in the meteorological screens, and a few fowls were housed therein.

Above this, the air-tractor was stored in a massive packing case, resting on the forecastle and two boat-skids. 'Tween decks did not escape similar treatment. There were 386 tons of coal in the bunkers, the tanks not used for fresh water were topped up with stores, and the cabins were so loaded with instruments that there was scant room for the forty men aboard. The main stowage areas had been organised to keep the equipment and supplies for each of the four bases separate, so that they could be unloaded without interfering with the materials for the next base or affecting the trim of the ship.

Even more room had to be found when the ship stopped several miles down the Derwent to pick up the remaining thirty-eight dogs from the quarantine station. Struggling and attempting to jump overboard, they were carried out to the ship in a fishing ketch, then hauled aboard and tethered on top of the deck cargo, just out of reach of one another. As soon as they were secure, all hands prepared for bad weather, because shortly before leaving Mawson had received a telegram from H.A. Hunt of the Commonwealth Meteorological Bureau warning him to 'expect fresh south westerly.'

After several miserable days, the storm reached its most dangerous. While Ninnis and Charles Harrisson, a biologist and talented artist from the Hobart Museum, were feeding the dogs, a wall of water swept them off their feet and nearly off the ship. It is remarkable that they were able to stay aboard because it also demolished half the bridge, smashed in the back of the motor-launch, and stove in the case holding the air-tractor, 'causing the machine to protrude through the far end some 4 ft, driving it through the inch planking and tin lining like a nail.'

Fortunately, the weather thereafter improved, and on 11 December *Aurora* arrived at Macquarie Island. The slow passage meant that *Toroa* was not far behind. She, too, had been confronted by a gale within hours of leaving the harbour, but that had not been the kind of thing to intimidate the captain, 'Roaring Tom' Holyman. A barrel-chested, spade-bearded master mariner of legend, Holyman had realised the night before they sailed that they might be forbidden to leave because *Toroa* was so heavily loaded that her Plimsoll line had disappeared beneath the water. His solution was simple: he had himself lowered over the side after dark and painted on an alternate line so that the port authorities would not know. Shortly after sailing, Holyman was forced to anchor for more than a day to wait out the gale, but then *Toroa* sped on, and on 13 December, she, too, reached Macquarie.

Two years before, Davis had stopped briefly at Macquarie Island on *Nimrod*'s return to England, so, although little had been recorded about its geography and no serious scientific studies had been made there, he was as familiar with it as almost anyone other than sealers. The sealers on Macquarie were employed by Joseph Hatch of Invercargill, New Zealand, who for several decades had leased the island from the government of Tasmania to obtain seal and penguin oil. Discovered in 1810, it had at that stage hosted an enormous population of fur seals, but within several years sealers had virtually exterminated them. Elephant seals became the next target, and when their decreasing numbers rendered 'elephant oiling' economically unviable, Hatch's men turned Macquarie into the centre of the world's penguin-oil trade, taking mostly the vast colonies of kings and royal penguins, although not forgetting that rockhoppers and gentoos could be used to 'top up' their quotas.

Macquarie is twenty-one miles long, between one and three miles wide, and consists primarily of a plateau 650–1,000 feet high, which drops sharply to the coast. In the north, there is a low spit running three-quarters of a mile north to an isolated flat-topped hill. After an initial visit to Caroline Cove in the southwest concluded with *Aurora* striking a submerged rock, Davis took the ship to Hasselborough Bay, west of the spit. Mawson and Ainsworth soon determined that, as the hill stood some 300 feet high, it would be the best place for the wireless station. The living quarters for the five expedition members would be located near its base, at the north end of the spit and not far from where several sealers lived throughout the year.

As soon as these decisions were made, the landing of equipment began, that destined for the wireless station being taken to a rocky cove on the west side of the lonely rise that became known as Wireless Hill, while the materials for the living quarters went to a beach at the northern end of the spit. The men aboard *Toroa* soon joined those from *Aurora*, and while they transported ashore everything needed for a year and a half, a motorboat slowly lugged ninety tons of coal from the steam-packet to *Aurora*. As the stores and coal were taken off *Toroa*, she steadily rose in the water, and soon the old Plimsoll mark reappeared; it had been submerged by more than two feet.

The most difficult part of the project was moving numerous large and heavy items to the top of the hill. Wild rigged a 'flying fox' that consisted of:

> two steel-wire carrying cables, secured above by 'dead men'
> sunk in the soil, and below by a turn around a huge rock
> ... For hauling up the loads, a thin wire line, with a pulley-
> block at either extremity, rolling one on each of the carrying
> wires, passed round a snatch-block at the upper station. It

was of such a length that when the loading end was at the lower station, the counterpoise end was in position to descend at the other. Thus a freight was dispatched to the top of the hill by filling a bag ... with earth, until slightly in excess of the weight of the top load; then off it would start ...

Unfortunately, the heaviest and bulkiest loads – including the wireless masts – were too much for one wire and had to be attached to both and hauled up by sheer muscle. After the greater part of the materials reached the top, the men started putting up the two masts – each of which was erected in several sections totalling approximately 100 feet – and building the two work stations needed, an engine hut (housing the engine, dynamo, and generator) and an operating hut.

Throughout this two-week period, Mawson worked as hard as anyone, leading from the front and encouraging his men by example. His efforts were made not only to establish his right to leadership, but because, as he wrote to Paquita, 'The last few days have been very strenuous ones but I like it – I am in my element. Hard physical work agrees with me.'

As the time drew near for the expedition to head south, the ship desperately needed water. During the gale, a deck plug from a fresh-water tank had fallen out, and so much seawater ran in that the contents became too brackish to drink, forcing rationing. On 21 December, an effort was made to obtain water from the east side of the island, but a series of mishaps not only forced the effort to be abandoned but resulted in the loss of the port anchor and damage to the starboard one.

On Christmas Eve, after farewells to the men remaining on Macquarie, Aurora sailed into Caroline Cove, hoping to resupply the dwindling water. It was an agonisingly slow procedure, as two 112-gallon puncheons had to be filled

by buckets from a stream approximately a hundred yards
away, towed back to the ship, emptied, and then taken
back to shore and the procedure repeated. At 11 p.m. the
operation halted, with the intention of finishing it in the
morning. But four hours later the ship again was driven
onto rocks. The water and the notion of a quiet Christmas
were forgotten, and Davis immediately took to sea, heading
for the Antarctic.

Davis' intention was to follow the 157th meridian south, a
course that runs west of Cape Adare. However, if they could
land, they would still be well set to make an attempt on the
Magnetic Pole from the north. Should they not be able to
land, they would work their way steadily west, hoping to
find a lead – a track of open water – through the ice to the
mainland.

For most of the men, the sights unveiling before them
were totally new, and on 27 December the ship was
surrounded by whales as far as could be seen. In the afternoon two days later, the first Antarctic petrel was sighted,
and the older hands, knowing from legend that those birds
were seldom far from the edge of the ice pack, assumed
they would soon be near the 'frozen stuff.' And so they
were, as within a couple of hours the first icebergs appeared
out of a heavy mist. 'Icebergs are eye-openers,' wrote Frank
Stillwell, scheduled to be the geologist for the Western Base.
'I had expected a huge white mass of ice . . . but not so.
The water line of the berg is a beautiful bluish green, and
all the joints and cracks of the bergs are filled with a rich
sapphire blue.'

Some of the men had never even seen snow before, and
the only thing that could distract them from staring was
Mertz, who, according to photographer Frank Hurley, stayed
up in the crow's nest, 'in high ecstasy . . . entertained us and
the denizens of the pack by warbling loud yodels.' The situation did not mean that Mawson and Davis let the crew or

shore party forget that there was still work to do, including
rotating through four-hour watches; taking care of the dogs,
several of which died after a series of fits; and repairing the
motor-launch, which had smashed bow-on into the ship at
Macquarie, springing some of its planking.

Those members of the shore party who had sailed aboard
Toroa, and therefore not observed Davis in action, now
began to understand why many of his men knew him simply
as 'Gloomy.' Although still only twenty-seven, his reserve
and intense awareness of his responsibility made him aloof
and at times almost unapproachable – even by Mawson.
'Davis says very little, this man thinks too much about how
to keep to the route, and about all his duties,' Mertz had
written on the voyage to Hobart. 'When his ship is in a
perfect state perhaps he will be different.' No one was to
find out, however, as not only did Davis never consider his
ship perfect, but at 2 p.m. on 30 December *Aurora* met the
first pack ice of the expedition, and Davis 'knew that my
responsibilities and those of my officers had begun in
earnest.'

By the morning of the last day of the year, they had
followed a course west and were skirting the northern edge
of the ice pack, seeking a lead to the south. In the next few
days they twisted and turned through the ice, but nowhere
could they find anything remotely resembling a landing place.
Then a long barrier of ice appeared in front of them, sixty
to eighty feet high. They followed it north, then west, and
finally coasted south along its western end, Davis and
Mawson both thoroughly confused by Wilkes' inaccurate
charting, which would later lead them, like Ross before, to
criticise the American's accounts.

Strong winds whipped up now, forcing Davis to stay
within the lee of the giant barrier for two days, and in that
time, with the supply of coal diminishing and the chance
of finding a location even for the Main Base – much less
two more – dwindling, Mawson made a crucial decision.

He resolved to consolidate the Main and Western parties, deciding that 'the Main Base would be increased in strength for scientific work, and the other party ... would be composed of men of specially good sledging calibre, besides being representative of the leading branches of the scientific programme.' To re-align the personnel, there was some last-minute shuffling, and then at lunchtime on 6 January, the new plan was unveiled to all. Wild would command the newly reorganised Western Base, taking with him Harrisson, medical officer Sydney Jones, magnetician Alec Kennedy, meteorologist Morton Moyes, cartographer George Dovers, and a pair of geologists, Andy Watson and Archibald Hoadley. All the others, for good or for bad, would remain with Mawson – if a place to land were ever found.

As it turned out, they did not have to wait much longer. On the morning of 8 January, they entered a broad coastal indentation that Mawson named Commonwealth Bay. Some forty to fifty miles ahead, but still visible, was an outcrop that near enough matched the location of Cap Découverte, the easternmost limit of Terre Adélie seen by Dumont d'Urville in 1840. Although Mawson adjudged that Commonwealth Bay and the region to its east had never before been seen or claimed, he immediately called the entire area 'Adelie Land.'

Mawson was becoming progressively more concerned as they sailed west. Not only were they increasing their distance from the South Magnetic Pole and possibly confounding the research related to it, but they were also making their wireless communication with Macquarie Island less certain. The problem was resolved shortly after noon, when Wild reported a rocky area some fifteen miles south. They made towards it, and near a fringe of low islets, Mawson and Wild took a whaleboat, along with Madigan, Bickerton, Kennedy, Webb, Hurley, and Bob Bage, and rowed approximately a mile to what turned out to be a tongue of rock projecting beyond the ice cap that towered high above.

'Doctor Mawson leapt ashore, the first man to put foot on Adelie Land,' wrote Hurley. 'We all wanted the honour of being second and jumped excitedly ashore in a bunch – I slipped and fell – gaining the honour of being the first man to "sit" on Adelie Land.' Mawson and Wild found the area to be 'about one mile in length and half a mile in extreme width. Behind it rose the inland ice, ascending in a regular slope and apparently free of crevasses – an outlet for our sledging parties ... To right and left of this oasis ... the ice was heavily crevassed and fell sheer to the sea in cliffs, sixty to one hundred and fifty feet in height.' There was also an appropriate place for a hut, a narrow cove that made a perfect boat harbour, and a series of fresh-water lakes. Moreover, large numbers of Adélie penguins and Weddell seals on both the mainland and what they called the Mackellar Islets – after a contributor to the expedition – promised an extra food supply, if necessary.

As soon as the party returned to *Aurora*, Mawson announced to all that they had found the site of the Main Base, or what he would call 'Winter Quarters.' Wasting no time, they filled the motor-launch and a whaleboat with mutton, eggs, other perishable items, and benzine. But before these were fully unloaded ashore, a strong wind sprang up, and by the time the party reached the ship, a gale was roaring. For the next forty-eight hours, it blew like the devil. Little did they know, but Mawson had selected as his base the windiest place on Earth, where katabatic winds dropping from the Polar Plateau average 45 miles an hour for the entire year. These winds, and the resultant drift – surface snow driven by the wind – affected virtually everything they did thereafter.

After two days the wind abated, and unloading began apace under the direction of Davis aboard ship and Wild ashore. The motor-launch was filled to capacity and, driven by either Bickerton or Gillies, the chief engineer, pulled to shore a pair of whaleboats – also full – as well as rafts of timbers for the huts or the wireless masts. In this way, five or six tons were landed on each trip. The gales came and went over the next eight days, but each time the wind calmed, unloading recommenced, with the men working eight hours on, eight hours off until stopped by the weather. Even Gloomy noted that all hands were working splendidly, with Mawson as usual leading the way.

By 18 January they had embarked 'twenty-three tons of coal briquettes, two complete living huts, a magnetic observatory, the whole of the wireless equipment, including masts, and more than two thousand packages of general supplies containing sufficient food for two years, utensils, instruments, benzine, kerosene, lubricating oils an air tractor and other sledges.' Nineteen of the twenty-nine surviving dogs were amongst the last things disembarked. The next day, after personal gear was taken ashore, there was a farewell party aboard ship, complete with speeches and toasts to Dumont d'Urville and Wilkes, who had first explored the region. Then 'Auld Lang Syne' was sung, three cheers exchanged, and the eighteen men of Mawson's party headed for shore, leaving the rest to travel west to find a place for the last base. 'I could have wept,' wrote Ninnis. 'All the second party, the ships officers, and many of the crew, were my friends, and they were leaving us and vanishing . . . into the unknown land to the west.'

Frustratingly, it took almost four weeks and more than 1,500 miles for Wild's party to find a suitable place, and even then it was not land, but ice. Day after day – through uncounted gales – Aurora continued west, Davis entering the pack to try to reach shore at every opportunity. But each time they failed, despite sailing south over where land had been charted by Dumont d'Urville and Wilkes. The coal was fast disappearing, and many men were down sick, when cliffs eighty feet high blocked their path. For sixty miles

Davis followed what appeared to be a vast glacier tongue or ice shelf, finally turning south at its termination into a never-before-seen sea thickly studded with icebergs and floes. And at the base of it, on what would be named the Shackleton Ice Shelf, Wild, in desperation, argued that his party should remain, rather than being taken back to Australia. Davis reluctantly acceded, and, after several days of unloading, Wild and the other members of the Western Base were left in that white, icy realm, where, for the next year, they would have no contact with Mawson, Davis, or any other person in the outside world.

Back at Winter Quarters – the location of which Mawson named Cape Denison in honour of an early sponsor – there was no doubt that the construction of the living facilities was of supreme importance, particularly as, until a hut went up, the men had only four tents in which to live. Therefore, the day after *Aurora* departed, 20 January, work began with a vengeance. 'As we were securely isolated from a trades hall,' Mawson wrote, 'our hours of labour ranged from 7 am to 11 pm.'

The huts for all four bases had been designed and prefabricated in Australia, and packaged so as to make reconstructing them in the Antarctic as simple as possible. But since Mawson had combined two of the shore parties, he now had two huts, and he and Alfred Hodgeman – an articled architect from Adelaide who had drawn up the original plans – had to rejig the notion of how these two huts would be organised. They decided that they would stand adjacent to each other, with the smaller in the lee of the larger. The former would serve as a workshop, engine room for the wireless plant, and vestibule to make the larger, living hut more secure from the weather.

Each hut had a pyramidal roof extending down past the walls of the main room to approximately five feet above the ground, creating a veranda outside that could in turn be walled in. This lent stability to the hut, kept it warmer, and added space away from the elements that could be used as a store-house, laboratory, or dog shelter. Because of the veranda, and Mawson's assumption that the building would be buried by snow for much of the year, the only windows were in the roof, one in each face. 'Round the outside of the three veranda walls boxes of stores were stacked, so as to continue the roof slope to the ground,' Mawson wrote. 'Thus, the wind striking the hut met no vertical face, but was partly deflected.'

The first stage of erecting the living hut was to blast foundation holes in the hard gneiss with dynamite. Three-foot wooden posts were then embedded into the holes, and fifty tons of boulders were used to fill completely the space beneath where the floor would sit. Within four days, this had been done, and the floor and outside walls for a room 24 × 24 feet with a veranda five feet wide were completed. The threat of hurricane winds prompted the men to lay steel wire cables over the roof, anchoring them in the ground.

As soon as the outer layer of the living hut was up, the foundations were laid for the 18 × 16-foot workshop, which housed the generators, petrol-motor, wireless plant, lathe, sewing machines, and another stove. Being adjacent to the living hut, it required numerous alterations by Hodgeman, particularly in the roof, and it had only two verandas, since on the north side – away from the prevailing wind – was Bage's auroral observatory.

While the workshop was raised, the living hut was made habitable: a stove installed, bunks built around the walls, Mawson's private bedroom and workspace set up, and a darkroom and library established. The stove proved exceptionally problematic, because during its assemblage several key elements were found to be missing. During the landing of supplies, one case had fallen in the water, and Mawson thought that it might contain the needed parts. Therefore, he and Charles Laseron went out in the whaleboat at low tide and located the case with a pole. However, they were unable to hook it and bring it to the surface. 'At last I went in,' wrote Mawson, 'and, standing on tip-toe, could just reach it and keep my head above water. It took some time to extricate from the kelp . . . The case turned out to be full of jam.'

On 30 January, the first day the stove was fully functional after the parts were found in another case, Mawson prepared the party's initial sit-down dinner, consisting of duck, new potatoes, peas, blancmange, nuts, and tea and coffee. Laseron, who was the messman for the day, later recalled how Mawson insisted on demonstrating the correct procedure for making blancmange.

> I looked on for a while and the Doctor explained the process, until, happening to look at a packet, I remarked: 'Why, here are the directions on the packet.'
>
> 'Oh, yes,' remarked the Doctor airily, 'those are what I am following, but what is most important is the technique of the thing.'
>
> Later, when the blancmange wouldn't set, the Doctor discovered he had just brought the stuff to the boil instead of boiling it for ten minutes, as the directions stated. Hannam came to the rescue with some cornflour and made a good job of it.

The stove was important for more than just cooking. It was also the main source of heat and was kept lit constantly, although the men were able to turn it down once the gales buried the hut up to roof level in snow, which proved an excellent insulator. At points, the snow covered the roof windows, but artificial lighting was supplied by an acetylene generator. The snow also made entering and leaving the hut complicated. The only door from the living quarters went into the workshop, from where a vestibule led to the west veranda. This not only covered a cellar where frozen meat was stored, but served as the main entrance and exit point. The men used either a door in the roof or a trap door into a tunnel dug through the snow, depending on the weather.

Within the hut itself, the different areas soon reflected their occupants, just as they had when Mawson had been a member of the BAE. For example, where the south wall, with Ninnis' bunk above that of Madigan, joined the east wall, where Mertz lived above Bickerton, the European connections caused Ninnis to dub the area 'Hyde Park Corner.' McLean's bacteriological lab table nearby was then nicknamed 'St George's Hospital.' The inside of the hut was also a home for some of Madigan's meteorological instruments. Others were placed at a met screen twenty yards east of the hut, and the wind and sunshine recorders, which had to be at a higher location, were set up 150 yards away, on Anemometer Hill.

Although under normal circumstances these were not huge distances, the hurricane-force winds meant that even leaving the hut briefly could be dangerous. One day in March, the wind was blowing 80 miles an hour when Madigan, Bickerton, and Hodgeman set out to Anemometer Hill. Hodgeman was quickly separated from the others, who continued and, after taking readings, returned to the hut, where they found he was still out. '[It] would have been the easiest thing possible for a fellow who was out in his bearings to have gone over into the sea,' wrote Ninnis. So eight men set out to find him, roping up in order not to be blown into the water themselves. But they could not locate him.

Meanwhile, Hodgeman had eventually reached Anemometer Hill, but, finding no one there, started back to the hut. He then became hopelessly lost, his prospects rendered more precarious by losing his mittens in the wind. Crawling on all fours, he suddenly came upon a rocky patch he recognised as a moraine near the hut. Guided by this, he reached safety after almost three hours.

A trek even longer than that to the meteorological instruments was made regularly by Webb – to the two buildings he and Stillwell constructed for the magnetic programme, the Absolute House and the Magnetograph House. The latter contained equipment that could be disturbed by other magnetic forces, so only copper nails were used; it was placed 400 yards north of the main hut in an area cleared with dynamite. However, it was damaged by the wind shortly after being built, so in early March thirty tons of boulders were piled around it as a protective shell.

Soon thereafter, work on the hangar for the air-tractor was begun, and efforts were made to erect the wireless masts. But the wind hampered any consistent progress on the masts, and it soon became apparent that contact with Macquarie Island would be unlikely. The weather also played havoc with the biological programme, as in mid-March the whale-boat disappeared, either driven out towards the Mackellar Islets or sunk.

In fact, nothing left outside, no matter how carefully anchored, was safe. 'Northward from the Hut there was a trail of miscellaneous objects scattered,' wrote Mawson. 'One of the losses was a heavy case . . . Weighted down by stones this had stood for a long time in what was regarded as a safe place.' This might have been the result of a 'whirly,' a violent whirlwind that could measure from a few feet to hundreds of yards in diameter. One of these picked up the 300-pound lid to the air-tractor case and tossed it fifty yards.

The greatest concerns were for the safety of the men, who could have been blown off their feet and carried great distances. The slick ice near the hut made the footing trickier, but, after experimenting on hands and knees and by wriggling like snakes, they learned never to go outside without crampons and found the best way to walk was to keep the body rigid and lean far forward, although a momentary lull would then drop one straight to the ground.

Mawson hoped that the weather would improve, but as March passed and the blizzards increased in both strength and duration, he realised that outside work would simply have to wait until the wind fell to less than 30 miles per hour. It was frustrating – and terrifying – to realise that only a month before, such winds had stopped all outside activity; now they were seen as lulls.

5

HURRICANE FORCE

'IT REALLY LOOKS,' wrote Ninnis in mid-April, 'as if there must have been a large surplus of bad weather left over after all the land had been formed at the Creation, a surplus that appears to have been dumped down in this small area of Antarctica.' He was writing in the teeth of a hurricane that was continuing a pattern of increasing wind speed and decreasing temperature each month since their arrival at Cape Denison. February had been bad enough, when the wind averaged 25 miles per hour for the entire month. But that was as nothing compared to the 49 mph average to which it suddenly increased in March. And now, in April, it was reaching more than 51 mph. So perhaps Ninnis could be forgiven for noting: 'It can't last forever.' But how wrong he was – for in the next six months the average monthly wind speed would never drop below 55 miles per hour. Truly they were in, as Mawson entitled his book, the home of the blizzard.

Nothing was more affected by the wind and the drift than the sledging programme. Mawson's plan included an early reconnaissance inland to discover and mark a safe route to the Plateau and to determine the possibilities of an extended sledging campaign. Since there were tentatively to be a dozen men in the field – two support parties of four in aid of a four-man main party that would be away for up to a month – almost anyone who wanted to engage in serious sledge work was supposed to get the chance. But after Mawson went out briefly with Mertz and Bage, the wind prevented for the time being any more attempts at going up the steep, crevassed passage of ice behind the base. With no sledging in sight and no contact with Macquarie Island because of the inability to erect the wireless masts, Mawson insisted his men stay busy with scientific work, preparing clothing and equipment for future sledge trips, or routine maintenance and duties around the hut.

However, the daily round of unceasing tasks and little time to themselves did not promote a positive mood among all the men. Mawson feared for morale, but he drove himself incessantly and did not seem in tune enough with his men to do anything different for them. But, harking back to Shackleton's decision to avoid frustration by making an ascent of Mount Erebus – while at the same time knowing that the weather made it too dangerous to leave the vicinity of the hut – Mawson determined to make 25 February a special day. First, he held the initial full Sunday service since they had been in the Antarctic, the men singing familiar hymns while Stillwell played a small organ. Then, leading everyone outside, he took possession of Adelie Land in the name of King George V. The Union Jack was run up the flagpole, the men gave three cheers, and photographs were taken. 'Simple as the ceremony was, it was impressive in its way,' Ninnis recorded. 'We have formally added our newly discovered land to the list of British possessions, and one more blot of red will be added to the map.' That night, the hut was decorated with flags, and a celebratory meal was followed by speeches.

But the weather still refused to give in, so at last Mawson decided to challenge it head-on. Late in the afternoon of 29 February, he, Bage, and Madigan braved the gusting winds and, with support from Bickerton, Hurley, and Mertz, began a slow ascent of the incline that led at a dizzying angle to the Plateau. They struggled on for a mile, and an increase of 500 feet in elevation, before anchoring the sledge and returning to the hut for the night. The next morning they collected the sledge and pushed on to a point about three and a quarter miles from base, where they planted a flag as a route marker. By 7 p.m. Mawson, Bage, and Madigan had travelled just short of five and a half miles, and had reached the brow of a rise at approximately 1,500 feet elevation. 'To the south nothing was visible but a great, wan, icy wilderness,' Mawson wrote. Turning around, he could see the sea, but not, due to the curve of the intervening ice, Winter Quarters.

They camped there on the edge of the Plateau, planning to head inland the next morning. That night Mawson awoke to find Madigan fumbling around in the tent. 'From inside my bag I called out to inquire if there was anything wrong, and received a reply that he was looking for the primus-pricker,' Mawson wrote. Madigan then returned to his sleeping bag, and all became quiet, leaving Mawson 'dimly wondering what use he could have for a primus-pricker in the middle of the night . . . In the morning . . . I found that Madigan knew nothing of his mid-night escapade.' It had been one of the first cases of sleepwalking in the Antarctic.

Looking outside the tent, the drift was so dense they could not proceed safely, so they erected another marker flag, froze the legs of a drift-proof box containing a thermograph into the ice, and anchored the sledge. They then returned to Winter Quarters, congratulating themselves on the importance of their route-finding operation, since the ice beyond their first flag was so broken and dangerous. On the way down, they observed that the wind and drift were distinctly heavier at higher elevations. There was plenty enough, however, at the base, where for five consecutive days it imprisoned them in the hut, confirming that there would be no more autumn sledging.

*   *   *

Mawson clearly was caught off guard by the fearful winds and weather, which were so different from those in McMurdo Sound and Victoria Land. They not only threatened the success of the sledging and scientific programmes, but were potentially matters of life and death. Yet, according to Laseron, Mawson knew a leader should keep such concerns to himself: 'He showed nothing of the anxiety which consumed him . . . while he was appalled at the weather conditions, he said nothing at the time, for our very inexperience caused us to accept this just as Antarctic conditions, and so the work was done in spite of it.'

However, decades later, Eric Webb remembered the situation differently. 'After his first sledge trip . . . to the site of our eventual 5-mile depot, he addressed us at dinner,' Webb wrote, indicating Mawson said, 'I have never met such conditions of wind & temperature before. You chaps know as much about it as I do so just get on with it!'

Such conflicting memories are typical of the contradictory impressions of Mawson. Some descriptions from the time portrayed him as austere, reserved, and aloof; others as annoyingly meddlesome, interfering in the kitchen or in recording scientific observations; yet others as a beloved father figure. He was undoubtedly a combination of them all. Certainly he had an area separate from the others in the hut, but this was because Shackleton had demonstrated the importance of a leader not being lodged in the main room, so the men would not feel constrained by him. And overseeing daily activities was only natural for a man who was both ultimately accountable and the only experienced Antarctic hand at Winter Quarters. Most of the men eventually realised that part of Mawson's manner was due to the responsibility he shouldered for the safety and success of the expedition. Certainly it is fair to say that Mawson generally fit in with the others. As Laseron wrote:

> though sometimes as stern as billy Oh! he is far more of a
> comrade than any of us thought he would be, and enters
> into all our jokes & sports . . . I think most of us would

follow him anywhere . . . this is because he is such a worker, for from the start he has done more than any two of us. And while we have always respected and admired him, I am sure we now like him much better than at first. This is of course all in spite of his faults of which he undoubtedly has a good many. One of his worst is a nasty sneery way he has of saying things at times, though perhaps he doesn't mean all he says and evidently forgets as soon after.

These were, of course, the kind of comments that could have been made about any of the party, as with eighteen men in a small hut, relations would invariably be strained at times. The only regularly negative impressions recorded came from Cecil Madigan – tall, athletic, intellectual, arrogant, and condescending – who saw himself as the best man on the expedition and was unable to forgive Mawson for being in command. It was Madigan who, 'in an outburst of Latin,' dubbed Mawson 'Dux Ipse' – the Leader Himself – not a friendly or generous term, and not one used to his face. Madigan also resented Mawson overseeing the work of the other scientists, when he had not taken charge of a single area of research himself.

This was, however, an issue carefully considered by Mawson. Frank Stillwell, the quiet but brilliant geologist, had been placed in a potentially difficult position. Originally scheduled for the third base, the consolidation of parties meant that he was reassigned to Winter Quarters, where his expertise coincided with that of Mawson. However, rather than turning a talented scientist into little more than an assistant, Mawson assumed the role of general helper, accompanying Stillwell on geological ventures while also taking meteorological readings, assisting biologist John Hunter in dredging, and participating in the hardest physical labour, which he relished. 'An occupation which helped to introduce variety in our life was the digging of ice-shafts,' he wrote about a task that most of the men did not think so enjoyable.

'[V]arious excavations were made in the sea-ice, in the ice of the glacier, and in that of the freshwater lakes ... Even a whole day's labour with a pick and shovel at the bottom of an ice-hole never seemed laborious.'

Such an attitude spoke much louder than words about Mawson's dedication to the scientific programme – which *he* had, after all, set up. It included the most comprehensive range of scientific studies that had ever been carried out in the Antarctic. Hunter – who, like Mawson, had attended the Fort Street Model Public School and the University of Sydney – was in charge of a broad biological agenda that included studies of marine mammals, birds, life forms dredged from both the waters of Commonwealth Bay and the local fresh-water lakes, and terrestrial biology. Day after day, he could be seen dissecting, bottling, or inspecting his specimens under the microscope. Laseron, officially the taxidermist and biological collector, had been a self-reliant youngster who worked his way through the Technical College of Sydney, earning a diploma in geology. However, his skills as a collector earned him a position on the expedition, and he worked closely with Hunter, skinning, preserving, and mounting seals, petrels, skuas, and a range of other birds. Chief medical officer Archibald McLean – fondly nicknamed 'Dad' from his habit of greeting other people with the phrase 'Hallo, Dad' – also ran bacteriological investigations, making 'St George's Hospital' the centre of examinations relating to microscopic cultures and blood samples.

Although each of these men had to conduct some research outside, several other scientists had to face the terrible weather conditions on a daily basis. Madigan was assisted by Hodgeman in compiling the meteorological data, which meant they both made regular trips to the met screens. They not infrequently returned to the hut with 'ice masks,' which developed when snow packed around one's face inside the funnel of the Burberry helmet. Changed by the warmth of the skin and breath into a covering of ice, it 'adhered

firmly to the rim of the helmet and to the beard and face'
and could cover virtually the entire opening of the helmet.
The mask had to be removed inside the hut, where one
'would first see that the ice was broken along the rim of the
helmet; otherwise when it came to be hastily dragged off,
the hairs of the beard would follow as well. As soon as the
helmet was off the head, the icicles hanging on the beard
and glazing the eyelashes were gradually thawed by the
fingers and removed.' In late May, Madigan had the unfortunate experience of an ice mask causing severe frostbite to
his face. 'Before discovering the fact,' Mawson wrote that
night, 'he endeavours to throw away part of his face, believing
it to be a piece of ice.'

Webb – who earned the nickname 'Azi' from his regular
use of the word azimuth – had to make even longer daily
trips to the Magnetograph House, frequently in the company
of Bob Bage. Every other week, Webb also made a 'quick
run,' an extended series of magnetic observations that were
taken synchronously with similar ones at Wild's Western Base,
Wilhelm Filchner's German Antarctic expedition in the region
of the Weddell Sea, and several observatories in the Southern
Hemisphere. For four hours Webb checked the readings while
an assistant recorded them. 'In a temperature of from 10°
to 20° below zero, there was no chance of movement in the
cramped space,' Laseron wrote. 'It was impossible to write
with mits on, so the hand had to be kept uncovered, and
got so stiff and cold that the pencil could hardly be held.'

On the return from one such trip with Mawson in April,
the drift was so blinding that they could not even tell they
had reached the hut, as so much snow had accumulated in
the vicinity that the top of the roof was even with the level
of the snow. 'No light from the Hut, it is difficult to tell
when one is on top of it,' Mawson wrote. 'Outside one is
in touch with the sternest of Nature – one might be a lone
soul standing in Precambrian times or on Mars.' Seeking for
the door through the roof, Mawson could continue only on

hands and knees, probing with an ice axe. '[C]annot see though clear my face of ice with mitt,' he wrote. 'At last, after probing in every direction, feel a space below and plunge in.'

Another man regularly braving such conditions was Bage, who was on leave from the Royal Australian Engineers. As well as assisting Webb, he was also in charge of the tide-gauge measurements, the chronometers, and auroral and astronomical observations. The last required building the Transit Hut thirty yards away from the living hut in order to make star sightings that would help determine Cape Denison's exact longitude.

In addition to the scientists, there were several men whom Mawson engaged for their technical expertise in specific fields, as well as to help with a variety of general duties. No one fulfilled this varied role better than Frank Hurley. Trained early on in metalworking, electrical fitting, and instrument-making, it turned out to be photography for which Hurley had both a passion and remarkable natural talent. When Mawson announced a position for an expedition photographer, Hurley, already well known commercially in Sydney, imme-diately applied, offering his services for free. Although Mawson took some convincing, Hurley finally succeeded and, once a member of the expedition, showed a willingness to take on whatever work needed doing. He also proved to be 'skilled at seeking out novel (but often dangerous) locations for his camera. It was his ability to recognise and use the pictorial potential of his surroundings which makes his work so notable.'

But seeking out such surroundings almost proved the end of him when Hurley walked to an area beneath the coastal ice cliffs at Cape Denison. 'I had just erected my camera, when, without warning, the ice gave way beneath me,' he later wrote. 'In an instant I was floundering in the sea. I threw my arms out, and saved myself from being swept beneath the ice, but the thin sheet, once fractured, would no more than barely support me, and broke every time I tried to climb out.' It was a desperate situation – and no one knew where he was. 'My muscles were contracting and my limbs growing numb,' he continued. 'Fortunately I espied a heavy piece of ice that had fallen from the cliffs and was frozen in some fifteen yards ahead. Pushing my camera along on the ice, I broke my way towards it. By good fortune I found a hand-grip, and laboriously I drew myself out.'

Thus saved from an early demise, Hurley went on to produce some of the most remarkable photographs in the history of polar exploration. His efforts were even more impressive considering that most of the cameras were large, heavy models that necessitated a tripod and used glass-plate negatives loaded into wooden plateholders, which had to be inserted into the camera individually with each use. Fiddling with plates and adjusting a camera with no focusing scale was difficult in freezing temperatures and gale-force winds, when one's hands suffered frostbite very quickly.

Although lacking Hurley's flair, the expedition's youngest member, Percy Correll, was also a highly competent photographer. A science student at the University of Adelaide, he possessed undoubted skills with engines and practical mechanics, and had given valuable assistance to Frank Bickerton with the aeroplane after its crash. Despite Correll being only nineteen at the time, Mawson hired him as the expedition's instrument-maker, a decision that proved to be a stroke of genius, as Correll showed exceptional talent repairing damaged equipment. He also kept the acetylene generator running like a charm, providing a necessary service that was widely considered the least pleasant indoor job on the base.

Correll's hiring was inspired, but that of another mechanic, Walter Hannam, proved much less so. Brought in to oversee the entire wireless operation and to serve as the Main Base operator, Hannam was considered by some the best practical engineer in the party, but he proved to be sadly overmatched by the challenges of establishing wireless communications in such a hostile environment. Beginning in April, whenever there was a calm spell all hands turned out to work on the masts – each of which consisted of three sections fixed together – and several fine days saw numerous anchorages placed and the two lower masts finally put up. Hopes soared that soon they would be in contact with Macquarie Island, but there followed only brief chances to work on the wireless set-up until late July, when two calm days allowed the topmast of the northern unit to be erected. Since the sixteen-stone Hannam could not be sent aloft, Bickerton worked three and a half hours dangling far above the others to attach it. By the next night, however, the blizzard had returned, and the second mast remained unfinished. Part of the problem was clearly the weather, but Mawson felt part was also that Hannam was not up to the task, an assessment that did not sit well with the wireless man. 'The Dr informed me that wireless was the biggest failure on the expedition,' Hannam wrote, 'which makes one laugh as he expects a thing to be put up & work without any testing out or anything.'

In comparison, the weather had not prevented Bickerton from moving ahead on his own endeavours, but it made sure they, like the wireless masts, remained unfinished. On 14 April he began repairing the air-tractor, which had been damaged during the voyage south, and in two months he finally had the engine running properly. Unfortunately, the machine's true capabilities remained unknown for the time being, as, with the wind averaging 58 mph through June, it could not be tested outside and had to wait until an easing of conditions.

Due to those same conditions, the final 'technician' was also rarely able to ply his trade. Xavier Mertz had been hired primarily as the expedition's ski expert. With the wind and drift – and the excessively steep ascent to the Plateau – Mertz instead found himself continuing his shipboard assignment of overseeing the dogs, in conjunction with Belgrave Ninnis. They had been the last two members of the expedition to be integrated into the land party, because they had spent so much time at the quarantine station outside Hobart with the dogs, while the others worked together at the dock. However, during the initial voyage to Australia they had become close friends, and, once thrown together with the rest of the men, they were quickly taken to their hearts as well. Mertz, with his impressive work ethic, splendid nature, idiosyncratic way of speaking, and amusingly shaky grasp of English, was both a role model and the target of many good-natured jokes. As his Christian name was unusual-sounding to Australians, it was soon abbreviated to 'X.' Ninnis was quickly christened 'Cherub' because 'of his complexion, which was as pink and white as that of any girl. He was tall [six feet three inches] and rather ungainly in build, and had more boxes of beautiful clothes than seemed possible for one mere man.' But he quickly fit into the laddish mentality of most of the twenty-something members of the expedition, although his cooking skills were such that more than one considered him a 'regular poisoner.'

These men were, to Mawson's way of thinking, an impressive and harmonious group, as he noted in his diary: 'amongst those here at Commonwealth Bay are a number of the very type of men who have made Great Britain what she is . . . and will, I venture to think, make Heaven out of Hell.' Unfortunately, as far as Mawson was concerned, there were three others at Winter Quarters who did not fit this assessment.

One of the first things Mawson did after the hut was made habitable was to set out routine duties and establish a rota for shared tasks. Every eighteen days each man served as cook, messman, and nightwatchman. They also were given individual duties, reflecting, for the scientists or technical people, their areas of specialisation. The men without such expertise were given other jobs – Ninnis shared responsibility for the dogs, Herbert Dyce Murphy was in charge of stores, Dr Leslie Whetter, the second surgeon, was to keep the hut supplied with ice, and John Close was to clear the snow from the veranda entrance and empty the rubbish box into the sea.

Regardless of the other duties, those of the cook, messman, and nightwatchman were inviolate. The cook's job commenced at 7 a.m. and continued until washing up was completed that night. In that period, he made breakfast for 8 a.m., lunch for 1 p.m., and dinner for 6.30 p.m., while keeping the stove filled to a point where the hut would stay above freezing but not exceed 45°F (7°C). He had great freedom in producing meals except that he had to follow a schedule for the main course at dinner – known as the 'pièce de résistance' – of penguin on Mondays and Thursdays, seal on Tuesdays and Fridays, canned meats on Wednesdays, mutton on Sundays, and a cook's selection on Saturdays.

There was, needless to say, a great difference in the interests and talents of the cooks. 'Hurley . . . always went in for very elaborate menus,' Laseron wrote. 'His fault was that he would at times sacrifice tastiness for effect, deliberately making pastry tough, so that it would stand up in the form of a ship or some grotesque shape. Hannam, Hurley, Hunter and I early formed "The Secret Society of Unconventional Cooks," classing the others under the plebeian stigma of "Crook Cooks."' According to Hurley, Crook Cooks accepted Mrs Beeton as the unchallenged culinary authority and passed the responsibility of selecting the menu to Murphy, who simply used the ingredients most easily fetched. Murphy did not face too much of a test initially, but after the penguins disappeared near the end of March, he could no longer select fresh or lightly frozen meat and had to use a hammer and chisel to break off parts of birds stored long before.

The grandmaster of the Crook Cooks was Ninnis, who produced what was universally accepted as the worst lunch of the expedition, a salmon kedgeree. Mrs Beeton's recipe read: 'Take one tin of salmon, 2 oz of butter, 2 oz of flour,

pepper and salt to taste.' Thinking that he had to produce
four times the amount, Ninnis used four tins of salmon, and
eight ounces of butter and flour, but instead of cayenne
pepper and salt to taste, he read it as use eight ounces of
those as well. The dish came out nicely browned from the
oven, but was, according to Ninnis, 'so hot that tears and
perspiration stream from the fellows as they seize pounds
of butter with which to anoint their scorching mouths.'

After the gasps, Ninnis' effort received enthusiastic yells
of 'championship!' – a term applied 'to a slight mishap, care-
less accident or unintentional disaster in any department of
Hut life. The fall of a dozen plates from the shelf … the
burning of the porridge or the explosion of a tin thawing
in the oven brought … a storm of derisive applause and
shouts of "Championship!" '

The day after being cook, one served as messman, with
responsibility for laying the table, warming the plates,
sweeping out the hut twice, filling the melter with ice, getting
the coal, taking the refuse to disposal sites, and washing the
table, dishes, and utensils after each meal. With eighteen
men in the hut, this was no easy task, and occasionally led
to significant errors, as Ninnis found when he had 'the
misfortune to put into the melting pot two ice specimens of
Mawson's.'

Around the time the evening clean-up was completed, the
nightwatchman came on duty. His primary chores were to
make that night's meteorological and auroral observations,
keep the temperature of the hut above freezing, and ensure
that the melting pots of water were kept full. This brought
with it the only chance to use the hot water to wash clothes
and take a bath, but even inside the hut it was cold enough
to make bathing unpleasant, and some men occasionally
rejected the opportunity – every eighteen days – to bathe.

Although everyone tended to carry out these duties with
at least a modicum of efficiency, there were, in Mawson's
opinion, men who did not adequately perform the tasks they

were allocated individually. Chief amongst these was
Whetter, who, according to Madigan, was assigned to collect
the ice because he was of little use for anything else. He had
been accepted onto the expedition only because Mawson
had been desperate for a surgeon for the third base, and,
despite being a large, strong man, he had proven chronically
lazy, even telling Mawson that he had come south to study
for exams and not to work hard. The situation erupted
publicly on 4 June when, at breakfast, Whetter demanded
to know when 'the winter routine' would come into force.
Mawson asked what he meant, and Whetter responded that
Mawson had promised they would only work half a day
and have the rest on their own. 'This is rot,' Mawson wrote
hotly that night. 'He has never had more than two hours
per day.'

The situation went steadily downhill from there. 'He sleeps
all day today though stating that he would get up and get
ice this afternoon,' Mawson wrote amongst a litany of
complaints. 'Whetter is not fit for a polar expedition ... Of
late he has complained of overwork, and he only does an
honest 2 hours per day.' The next week brought more conflict
when Mawson told Whetter to relieve Close outside. Several
hours later, he found Whetter reading in bed. 'I showed him
that he was entirely unfit for an expedition, chiefly through
lack of determination in character and failing to do his level
best,' Mawson wrote. 'As usual he attempted to make light
of all the charges and seemed inclined to think my opinion
of little value.'

Whetter was not Mawson's only nemesis, however. He
was exasperated by both Murphy and Close, at thirty-two
and forty, respectively, the oldest men on the base. Murphy's
claims of extensive appropriate experience had initially
impressed Mawson, but once down south Murphy evinced
no strengths or talents other than being a remarkable story-
teller who provided immeasurable light relief for the others.
But Madigan expressed the belief that Murphy was hopelessly

impractical and unfit even to be in charge of stores, and
Mawson ultimately agreed. 'Murphy's work appears to be
the most arduous,' Mawson wrote sarcastically, 'for his
utmost efforts in getting in the stores for the day succeed
only a few minutes before they are required.' He was no
more impressed by his performance in the kitchen: 'Murphy
is an outrageous cook – boils the French beans with water
and butter, then pours off the liquid through colander.'

Yet even Murphy was not as maddening as Close, who
day after day proved incompetent, fussy, or in a state of
panic. 'Once again "D.I." [Dux Ipse] showed Close the
method of light kneading of the self-raising flour, and again,
as always, old Close punched and pummelled the offending
dough as if he had been at a boxing match,' Ninnis wrote.
'At length Mawson lost all patience and exclaimed "You'll
never learn, Close". "But Doctor," said J.C. "I do not properly comprehend the manner of manipulation", interlacing
his speech with the usual lengthy words.'

But whereas Mawson found him bothersome, the others
simply made him the main butt of their jokes. 'Close is
watchman tonight, and we have fixed up an apparatus, the
simple tube with its end under water, leading from Hurley's
bunk to a billy can of water on top of the acetylene generator
which will, when blown through, cause a bubbling as if the
generator was about to explode,' wrote Ninnis. As expected,
the trick gave Close 'blue fits,' and Ninnis reported: 'The
acetylene gas trick last night was highly successful, Hurley
bubbling at intervals, and Close calling Correll twice, being
in fear of an imminent explosion, and announcing it as his
opinion that, after that night, Mawson ought to abandon
acetylene lighting and stick to hurricane lamps!'

Such pranks helped bring most of the men closer to each
other, which would prove beneficial when sledging started.
Even Close could not bear grudges against the instigator,
Hurley, who was, he wrote, 'The life and soul of our party,
he exhaled humour at every pore, possessing a large fund

of inoffensive wit, and a weakness for practical joking from which no one of us, his seventeen comrades, wholly succeeded in escaping.'

Hurley's masterminding such mischief also kept up spirits and made the long, dark winter more bearable in what Mawson called an 'accursed country.' The drift became so heavy that a man could not see his feet. And the wind continued to get even worse. On 15 May it averaged more than 90 miles per hour for the entire day. Within several weeks, the puffometer showed gusts of 200 mph. And this came *after* Mawson noted, 'The vista is a chaos and I am quite sure that anybody who has been out in it for a few minutes would gladly exchange for hell.'

And so they finally reached Midwinter Day. The hut was only just able to be kept above freezing, five inches of ice covered the ceiling windows and several inches more were under the bunks, and the dogs froze to the icy ground by their fur and could not move until pulled up by the men. But it marked the beginning of longer days – and the promise of a sledging season to come.

6

Start the Sledging

By midwinter, the inhabitants of Cape Denison had already started preparing for sledging. Considering that any flaw in preparation might cost lives, they were extremely particular with their clothing, tents, sledges, and rations. Nothing was more important than one's harness for hauling sledges, an implement that would determine survival in a fall down a crevasse and that therefore needed the ultimate care in production. Mawson recommended a triple thickness of canvas encircling the hips, sewn to narrower braces that passed over the shoulders. 'Any one who was not a practiced needleman and machinist was handicapped,' he noted, 'until he fell into the ways of the through-and-through and blanket-stitch, thimbles, shuttles, spools and many other things he had once affected to despise as . . . women's work.'

Each man was also in charge of making any purely personal alterations to his clothing. Everyone had received a collection of sledging clothes, including two sets of Burberry outerwear, each with trousers, but one in which the helmet and blouse were in one piece and the other in which they were detached. Underneath these they would wear thick suits of Jaeger fleece, including singlets, shirts, underpants, sweaters, pyjamas, stockings, and socks. They also were issued a variety of other clothing components, such as finnesko, ski boots, crampons, gloves, and three kinds of mittens: felt, lambskin, and wolf-skin.

The weather at Winter Quarters quickly exposed any gaps in the clothes through which snow or wind could creep, and this allowed the men to address such problems long before serious travelling started. The lanky Ninnis, for example, sewed a length of canvas onto the top of his boots, so that his Burberry trousers could not work their way off them. Whetter was known as the 'Toggle King' because of his continuing efforts to connect his trousers and blouse with small stick-and-cord fastenings so that the blouse would not slip up during man-hauling. And Murphy made unique alterations to his boots, causing Mawson to note with some exasperation, 'Murphy was engaged spoiling his boots today in the belief that he was mending them.' Despite many efforts, no one came up with a successful way to protect the face, which remained uncovered inside the Burberry helmet, the front of which formed a funnel stiffened by rings of wire.

The men were not the only ones who received individual tailoring. Ninnis and Mertz measured the adult dogs and sewed harnesses for each. They then put the animals into teams affixed to sledges, studied the movements of each, and made final alterations as carefully as they did for themselves.

As well as clothes and sledging equipment, the party worked together to produce forty-eight weeks' worth of field rations. These were based on lessons Mawson had learned on Shackleton's expedition and his subsequent studies of dietary requirements, and he set the daily sledging ration at slightly over thirty-four ounces per man per day, almost exactly the same as used by Shackleton and by Wild at the Western Base. The main components of the daily allowance were pemmican – a concentrated mixture of dried meat and lard – and Plasmon biscuits, made of seventy percent wholemeal flour and thirty percent Plasmon powder, a trade-name for a protein in milk. These would be mixed with water and boiled to form 'hoosh,' which, depending on preference, was either stodgy and similar to porridge or thin, like soup. The other parts of the daily package were Glaxo – a dried milk with high butterfat – sugar, butter, Plasmon chocolate, cocoa, and tea.

To produce these items required many weary hours. Two men worked on the Plasmon biscuits simultaneously, one smashing them into crumbs with a hammer and then feeding them into a grinding machine, while the other turned the machine's handle continuously, converting the crumbs into powder. Countless tins of Bovril pemmican were opened, chopped up, and remixed because the fat had separated out. These components then went to men spread along the eighteen-foot dining table. Some mixed cocoa, Glaxo, and sugar together into one compound, and others mixed the pemmican and biscuit together. These were then weighed – as were the other food items – and repacked in small calico bags that contained the ration of a specific item for three men for one week. Although most of these bags were produced during the winter, some had been sewn earlier by Mawson's fiancée and her mother – each in a bright colour matching those established for the different bases – and were therefore known as 'Paquita bags.' One of these small bags would play a greater role in the expedition than Mawson or Paquita could ever have imagined.

On 31 July, long before the sun was in regular evidence in the sky, Ninnis, Mertz, and the dogs braved winds of 70 miles per hour to haul loads of provisions part way up the ferocious rise that served as a backdrop to Winter Quarters. About two-thirds of a mile behind the hut and 370 feet up was a cavern known as the Magnetic Cave or Azimuth's Cave. This had been excavated into the ice far away from any metal, so that Webb could make comparisons with the magnetic observations taken at the Magnetograph House and the Absolute House, but now it was to serve as the first stage in moving provisions and equipment onto the Plateau.

The next preparatory step was to take provisions to the depot where the sledge had been cached the previous March. As this was located at a point where the steepest grades had been passed, it was a logical springboard for sorties onto the Plateau. On 9 August, Mawson, Ninnis, and Madigan packed a sledge at the Magnetic Cave and, with the help of eight dogs, struggled up the icy slope to the three-mile flag. The next day, they pushed on against a wind so heavy that they were exhausted at the end of only a hundred yards. Nevertheless, by late afternoon they had reached the five-and-a-half-mile depot, finding the sledge, equipment, and supplies still there, including part of a plum pudding, which did not survive their dinner.

Since prevailing winds made the area difficult to camp in, Mawson decided to excavate a cave in the ice to save wear and tear on the tents, allow for secure storage, and provide a permanently safe haven. They dug a deep vertical trench and at the base of it a room large enough for the three of them. 'We call it Aladdin's Cave – a truly magical cave for in it perfect peace whilst outside a roaring blizzard, even the sound deadened,' Mawson wrote. Named for a fairy grotto in the book *Lady Betty Across the Water* – which was popular with the expedition members – according to Mawson it equalled the crystal-like feeling of its fictional namesake: 'The walls sparkle like diamonds as our breaths freeze on them and cause them to scintillate.' It also had practical aspects, as ice for water could be hacked from the walls, equipment placed in niches located wherever convenient, slops emptied down a crevasse connected to the cave, and clothes hung up by licking them and pressing them to the wall.

The next day, they pushed slowly into a ferocious wind, while ascending farther onto the Plateau. At a little more than eight miles from the hut and 1,800 feet above sea level, they finally stopped, as dark clouds threatened a heavy snow that might trap them. Overriding Madigan and Ninnis, who wanted to continue, Mawson ordered a retreat after they cached a pick, shovel, and a large amount of biscuit and dog food. They were lucky to find Aladdin's Cave in the fading light, and the next day increasing wind and drift forced them to remain there.

On 15 August, with Ninnis and Madigan both now anxious to reach Winter Quarters, Mawson acceded to their wishes and, despite a blinding drift, they started back. After half a mile they realised that the dogs – which they had not put in harness due to the conditions – had not followed, as they had assumed they would. They discussed returning, but the wind and drift made it unlikely they would find the cave, and they would need to pull the sledge uphill against the terrible wind. As 'there was plenty of food in the bags which they [the dogs] could get at, Mawson thought that they would be all right,' wrote Ninnis. So they continued their descent, arriving at the hut in time for lunch.

Early the next morning Mertz, Bage, and Hurley set out with five more dogs to collect those left behind. But the wind reached 80 miles per hour, and gusted up to 140. 'We slowly moved forward one metre after another,' wrote Mertz. 'For a while, on the steepest icy slope uphill, the dogs, the sledge and us, moved backwards . . . My comrades often walked on all fours . . . A particularly strong gust knocked down the five dogs . . . Two hours later we arrived at Azi's cavern, at a distance of about one kilometre from the hut.' Hurley and Bage had both received particularly nasty frostbites, so, with good sense overcoming their misgivings, they returned to the hut.

The weather was even worse the next four days, so they all remained in the hut, although Mertz anxiously wrote that 'If it depended only on me, we would be in our sleeping bags outside in the snow, and we would at least try to find the dogs. Mawson is definitely too cautious, and I wonder if he would show enough gumption during the sledging expedition.'

Finally, on 21 August, with the wind having dropped to 'only' 61 miles per hour, Mertz, Bage, and Hurley forced a path to Aladdin's Cave. It was a heartbreaking sight: six of the dogs were frozen by their fur to the ice and unable to stand up, and they were all extremely weak, having not eaten for a week, as they had not broken open the food supplies. 'I fed them with pemmican, and to some dogs I gave the food directly in the mouth,' wrote Mertz. 'One could see the weakness ... in their eyes which seemed to ask us why we had come so late.' A dog named Grandmother died that afternoon, and the men felt they had to wait for the others to recover. Before they could return, however, another blizzard trapped them for three days, which they spent enlarging the cave for future occupants – some would desperately need it.

It was one of the strangest sensations of the entire expedition. Through its first thirty days, August had equalled May as the windiest month, with an average of 61 miles per hour. But the final day dawned clear and calm, and that lasted into another day, and then another. In all, it was a tranquil period of almost five days, 'with the sun shining brightly,' according to Laseron, 'and the temperature steadily rising until it attained no less than 18°F [-8°C] ... Not a soul remained in the hut ... Burberries were dispensed with, mittens were no longer necessary, and balaclavas were rolled up to leave the ears bare.'

One of the first items of attention was the wireless. Earlier in August the south wireless mast had finally been erected, and on that last glorious day of the month, the aerial was raised between the two masts. Soon thereafter, Hannam started transmitting messages, but, much to the company's chagrin, nothing came back from Macquarie Island. Hannam argued for yet higher masts, but Mawson had begun to believe that Hannam simply was not up to it. In fact, although they did not know it, the messages *were* getting through. Arthur Sawyer on Macquarie heard Hannam tapping out: 'Having a hell of a time waiting for calm weather to put up more masts.' Sawyer immediately responded, but it soon became obvious that Cape Denison could not receive anything.

Meanwhile, other work continued at a frenzied pace. Each day different parties hauled food and supplies to the Magnetic Cave or from there to Aladdin's Cave, in the process caching more than half a ton on the Plateau. Stillwell made a topographical survey of Cape Denison, Bage worked on his astronomical observatory, Bickerton fitted runners onto the air-tractor, and Hurley photographed near and far. Several times Mawson, Hunter, and Hurley trekked out on the sea ice for dredging, with each of them breaking through at points. Perhaps the fine conditions encouraged carelessness, because late on 4 September, Madigan, Bickerton, and Correll went the farthest yet out on the sea ice. Then, within an instant, whirlies poured down the slopes, followed immediately by a full-fledged blizzard. The three men turned and dashed back. 'It was literally a race with death,' wrote Laseron.

> Nearer and nearer they came, and harder and harder blew the wind . . . cracks were already beginning to open in the floe, and it seemed as if they would never make that last hundred yards . . . Now they were fifty yards away, now twenty, then willing hands reached out to pull the cart across the fast-opening gap between the sea ice and the shore . . . Within a few minutes . . . not a vestige of ice was in sight.

The period of fine weather was over, but the proof that such spells existed fired Mawson with renewed hopes for an extended sledging season. He decided that at the first opportunity three parties would go out, both to break in the men to long-distance man-hauling and to determine if the weather at Cape Denison was more than a local phenomenon.

On 7 September, despite facing a wind of 56 mph, Webb, McLean, and Stillwell set out for Aladdin's Cave. After being held there for a day by even stronger winds, they proceeded to where Mawson had left the pick, shovel, and supplies, only to be forced to wait until the drift cleared to find the cache. With the items secured, they continued due south, but winds increasing into the eighties forced a stop a little less than twelve miles from base. Unable to move, and concerned that the tent might be destroyed by the heavy gusts, they dug a sloping tunnel down to the edge of a narrow crevasse, and, while forced to stay there for three days by the gales, expanded it into a cave that they named Cathedral Grotto. There seemed little hope of going farther south, so they cached two weeks' provisions and kerosene behind a wind break and returned to Winter Quarters.

Ninnis, Mertz, and Murphy had an even rougher time after leaving on 11 September. Heading southeast from Aladdin's Cave, the wind measured in the seventies, so strong that it 'often pushed Murphy backwards against me,' wrote Mertz. 'Many times he hung in the man-harness like a gallows, with his back in the snow, and his hands and legs up in the air.' After three days they were only twelve and a half miles beyond Aladdin's Cave, but being in a place no human being had ever stood so inspired Mertz that he 'yodelled with joy, and danced on the smooth snow.' The next morning, a gale roared at 90 miles an hour and the temperature plummeted to −30°F (−34°C). Holes were torn in the tent, part of the primus blew away, and they could do nothing but stay in their sleeping bags, crampons and ice axes at the ready in case the tent blew away. When the gale finally broke, they raced back towards Winter Quarters, where everyone else was virtually brought to tears of laughter by how Murphy's already legendary ability to spin tales turned a horrifying experience into a diverting yarn of 'Three men in a bag,' with him squashed in the middle.

There was nothing funny about the third party's experiences. Madigan, Whetter, and Close left on 12 September, and once at the Plateau travelled west across numerous crevasses and large sastrugi. The winds reached the seventies and the temperature dropped to $-35\,°F$ ($-37\,°C$), causing Close's hands to be so severely frostbitten that Madigan had to toggle and tie his clothes for him. After a week they reached the limit they were allowed to travel – fifty miles – and depoted food and kerosene. On their return, the heaviest gusts of the journey struck, ripping the poles away and splitting the tent right up one side, forcing them to repair it temporarily with Alpine rope and then to dash back to base just in time.

The three journeys proved to Mawson that conditions were not yet conducive to major sledging trips. They also showed that the tents, amongst other gear, still needed much improvement before they could successfully face the elements. 'Tents similar to those used with such success by British expeditions in the Ross Sea area were found quite impossible,' he later wrote. 'Even when greatly strengthened their life proved very short. Three reconnaissance parties . . . had their tents torn to ribbons and were fortunate in reaching the hut without serious accident.'

The men who had experienced the conditions came back with even firmer views. 'I was talking, in confidence to Madigan this evening, re, our two sledging experiences, and he says that he never had such a fortnight of absolute Hell, and has had pretty nearly a bellyful of sledging,' wrote Ninnis. 'Now, although I have . . . felt rather ashamed to acknowledge it even to myself, I have had the same feeling. Sledging in calm weather must be lovely, but sledging in a 60 to 80 mile gale in your teeth, with a temperature between $-15\,°$ and $-30\,°F$, with the tent never safe, and an ever-present uncertainty as to what will happen to it next, is utter Hell.'

*   *   *

As it turned out, none of the men had to worry about sledging again too soon. October proved to be the seventh successive month in which the wind speed averaged more than 50 miles per hour (56.9), and there was no period during it that remained stable long enough to convince Mawson that serious operations could begin. In fact, to Mawson it was probably more memorable for a variety of frustrations than for anything else.

These started at the beginning of the month, when the spectre of Whetter again surfaced. Mawson already had a list of Whetter's transgressions, including indolence, secret drinking, refusal to follow orders, and disregard for his duties. But the situation reached a head on 3 October when, after Mawson directed him to dig out the front of the hangar, Whetter showed up in the hut, planning to read. 'I was very wroth about this and asked him why he was coming in under the circumstances,' wrote Mawson. 'He said he had done enough. I asked him what had he come on the expedition for. He said "not to do such kind of work." I said he was a "bloody fool to come on the expedition if that was the case." He said "Bloody fool yourself" and "I won't be caught on another one." ' Finally realising that such a confrontation should not occur in public, Mawson took Whetter to his room, but the change of venue did not change either's position. 'He stated that I found work for anyone who did not appear to be busy,' Mawson continued, 'consequently he and certain others had been in the habit all the winter of drawing out their work so that they would not get additional . . . I pointed out that I had been fully aware that 3 of the men had done so and . . . despised them for it . . . Laseron of late has been doing [Whetter's work] . . . and he has always accomplished it in one hour.'

The conversation did not have a great impact on Whetter, but it did influence Mawson, who that night, perhaps realising the surgeon's comments were indicative of a wider dissatisfaction, revealed a new work regime, in which after 'a fair day's work done in 6 hours,' the men could halt at 4 p.m. except for set duties. He also announced that they would have Sundays off other than when major outside work could be accomplished.

Four days later was one of the few times such work was possible, as the wind dropped to a mere 40 miles per hour. The men jumped to complete scientific jobs, move provisions, and work on the wireless masts. Bickerton spent five hours ninety feet up, protected only by a rope around his chest, fixing a new top section to the northern mast, which was thereby increased to 115 feet. It could have proved at great cost, however, as at one point he dropped a hammer, which fortunately fell harmlessly in the middle of a number of men.

Less than a week after that – on a day called 'Black Sunday' by Hannam – those efforts proved for nought. During dinner there was a rending sound audible over the shriek of the blizzard. Terrified that part of the roof had been damaged, Hodgeman went outside and discovered that the northern mast had collapsed, the higher pieces having split into fragments. The cause of the collapse soon became apparent: the puffometer had registered gusts of 202 miles per hour before being damaged itself. But Mawson was certain that the wind had actually been considerably stronger after that, and he projected that the gusts had reached *at least* 250 miles per hour.

For most of the next two weeks the blizzard continued, and finally everyone realised that if the sledging journeys were to occur at all, they needed to go ahead regardless of conditions. Since Davis and *Aurora* were expected on 15 January, all parties had to return by then, so the sledging season would already be considerably shorter than Mawson had originally planned. Therefore, 'Mawson says no matter what the weather,' Ninnis wrote, 'the main parties start . . . and let the winds of Hell do their worst.' Throughout the second half of the month, speculation about the make-up of

those parties was rife. On 27 October, the rumours finally
ended when Mawson outlined the programme, which was
scheduled to begin in just ten days, with *seven* sledging
parties.

It had been only the previous week that a decision had
finally been taken by Mawson that helped make all of the
pieces fall into place. He had originally planned for Webb
– described as the most energetic man on the expedition but
also the least popular, since he was self-centred, domineering,
and unbearably superior – to be the leader of the Magnetic
Pole party, but as he came to know the New Zealander
better, Mawson had vacillated about whether such a decision
was the correct one. Then, towards the end of the month,
annoyed by Mawson's insistence that he calibrate the second
'dip circle,' Webb exploded at the leader. 'He states that
Madigan is weak in his astronomical work,' Mawson wrote,
continuing:

> I find that he is disappointed with the Expedition. Thought
> everybody was a greater specialist in their line than they are.
> He thinks he is practically the only one on the Expedition
> who is properly fit. He says he has never seen me observe
> with a theodolite and doubts my accuracy. States that there
> was nobody on Shackleton's expedition capable of instru-
> ment work . . . I size him up again and, in conjunction with
> roundabout information from others with him on late
> sledging journey, decide that he had better go second on
> the inland party.

There was no question that Webb *had* to be a member of
what Mawson called the Southern Party, but he so evidently
lacked the necessary leadership skills that Bage was put in
command. It was a wise decision, even according to Webb:
'After trying me out on a preliminary spring journey, Mawson
decided (quite unknown to me) that I was not sufficiently
mature to lead the magnetic polar party . . . Events showed

how right he was.' It also allowed Mawson to finalise the membership of the other parties, now that Bage, whom he had planned on leading a party all along, was accounted for.

Mawson still considered the Southern Party the key scientific one, and Bage, Webb, and Hurley were ordered to head directly towards the South Magnetic Pole, making a series of magnetic measurements along the way. Realising that their delayed departure meant they would be unlikely to reach the Pole itself, Mawson assigned a support party of Murphy, Laseron, and Hunter to help speed them along.

The majority of the other journeys were to head east, as the voyage to Adelie Land had shown inadequacies in Wilkes' mapping, and Mawson hoped that the coastlines to the west had been charted from *Aurora*. An East Coast Party of Madigan, McLean, and Correll would explore the coast east of the giant glacier tongue they had sheltered off the previous January. Meanwhile, a Near Eastern Party of Stillwell, Hodgeman, and Close would first serve as a support team for the East Coast Party and then turn off to map and make a geological examination of the area between that glacier tongue and Winter Quarters. They would then return to base, after which Stillwell would lead Close and Laseron (the latter of whom would have returned from the Southern Support Party) to the same region for a detailed reconnaissance and mapping of the coast.

The last group to depart – Bickerton, Hodgeman, and Whetter – would not leave until December, so that hopefully the air-tractor might face lesser winds and drift. The three would travel west on the Plateau, and, since no significant performance tests had been made on the machine, if it failed, they were to proceed by man-hauling.

Finally, making the longest journey of all was the Far Eastern Party, consisting of Mawson, Ninnis, Mertz, and the dogs. Racing over the Plateau, they hoped to travel some 350 miles, in the process reaching Oates Land, where mountains had been reported from *Terra Nova* in 1911. This trip would thereby link the AAE's discoveries with those of Scott's expedition, and would therefore hold the most glamour of any of the journeys; at the same time, it was potentially the most dangerous.

7

A FAR EASTERN TRAGEDY

Mawson's plan dictated that several sledging parties leave on 6 November and that more go the following day, so with 5 November seemingly the last chance for everyone to be together, a special farewell celebration was held. As usual, however, the weather had the final say, and a blizzard kept the entire expedition indoors for two days. It was not until the 8th that the East Coast Party and the two support parties finally left.

The Far Eastern Party was scheduled to depart after the others, because the dogs would quickly catch up with those man-hauling towards the east, and Mawson wanted to travel for a while with Madigan's and Stillwell's groups. But his exit from base was also weather-delayed, giving him time for extra reflection. 'I am writing this note in case anything may happen which will prevent me reaching you as soon as the mail from here, which is expected to be picked up next January,' he wrote to Paquita on the night of 9 November. 'So many things may intervene for truly one lives but day to day here and then our sledging journey is about to commence.'

Expressing such reservations was commonplace amongst men leaving on long sledging journeys, and Ninnis followed suit. 'I must close my writing now, maybe for two months, maybe for good and all,' he wrote, 'for who knows what may happen during the next two months.' For Ninnis it was just one of numerous times that he had expressed concerns about his future. Even when he was still in London, he had been plagued by apprehensions about personal disaster. 'During this expedition, when sledging, any accident may take place,' he had confided to his diary the day after first meeting Mawson. 'I might go over a crevasse and be badly smashed up, absolutely out of reach of help . . . in my humble opinion, the same course [suicide] would be right . . . Taking all these chances into consideration, I intend to take a small packet of cyanide of potassium tablets, to use in such an emergency.'

Mawson divulged no such fears, although the next morning he did hedge his bets in his letter to Paquita. 'The weather is fine this morning though the wind still blows,' he wrote, 'we shall get away in an hours time. I have two good companions Dr Mertz and Lieut Ninnis. It is unlikely that any harm will happen to us but should I not return to you in Australia please know that I truly loved you . . . I must be closing now as the others are waiting.'

In fact, most of the others still at Winter Quarters were being treated to penguin-egg omelettes for lunch, one of Mertz's specialties. They were not the only ones 'priming' themselves for a long journey; like the men, the dogs seemed to be building up their reserves. Not long before, Ninnis had noted:

At the evening feed, old 'Basilisk' [the lead dog] was jolly funny. I had given him a large piece of meat, but when I looked round a few minutes later, no sign of the meat and he was croaking piteously as if hungry, so I went back, but, suspecting cunning, dug among the snow by him. He at once took on a most woebegone air, and almost at once I unearthed the greater portion of his feed, which I returned to him, much to his disgust. He hoped to get some more.

Now, the dogs were definitely ready, and after lunch they high-stepped their way out of camp. Indeed, moments before, when Hurley set up the cinematograph to film them, they were attached to a sledge not fully loaded, and such was their uncontrollable energy that they bolted forward so suddenly that the sledge-meter – a bicycle wheel that ran along the ground to measure the distance travelled – was damaged.

Mawson's party was at last on its way, and with seventeen excited dogs pulling two sledges, they reached Aladdin's Cave by mid-afternoon. There, Mawson, Mertz, and Ninnis reorganised their loads. On the way up the steep, hard-pitted glacier ice, they had carried a third sledge on the second in order to save its runners for future use. Taking additional supplies from those at Aladdin's Cave, they distributed the weight, which totalled 1,723 pounds. Approximately half the total was placed on two sledges that would be pulled in tandem by the first team, while the third sledge, with the other half of the weight, was hauled by the second team.

The Far Eastern Party's principal sledge was organised similarly to those of the man-hauling groups. It had a bamboo mast and spar, immediately in front of which was a cooker box made of three-ply Venesta board, using a hinged lid and containing the primus stove, a bottle of spirit for priming it, a funnel for pouring kerosene, a repair outfit, and a variety of related articles. The Nansen cooker – designed originally by the Norwegian Fridtjof Nansen and subsequently adopted on all polar expeditions – was secured on top of the cooker box. A similarly constructed box was located near the rear of the sledge and contained navigating instruments, a hypsometer, a set of thermometers, binoculars, photographic gear, and a medical kit. Next to this, at the far back of the sledge to prevent leakage into any food, was a tray upon which were secured one-gallon, screw-topped tins of kerosene. Behind all else was a shaft running to the sledge-meter. In the middle of the sledge was an assortment of other necessary items, such as tent, sleeping bags, extra clothing and footwear, rope, theodolite legs, rifle, pick, three spades, a pair of skis, crampons, and food tanks. These last were large, squat waterproof bags with a square base the width of the sledge, which held sledging rations. At this stage, the other two sledges carried mostly food tanks, fuel, and approximately 700 pounds of dog food. This consisted of seal meat, blubber, and pemmican that had been dried over the stove to remove excess water.

When Mawson left Aladdin's Cave, he intended to rendezvous with the parties under Madigan and Stillwell some eighteen and a half miles to the southeast. However, his group had gone only about half the distance when the wind picked up and a heavy snow commenced. As it was impossible to locate either the other parties or the depot for which they were heading, they pitched their tent to wait.

In those conditions, raising the tent was not easy, and the operation took all three men. The tent was conical, with a flap that spread outwards on the ground so that ice blocks could be placed on it to keep it from blowing away, and with a short, tunnel-like entrance that could be gathered and securely tied on the inside. It had been designed so that the five bamboo poles would be erected in tepee-like fashion and then the heavy drill fabric lifted over the top. However, the gales of Adelie Land made this impossible, so the poles were affixed to the inside of the tent, hinged into a metal top-piece. When pitching it, the first step was to cut ice blocks. Then the tent was laid down with its top into the wind. One man crawled inside and, according to Laseron, 'spread the three windward legs, one directly upward, the others far enough apart to keep the material taut, and at the same time give sufficient room for the leeward legs to fall into position.' The other two held on for dear life while the inside man adjusted the final two legs. 'If the legs were too close, not only did the material flap annoyingly, but it was likely to be torn, and the space inside also became uncomfortably restricted.' Finally, the ice blocks were placed on the outside flap, and the canvas floor was laid down.

And that 'palace of the snows' is where Mawson and his companions remained for most of the next five days, although for one brief period the wind dropped, the sun broke through the clouds, and they moved as near to the depot as they could, to a place, according to Mertz, that 'seems to have been forgotten by God.' Then they again waited, the only extended departures from the tent being to feed the dogs, which seemed quite content being buried by drift and remaining under it except for their noses. 'Other animals, including wolves, would hardly bear such condition,' Mertz wrote. 'Our Eskimo dogs are always happy. They jump around when I give them food. They look like snowballs with the ice and the snow lumps which hang on their fur.' But their behaviour did not always endear them to the explorers. One night Pavlova – named by Ninnis after a famed Russian dancer who had visited *Aurora* in London – became the first of several pregnant bitches to give birth. She and the other adults quickly ate the pups.

Finally, on 16 November, the weather cleared and the other parties, which had also been kept in their tents, joined them. Madigan's threesome had proven much stronger than Stillwell's group, and frequently one of them had gone back to help the support party. That night the three parties camped together for the final time, and Correll was able to repair the damaged sledge-meter. Acting as if they were back in Hyde Park Corner, Mertz and Ninnis visited Madigan's tent, Mertz as always raising his colleagues' spirits by singing an old favourite German student song. The man-haulers also said goodbye to the dogs, one of which, Blizzard – the oldest of the pups born at Winter Quarters – was treated with particular affection. 'Blizzard had always been a special friend of mine, and used often to follow me up to the anemometer,' wrote Madigan. 'By special request she was let loose, and lay at our tent door. She further showed her devotion by chewing through the strap holding the cooker to the sledge.'

*   *   *

The next morning the man-haulers made an early departure, while Mawson's party re-stowed their sledges, having taken on 200 pounds more food and three extra tins of kerosene from Stillwell. They also made the first reduction to their team. Gadget – Blizzard's mother – was again pregnant and had not been able to keep pace; in fact, the previous day she had been carried for a while. So she was shot and cut into rations; together with the unborn pups, she totalled twenty-four future meals for the other dogs, who showed a distinct lack of interest in eating what smelled of their comrade that evening, but the next night 'ate "Gadget" meat voraciously, except "Shackleton", who turned up his nose.'

The dog teams soon drew level with the other parties, and for part of the day they travelled together, Mawson's group occasionally racing ahead so that they could stop and prepare tea for everyone. Late in the afternoon, from a high ridge, Mawson, Mertz, and Ninnis were treated to a remarkable panorama. Far to the northeast they saw the huge barrier *Aurora* had steamed along before reaching Commonwealth Bay. East of this feature – that would later be named the Mertz Glacier Tongue – was a deep indentation of the coast-line, which made Mawson realise that he would need to change his course to one farther south. Again they halted so that the man-hauling teams might catch up and he could outline his new plan. And then they were off again, waving goodbye for the final time.

The morning of 18 November brought beautiful weather, and any doubts about the capabilities of the dogs were put behind them, along with fifteen miles and two rocky outcrops. The first, which they had already passed but had been hidden by undulations of the ice, was named Madigan Nunatak; the second, a high feature still in front of them, Aurora Peak. Without the man-haulers plodding ahead, the three also settled into the pattern that they would follow for most of the next month. 'In sledging over wide, monotonous wastes with dogs as the motive power, it is necessary to have a forerunner, that is, somebody to go ahead and point the way, otherwise the dogs will run aimlessly about,' Mawson wrote. Mertz now filled that role, skiing in advance while Mawson and Ninnis drove the first and second teams, respectively.

All three men had become respectable dog-drivers, giving Mawson an advantage over many earlier Antarctic expeditions, such as Scott's first, where no one had any real expertise, or Shackleton's in *Nimrod*, where only Ernest Joyce proved capable. In fact, Mawson had given so much thought and study to dog-driving that it became a rather contentious issue. During the winter, he expressed doubts about the 'Eskimo fan' method of hitching the dogs to the sledge, which Ninnis and Mertz were using. 'He thought the Yukon method would be the best in crevassed country,' wrote Ninnis, 'with a man pulling in front, and the dogs in pairs on the rope as, with fan-shaped business, the whole show – sledges, dogs and men – would be more likely to all go down together, whereas by the first method only the man would go, and could be hoicked out again.'

Through the winter and spring, Ninnis and Mertz tested both, and Ninnis held to his reservations about the Yukon method: 'at times the leader, turning on the rear dog, is apt to cause a ghastly tangle of the long line ... the front dogs are out of reach of the whip and, having been used to the Eskimo method, the dogs are apt to look round to right and left for the accustomed neighbours. On the whole I do not think they pull so well.' But Mawson remained adamant, and in late October he announced that they would use the Yukon method. Ninnis and Mertz quickly changed to it full-time with the sixteen adult dogs, while concurrently breaking in Blizzard as a spare. 'At the start, "Blizzard" was a curse,' Ninnis wrote, 'lying down and being dragged along screaming, despite belabourings with the whip and, after a time, slipped her harness.' It was almost as if she knew that going on the journey was not a good idea for her or anyone else with four feet. The notion was soon to prove deadly accurate.

After oversleeping on 19 November, the three men soon found the tempo of the previous day greatly slowed by a steep descent into the valley carved by the Mertz Glacier. Mertz was excited because the scenery reminded him of Switzerland, but Mawson was concerned that their sledges or other equipment would be irretrievably damaged because several times they capsized and rolled sideways down the slope. The sledges also began to overrun the dogs, which, pulling frantically in different directions to avoid the careening loads, became entangled in the traces and were dragged downhill until the slide could be arrested. After Blizzard's forefoot was injured, most of the dogs were allowed to run free as long as the course continued downhill.

The next day proved more of the same, and worse. With Ninnis suffering from snowblindness, they reached a grade so steep that they tethered the dogs to ice axes while lowering the sledges hand over hand for more than 300 feet, all the while keeping rope brakes around the runners. Reaching a large snowfield, they were relieved to think that they were at the bottom of the valley, but a better view soon showed them they still had farther to descend. Then, suddenly, half of Mawson's dogs dropped out of sight. 'Next moment I realized that the sledges were in the centre of a bridge covering a crevasse, twenty-five feet wide,' wrote Mawson. 'We spent many anxious moments before they were all hauled to the daylight and the sledge rested on solid ground.' Shortly thereafter, more dogs broke through into a fissure, and when Ginger Bitch, one of the best pullers, abruptly lay down and gave birth to a single pup, they decided to camp.

Once to the actual surface of the glacier on 21 November, they faced continual crevasses into which the dogs regularly fell to the length of their harnesses. Having bypassed a gigantic ice hole that Mertz likened to a geyser, they were camped for lunch when a loud bang rang out. Mawson and Mertz swung around to find Ninnis hanging onto the edge of a crevasse, nothing showing but his head and arms. As they pulled him to safety, they realised to their horror that the tent was pitched on the lid of that sheer-walled hole, and, according to Mawson, 'Looking down into the black depths we realized how narrowly we had escaped.'

That same day, Ginger Bitch stopped three different times in the midst of sledging and produced an additional thirteen pups, which soon served as dog food, along with the remains of Jappy, the second dog to be shot.

The next morning they set off through a chaos of precipitous ice falls and deep cauldrons, but they still made excellent time, and by late afternoon they had covered more than sixteen miles, passed through the last of the sérac ice, and begun heading up the far side of the glacial valley, back towards the Plateau. While crossing a surface of large, pimply masses surrounded by wide fissures, the rear sledge, driven by Ninnis, suddenly broke through a snow bridge and became wedged below the surface. It took several hours to unpack the sledge – with one of them suspended over the edge on a rope hauling everything up item by item – in order to raise it. The next morning, after being on the move for less than an hour, the same thing occurred again, except that Ninnis almost disappeared into the nothingness, just managing to grab a sledge rope to save himself. They again unloaded slowly and carefully, to make certain the sledge did not vanish into the depths.

Ninnis had now gone into a crevasse three times in relatively close succession, but under the circumstances there was little the men could do except try to be even more conscious of hazardous crossings. The usual procedure was that the forerunner tested the crossing over a crevasse with the ski pole. With the dogs halted at the edge of the crevasse, he then went over a snow bridge and sufficiently far onto the safe ground to allow the first team to clear the crevasse by reaching him. Only then was the second team allowed across following the exact same path. 'This precaution was very necessary,' wrote Mawson, 'for otherwise the dogs in the rear would make a course direct for wherever the front dogs happened to be, cutting across corners and most probably dragging their sledge sideways into a crevasse.' All in all, it seemed relatively safe.

For the next three days the dogs virtually flew across the ice. 'Their desire to pull is doubtless inborn ... We found that the dogs were glad to get their harnesses on and to be led away to the sledge,' Mawson wrote. '[A]s soon as its harness was in place, the impatient animal strained to drag whatever might be attached to the other end of the rope. Before attaching a team of dogs to a sledge, it was necessary to anchor the latter firmly, otherwise in their ardour they would make off with it before everything was ready.' Even an ascent back to the Plateau did not stop them, although one, Fusilier, was shot after his stamina waned.

Back again on the heights, spectacular vistas occasionally opened up, once showing through the shifting mists an unmoving dark area more than sixty miles away, which they correctly guessed was a rocky outcrop. But much more amazing was the view to which they awoke on the clear, sunny morning of 27 November. '[W]e saw the whole region,' wrote Mertz. 'In front of us there was a huge glacier with crevasses in the depths. In the distance there were broken ice blocks, and low hills, everything in white.' They had found, totally unexpected, a second giant glacier running out to a long tongue, even broader than the last.

They had no choice but to descend again, but although several hours were spent reconnoitring for the best route, their advance was a nightmare. The sledges capsized and the dogs' traces tangled uncontrollably, leading them to unhitch most of the animals. They eventually had to let everything down on ropes, their arms aching from holding back the sledges so they did not careen down the slopes to destruction. To top it off, when they reached the bottom they found that Betli, one of the stronger dogs, had disappeared, most likely into a crevasse. The next day they lost another, as Blizzard could not keep up and was shot. They were now down to a dozen dogs, and none was in prime condition any longer, the rapid drop to the glacier having been matched by a sudden drop in their performance and stamina. 'Dogs very done – things are looking serious for onward progress,' Mawson wrote. 'If only we could have a straight-out proposition instead of these endless snow hills and crevasses.'

But nothing was easy about crossing what would later be named the Ninnis Glacier. For four days they struggled on, starting and stopping due to the on-again, off-again vagaries of a gale that blew 65 miles per hour and to bad light, which prevented them from seeing crevasses. Problems arose whether they remained in camp or continued on. One evening Shackleton, one of the two lead dogs, broke into a provision bag and ate two and a half pounds of butter, the men's entire ration for a week. Then, shortly before lunch one day, in a heavily crevassed area, Mawson was running next to the dogs when suddenly the sledge began moving backwards. The dogs had swung sharply after crossing a crevasse, and the second sledge had dropped through a rotten snow bridge and was hanging vertically, pulling everything attached to it towards an icy end. 'Exerting all my strength I held back the front sledge,' he wrote, 'and in a few moments was joined by Ninnis and Mertz, who soon drove a pick and ice-axe down between the runners and ran out an anchoring rope.' The sledge was no longer sliding into the crevasse, but they could not pull it out because its bow was caught on a V-shaped cornice from a mass of overhanging snow. And they could not approach it because the covering was so thin that a man would fall through. Eventually, Mawson was lowered and swung over, so he could attach a rope to the aft of the sledge. With ropes at either end, they finally manoeuvred it to level ground.

By the last day of the month they had reached the eastern border of the Ninnis Glacier and looked forward to the highlands ahead. However, December brought with it a whole new set of problems. The temperature suddenly soared to 34°F (1°C), making the snow so slushy that the dogs could not pull effectively, and leading Mawson to decide to travel in the cool of the night. Even then the surface remained atrociously bad, with hard, sharp sastrugi that were constantly more than two feet high and often as much as three and a half feet from crest to trough.

When they did reach the heights, the view made Mawson's heart sink. 'It is obvious that we have been deluded by Wilkes' reports . . . for it appears that no land exists in that direction [northeast],' he wrote, 'and if Wilkes saw anything it can hardly have been more than a barrier edge. We now appear to be off the real continent edge.' That discovery required another annoying change of direction, since Mawson had instructed Madigan to follow the coastline, meaning the East Coast Party's route would be not far north of them. So for the next two days they struggled south, away from the coast.

On 4 and 5 December, the dogs seemed a little regenerated, and, turning due east, the party totalled twenty-six miles, while rising to 2,800 feet in elevation. But hard on the heels of that success came the first extended blizzard in three weeks, blowing drift at 70 miles per hour. 'One day in the sleeping bag does not come amiss after long marches,' wrote Mawson, 'but three days on end is enough to bore any one thoroughly.' Nor did any of them prove better for the lay-off: Mawson was in agony from neuralgia on his left side and a burst lip, Ninnis suffered continually from a throbbing whitlow – a suppurative, inflamed sore – on the base of one of his fingernails, and Mertz's back bothered him from lying on the hard ice too long.

Finally, on 9 December they set off again, despite continuing heavy drift. Three long days took them forty miles east over a long, gradual descent before they were halted by ice falls, beyond which coastal cliffs tumbled to a frozen sea. Almost due north, at an ice-capped peninsula Mawson named Cape Freshfield, the coast had made a sharp turn south, necessitating the three heading southeast yet again to avoid the crevasses and sérac ice ahead.

On 13 December, with the time nearing when they would have to turn back in order to catch the ship, the three made their final plans. In recent days, it had become apparent that the coast continued towards Oates Land in a nearly west-to-east direction. Therefore, they decided to follow that line, but sufficiently far inland from the coastal margin to be generally free of crevasses. This would allow them to make the best possible progress for one more week. Initially they would proceed to a point high on the Plateau, approximately thirty miles southeast. There they would establish a depot, leaving behind the supplies for their return to Winter Quarters. They would then race east as fast as possible for five days, before returning to the depot and making for Cape Denison in a straight line that would 'provide a guaranteed good (so far as the Plateau is ever good) all-weather travelling surface with the prevailing wind in our favour.'

Meanwhile, Ninnis had become unable to endure any longer the excruciating pain from the whitlow on his finger. For days, it had given him continual agony and had prevented him from sleeping regularly, although he had never let it affect his performance. Unable to tolerate it any longer, he asked Mawson to lance it. The minor surgery successfully accomplished, Ninnis rested while Mawson and Mertz reorganised the sledges and their loads.

Ninnis' sledge, which was the most worn due to carrying heavy tins of dried seal meat, was abandoned, the hide on it being given to the dogs to eat. The remainder of its load was divided between the other sledges. The dogs also were split into new teams, with the six best – which the men hoped to take back to base – assigned to the new rear sledge, which Ninnis would drive. This would be overloaded with the most vital equipment and most of the food. The front sledge, to be driven by Mawson, would carry less important equipment and would be pulled by the six dogs already in poor condition, which would eventually be fed to the others. Thus, if anything were lost in a crevasse, it would be the less-important, leading sledge.

Preparing everything for departure took until 2 p.m., as there were still a number of repairs to make, including finding an alternative to the leather strap off the cooker box, which one of the dogs – now with a taste for hide – had promptly pilfered. Nevertheless, they were able to make almost fourteen miles before calling it a day. On the way, they suddenly heard a loud booming. Although Mawson later gave a scientific reason for this phenomenon, he and Ninnis were not so calm when it occurred. 'At 8 pm, it suddenly cracked a few times under us,' Mertz recorded. 'The vault of the ice masses seemed to break. The sound was similar to far cannon shots. My comrades were a little afraid, as they never heard before the sound when huge ice masses broke off.'

By the time they camped, not only had they covered half the distance to the proposed depot, they had climbed back to 1,900 feet. They also felt that they could congratulate themselves for reaching a point well south of the dangers from crevasses.

Saturday, 14 December, dawned perfect for travelling, with a sky dotted only by a few altostratus clouds, a wind of but 10 miles per hour, and a crisp surface made ideal for sledging by temperatures that had dropped into the teens. Ninnis had enjoyed his first good sleep in several days and experienced relief from pain for the first time in more than a week, and all three were looking forward to that evening, when they would cache their supplies for the return home. At noon they stopped in an area of smooth névé so that Mawson could make the daily latitude observations, and when they moved off again, the dogs were pulling eagerly and Mertz could be heard singing songs from his student days.

They had not gone too far when, on a level and unbroken surface, Mertz unexpectedly came across a crevasse, 'similar to the hundred previous ones we had passed during the last weeks. I cried out "crevasse!", moved at right angle, and went forward.' Mawson was surprised by Mertz's signal, since they seemed far from the dangers of the broken coastal slopes. When he reached the spot, he saw only a faint indication of an underlying crevasse, but called out a warning to Ninnis, who, walking next to the rear sledge, turned his lead dogs to cross the crevasse at right angles rather than diagonally. As Mawson's dogs moved forward, he jumped on the sledge to figure out the latitude from his observations. 'There was no sound from behind except a faint, plaintive whine from one of the dogs which I imagined was in reply to a touch from Ninnis's whip,' Mawson wrote. 'I remember addressing myself to George, the laziest dog in my own team, saying, "You will be getting a little of that, too, George, if you are not careful." '

After a quarter of a mile, Mawson looked up from his figures to see Mertz halt and nervously scan the area behind them. Following his gaze, Mawson turned around, and, seeing no sign of Ninnis, immediately jumped out of his sledge, and rushed back. For a moment as he ran he thought that a rise in the ground had obscured their view, but then he quickly signalled to Mertz, who brought back the sledge.

In front of them was a gaping hole eleven feet wide, with two sets of tracks running to it on the far side, but only Mawson's continuing. Looking down through a light blue haze with tiny flecks of snow still hovering in the air, they could see clean-cut perpendicular walls of ice changing as they descended from brilliant cobalt to navy blue – and thence to blackness. For a moment, there must have been total disbelief. Then they began to shout for their comrade, but in response there came only the faint moaning of a dog. 'From the other side, by hanging over on an alpine rope, we caught a glimpse of what appeared to be a food bag and one dog partially alive moaning,' wrote Mawson, 'and part of another dog & dark object, apparently the tent, caught on a ledge.' The dog, named Franklin, tried to raise the front of his body, but his back was broken, and he lay back, whimpering. 'We heard no other sound,' wrote Mertz. 'I wanted to put the remaining sledge across the crevasse, and then climb down, but this was impossible, the crevasse was too wide, and our ropes too short. We absolutely wanted to do something, but what could we do?'

Again they listened and called, over and over, but no answer came back. They used the binoculars to try to make out something – anything – but were unsuccessful. Then Mawson fetched a furlong fishing line, and, lowering it until it actually touched the dog, they determined the ledge to be 150 feet down. They tied together all their rope and anything else that might be able to hold them, but it was far too short to reach the ledge. Franklin stopped whining, and all was quiet. They yelled yet again for their friend, but the truth could not long be ignored. 'Ninnis certainly died instantly,' wrote Mertz. 'He would not survive, if he was only seriously injured and unconscious. In a glacier it is too cold at a depth of 150 feet.' But that depth was just to the ledge, and 'the crevasse goes down deeper, and Ninnis must have crashed lower.'

They would still not give up, however; for three hours they called and listened, hoping beyond hope, but they heard nothing, and could feel only a chill draught blowing from the horrible opening. Late in the afternoon, needing some form of action to deal with their stunned grief, they decided to proceed a short way up the rise ahead of them to gain a wider outlook over the surrounding area and the continuing coastline. Once going, they actually travelled five miles, reaching the limit of their journey at 315 ¾ miles from Winter Quarters. From the heights, they saw that the broken ice cliffs of the coastline continued to the horizon, and they also found that it was not just a single rogue crevasse that had taken their friend; the ice cap and the route to it were riddled with them.

Forlornly, they retraced their path to the scene of the disaster and called to Ninnis for another hour, hoping desperately that he had not been killed and that in the interim he had regained consciousness. But no movement or sound came from the black depths of the malevolent gash in the ice. 'We could do nothing, really nothing,' wrote Mertz. 'We were standing, helplessly, next to a friend's grave, my best friend of the whole expedition. We read a prayer in Mawson's prayer book. This was our only consolation, the last honouring we could do for our beloved friend Ninnis. Our only comfort was the thought that the death was a straight path from a happy life. The ways of God are often difficult to explain.'

Part of this despair and bewilderment clearly came from not comprehending the causes of the disaster, which occurred despite the efforts to ensure that nothing would happen to the second, more valuable, sledge. 'Why had the first sledge escaped the crevasse?' Mawson later wrote, asking the question that was then very much on their minds. 'It seemed that I had been fortunate, because my sledge had crossed diagonally, with a greater chance of breaking the snow-lid. The sledges were within thirty pounds of the same weight.' In fact, Mawson's sledge was actually heavier, since he was riding on it. And although the first sledge might have weakened an all-important snow bridge, it is unlikely, since Mawson and Ninnis went over the crevasse at different angles. No, the explanation was simply that 'Ninnis had walked by the side of his sledge, whereas I had crossed it sitting on the sledge. The whole weight of a man's body bearing on his foot is a formidable load, and no doubt was sufficient to smash the arch of the roof.'

The tragedy was that it was totally preventable. Nansen, Otto Sverdrup, and Roald Amundsen, the three greatest Norwegian polar explorers, had proven beyond question the value of skis in the polar regions, not only for ease and speed of travel, but for safety. Skis distribute body weight about ten times more widely than a man's foot and therefore minimise the downward pressure per square inch that is exerted. Had Ninnis, like Mertz, worn skis or, like Mawson, ridden on the sledge, it is unlikely that the catastrophe would have occurred.

But now Mertz and Mawson had to tear their thoughts away from their friend and consider themselves. Their situation did not make for happy prospects: 'practically all the food had gone down,' wrote Mawson, 'spade, pick, tent, Mertz's burberry trousers & helmet, cups, spoons, mast, sail etc. We had our sleeping bags, a week and a half food, the spare tent [cover] without poles, & our private bags & cooker & kerosene.' In addition, the six best dogs were gone, with *all* of the dog food. Those left were in poor condition and gladly devoured the worn-out finnesko, mittens, and hide straps that were thrown to them.

Despite such overwhelming adversity, Mawson and Mertz agreed that by taking as direct a route as possible, and feeding the dogs to each other and to themselves as they went, they might – just might – reach Cape Denison. Their first stop needed to be their camp of 12 December, where they had discarded the sledge and a number of other items – including a broken shovel – which were suddenly of considerable value. Then, it would be a race against death. 'Mawson and I have to hold together,' Mertz wrote, 'and with the few remaining things, to do our best to find the way back to the Winter Quarters.' Meanwhile, after finishing his account of the calamity in his diary, Mawson paused, and simply added: 'May God help us.'

8

RACING WITH DEATH

AT 2.30 IN THE morning of 15 December, having travelled twenty-five miles since they had last rested,
Mawson and Mertz saw their discarded sledge and knew
they had reached their campsite of two nights before. On
most long sledging trips, being homeward-bound brought
excitement – or, at very least, relief – to weary explorers.
This time, however, there was no such elation: 'we were on
our way back, but without our friend Ninnis,' wrote Mertz
with a heavy heart. 'Our dear old Ninnis is dead. This change
is so rapid, that I can hardly believe it.'

The journey over the previous hours had been carried out
in something of a stupor, with little conversation and even
less concern for safety. While Mertz zoomed ahead on his
skis, Mawson rode on the sledge, neither of them caring
much that each reckless careening down crevassed slopes
might deposit them in a position like that of their late friend.
They experienced, wrote Mawson, 'a languid feeling that
the next one would probably swallow us up. But we did not
much care then, as it was too soon after losing our friend.'

Before they could even rest, the first task was to construct
a new tent. Mertz cut a runner from the abandoned sledge
into two pieces; together with his skis, these could serve as
a framework for the tent cover, which was being rushed into

service since both the tent itself and the poles had disappeared down the crevasse. It was far from ideal, as each time the shelter was set up the four supports had to be slowly and painstakingly lashed together at the peak. The inside allowed just enough room for two sleeping bags, and only one man could move at a time, with neither able to rise above a sitting position. But at least it provided protection from the elements.

Then they turned in, but any thought of sleep was replaced by a deliberation on what to do. The first of their two options was to descend to the coast and follow it back to base. This would eliminate the concerns for food, both for themselves and the dogs, because they would be able to kill seals or penguins. However, it would entail crossing more heavily crevassed areas, which would not only increase the dangers, but might cause delays, as would the journey along the coast, since it would both add to the distance and expose them to the risk of the sea ice breaking up, a situation Mawson had experienced on the BAE.

Their other option was, as already considered, dashing straight over the Plateau, taking the shortest possible course to Winter Quarters. By doing this, they would travel over some country with which they were familiar, and they would be forewarned of certain areas they should avoid. They still had the cooker, kerosene, and one and a half weeks' rations – giving them eight ounces a day for five weeks – so, with fewer delays facing them, and by eating the dogs to bulk out their provisions, they felt they could make their supplies last.

After much consideration, the latter plan was adopted, sadly not only condemning Mawson and Mertz to extremely short fare, but eliminating any chance of meeting the members of the East Coast Party. Madigan, McLean, and Correll were at that very time trekking quickly across impressively solid sea ice, heading towards Cape Freshfield – where the bend in the coast had forced Mawson and his companions to turn south. Within several days they would make landfall at a set of stunning red dolerite columns no more than twenty-three miles from where their desperate colleagues would pass. It was a distance the two men could easily have covered, but there was no way to contact Madigan's party, and this lack of communication would help account for yet more tragedy.

It was nearly midsummer, and, as if in response, the afternoon temperature rose to 30°F (−1°C), making the surface too soft and sticky for effective travel. But that did not prevent the two men from advancing their preparations. They discarded a number of objects and reorganised others. Mertz lashed splints from the sledge to the broken shovel to form a handle, and then carved wooden spoons from other sledge pieces. Meanwhile, Mawson made two pannikins from small storage tins in which cartridges and matches had been stored. The dogs were terribly hungry and noticeably weakening, so George, who was in the worst condition, was killed and divided between the other five and the two men. 'The meat was roughly fried on the lid of the aluminium cooker,' wrote Mawson, 'an operation which resulted in little more than scorching the surface. On the whole it was voted good though it had a strong, musty taste and was so stringy that it could not be properly chewed.'

By evening, the temperature had dropped to 21°F (−6°C), and the surface had become harder. All was ready, except one final formality. 'We forgot to hoist the Union Jack flag, because the misfortune gave us enough to do,' Mertz wrote about their time at the farthest point east. So 'when we had carried out all the repairs, Mawson hoisted the flag.' Then they were off, advancing mainly to the west while ascending to 2,500 feet, regaining the height they had only just dropped from that morning. For more than ten hours they kept up a strong pace, broken only by one stop to melt snow for water. But raising their makeshift tent to prepare their 'boil-up' was so tedious that they agreed not to stop again for

refreshment during their night marches. When they finally
halted, they had covered more than eighteen miles and were
quite pleased with their start.

Sadly, things did not continue so well. During the day,
Mawson slept very little, as he suffered badly from the pain
of snowblindness – brought on by the strain of navigating
the previous night during several hours of white-out conditions. Mertz treated him three times with cocaine and zinc-
sulphate medication, but when they finally continued that
night, Mawson had to keep one eye bandaged. As they discovered, it mattered little because the snow fell so thick that
they could see virtually nothing; in addition, their proximity
to the South Magnetic Pole made their compass of little use.
The snow also buried the old sastrugi, making impossible
the usual practice of steering by the direction in which the
features were blown, and increasing the difficulty in maintaining the correct direction. Worse yet, the dogs helped only
marginally. After five miles, Johnson collapsed in his harness
and was placed on the sledge. Four miles later, Mary faltered,
forcing them to camp, particularly as Pavlova also appeared
done in. 'Great disappointment to halt before 15 m but must
do so and feed up the dogs,' Mawson wrote. But feeding
four of them meant killing another, and that night it was
the turn of Johnson, who was shot and cut up by Mertz.

The night of 17 December seemed to offer hope in one
respect but to steal it away in another. Despite the sky being
a blanket of white that made trying to hold a straight course
wretchedly difficult, they still managed an impressive seventeen and a half miles. But about half-way along, Mary, whom
Mawson noted with sadness had been a 'splendid dog,'
collapsed again, leading to her being shot when they eventually camped. Only three dogs were left, and only Ginger
continued to pull well, so Mertz was forced to stop breaking
the way in order to go into harness with Mawson. 'The most
uncomfortable thing was the bad light,' Mertz wrote. 'Over
the sastrugis, I often had the impression of walking like a

drunkard, and more than once each of us fell onto his face. The diffuse light is terribly nasty.'

The light had not improved by the ensuing night, when they began to descend through an area of large sastrugi with hard, polished surfaces. Although the sledge moved more easily than usual, the men continually fell, as it was impossible to see ahead. Near midnight, after almost seven miles, they camped, hoping that the better light during the day would allow them to progress with less punishment. However, that afternoon their advance was impeded instead by warm weather, which made the surface like a mire. After five slushy miles, their experiment came to an end, and they decided to go back to sledging at night.

Everything now began to merge into one interminable nightmare, as they tried to hold a course through every miserable type of weather and surface. At points they had desperately difficult pulls uphill, only immediately to descend, the downward slopes invariably being slick and mercilessly hard. They rarely could see the sky – with fog lasting all day and drift blowing at night – and often they could not even distinguish their feet, making every stride treacherous. It remained too warm during the day, and a sudden drop of temperature at night particularly bothered Mertz, whose burberry trousers had been on Ninnis' sledge. They must have thought it could not get any worse – but it could.

Early one morning, soon after surface changes and increasing crevasses made them realise they were nearing the head of the Ninnis Glacier, Haldane, the grey, wolf-like brute that was the biggest of the remaining dogs, dropped down a crevasse of exquisite blueness, halted only by the traces connected to the sledge. Having lost so much weight, he no longer fit well into his harness, and it slipped off just as he reached the surface. Fortunately, Mertz was able to grab the animal's long hair, by which he pulled him to safety. A loss of such potential rations would certainly have doomed the men.

Soon thereafter, Haldane became shaky on his feet, staggered, and simply fell over. He was put on the sledge, but several hours later the other dogs played out as well, so the men camped to let them recover. Haldane was by far the weakest – he could not even eat the food he was given, only holding it between his paws and licking it. 'Outside, the hungry huskies moaned unceasingly until we could bear to hear them no longer,' Mawson wrote. 'The tent was struck and we set off once more.' Haldane was put on the sledge for his final trip, then shot at the next camp.

Despite his large frame, Haldane seemed little more than fur. 'All the dogs were miserable and thin when they reached the stage of extreme exhaustion,' wrote Mawson. 'Their meat was tough, stringy and without a vestige of fat . . . Only a few ounces were used of the stock of ordinary food, to which was added a portion of dog's meat, never large, for each animal yielded so very little, and the major part was fed to the surviving dogs. They crunched the bones and ate the skin, until nothing remained.' The seemingly more desirable pieces were put aside for the men. Even so, most of it was stringy and hard to chew. 'It was a happy relief when the liver appeared,' Mawson wrote in a later edition of his expedition account, 'which, even if little else could be said in its favour, was easily chewed and demolished.' Although pleasurable at the moment, the soft meat would soon have dire consequences.

Sometimes faster, sometimes slower, Mawson and Mertz pushed on, cutting steadily into the distance to Cape Denison. By early on the morning of 23 December they had covered about 115 miles from the scene of Ninnis' death. But after a laborious pull up a steep slope – with Pavlova on the sledge – everything began to go pear-shaped. It had been snowing heavily when, in a brief moment of clear weather, they saw to their horror that they had stumbled into the midst of a vast cluster of crevasses. They had no choice but to stop immediately and camp until clearer weather came. But even as they set up their tent, they were left with the distressing knowledge that going ahead might prove unfeasible, forcing them to backtrack. 'Are we at the west or east side of the glacier?' Mertz asked his diary. 'The obstacles could take us far backwards, and the provisions wouldn't be enough ... We both realize that hard work and little food don't go well together.'

They did their best to address Mertz's unfortunate equation that evening, after awaking to find they were still unable to move either way safely. First, Pavlova was killed, in a particularly distressing manner because the rifle and ammunition had been discarded during a heavy uphill pull two days before. Then, after skinning her, they set to boiling all of the dog meat, in order not only to save time later but to cut back on the weight of both kerosene and bones. 'We found that it was worth while spending some time in boiling the dogs' meat thoroughly,' wrote Mawson. 'Thus a tasty soup was prepared as well as a supply of edible meat in which the muscular tissue and the gristle were reduced to the consistency of a jelly. The paws took the longest of all to cook, but, treated to lengthy stewing, they became quite digestible.'

Soon, off the sledge went all but the most necessary items. The garment box, the camera, photographic films (exposed and not), the hypsometer, thermometers, the scientific equipment other than the theodolite, and the heavy sledge runners that had served as tent poles – which were replaced by the lighter theodolite leg poles – were all unceremoniously dumped. Yet even all this planning could not balance the vagaries of the weather.

Celebrating at the return of the sun and a clear view, first thing next morning they were off without having to retreat. But by noon, after less than four miles zigzagging through the crevasses, they were forced to camp because the warmth of the sun made the snow too sticky for them to pull even the lightened load. They took the opportunity again to run the primus for an extended period: 'We cooked a soup with "Pavlova" legs,' wrote Mertz, 'so the meat was nearly soft.' Even such a delectable treat, however, did not stop Mawson from dreaming that: 'I visited a confectioner's shop. All the wares that were displayed measured feet in diameter,' he wrote. 'I purchased an enormous delicacy . . . but something happened before I received what I had chosen. When I realized the omission I was out in the street, and, being greatly disappointed, went back to the shop, but found the door shut and "early closing" written on it.'

Mawson had experienced similar dreams while sledging in less desperate situations on the BAE, so it is not surprising that both he and Mertz did now. After all, at this time, according to Mawson, they 'were eating largely of the dogs' meat, to which was added one or two ounces of chocolate or raisins, three or four ounces of pemmican and biscuit mixed together, and, as a beverage, very dilute cocoa. The total weight of solid food consumed by each man per day was approximately fourteen ounces.'

However, a little extra – very little – was shared out at one o'clock the next morning, when Mawson woke up Mertz to wish him merry Christmas. After splitting two bits of biscuit Mawson had found in his bag, they pounded out ten miles, reaching the middle of the Ninnis Glacier, where, Mertz wrote, 'have a Christmas party on snow and ice, we demolished some dog meat with a little butter. I hope to live to share many merry Christmases with my friend Mawson.'

That evening, Mawson's computations put them only 158 miles from Winter Quarters. As if buoyed by the news, each of the next two days they pushed forward at least ten miles. But at the same time, Mertz, until then totally stoic, began to note his suffering in his diary. 'The drift is uncomfortable, because everything gradually gets wet,' he wrote. 'Without wearing mountain pants, the snow can penetrate into my underpants. At night, when I lay in my wet sleeping-bag, I realise how slowly a piece of clothing, after the other one, thaws on my body. One can't say that such conditions are comfortable.' Mertz was not the only one feeling the severe conditions: after lasting long beyond the other dogs, Ginger collapsed and was placed on the sledge on the 28th. Her weight and an extended steep grade led to an early halt after only five miles, at which point she was slain, cut up, and cooked. The next morning, after a seemingly unending slog uphill finally took Mawson and Mertz off the Ninnis Glacier, they said their final goodbye to their companion: 'Had a great breakfast off Ginger's skull,' wrote Mawson, 'thyroids and brains.'

Now back on the Plateau, the two men again picked up the pace and, despite an increasing wind, dashed fifteen miles in ten hours during the night of 29–30 December. But the effort sharply affected Mertz, who, as soon as the tent was up, disappeared into his sleeping bag. 'Xavier off colour,' wrote the concerned Mawson. 'He turned in – all his things very wet, chiefly on account of no burberry pants. The continuous drift does not give one a chance to dry things.'

It was not only the wet that dampened Mertz's outlook. He somehow sensed that the dog meat was not agreeing with him, and asked if they might temporarily give it up in favour of ordinary sledging rations. Hoping to buck him up, Mawson readily agreed, and on the morning of the last day of 1912 – having not travelled the previous night – he prepared a breakfast of biscuit, butter, and tea. Afterwards, they tried their luck in the dangerously tricky light, but white-out conditions put a stop to that after only two and a half miles. Once again trying to revive Mertz, Mawson dug into their larder for pemmican and cocoa. It temporarily worked, and that evening they struggled on, but falling snow, drift, and heavy wind made their direction so uncertain that after only five miles they had to camp yet again.

Confined to the tent on New Year's Day, Mawson became extremely worried because, although Mertz 'did not complain at all except of the dampness of his sleeping-bag . . . when I questioned him particularly he admitted that he had pains in the abdomen. As I had a continuous gnawing sensation in the stomach, I took it that he had the same, possibly more acute.' Meanwhile, Mertz, although not mentioning any specific disabilities in his diary, noted: 'The dog meat looks indigestible for me, because yesterday I felt a little weak.' He had hit the mark directly, but, tragically, would not live to confirm the reasons behind his symptoms.

Three days into 1913, Mawson could see the chances for survival slipping away. The terrible weather that had stopped them from travelling on New Year's Day did so again on the 2nd and much of the 3rd, and the longer it lasted the less they allowed themselves to eat – no progress, no food. The reality was that evening meals consisting of only two ounces of chocolate were not going to give them enough strength to sledge great distances, and when they did share a portion of cocoa and biscuit, Mertz found the latter made him ill. Mawson agreed that Mertz could have the Glaxo, and he would take more of the dog meat – anything to get his friend over the low spot.

Finally, late on 3 January, the sun gleamed through the clouds, and they struggled out of the tent. 'Did 5 miles but cold wind frost-bit Mertz's fingers, and he is generally in a very bad condition,' Mawson wrote with disappointment after Mertz's state forced them to camp despite a good surface. Perhaps, Mawson hoped, it would be a case of 'early to bed, early to rise,' but the next morning Mertz was still unable to proceed. Mawson spent the day doctoring his friend, mending gear, and hoping for improvement, but, to his growing alarm, 5 January was no more productive: 'I tried to get Xavier to start but he practically refused, saying it was suicide and that it much best for him to have the day in bag and dry it and get better, then do more on sun-shining day. I strongly advocated doing 2 to 5 miles only for exercise even if we could not see properly. Eventually we decided to rest today but every day after that he would shift.'

To further encourage him, Mawson prepared 'a rattling good meal' of half a tin of hoosh, cocoa, and half a biscuit. But it seemed to have little effect, as on the next morning Mertz was unable to contribute to any preparations, leaving Mawson – weak himself – to cook, pack, and lead the way downhill. Despite a good surface, Mertz caved in after only two miles and refused to go farther. Both men had been worn down by 'starvation, refrigeration and toil,' and Mertz was obviously in great pain, but Mawson could see that stopping was tantamount to suicide, so, by force of will, he persuaded his friend to lie in his sleeping bag on the sledge while Mawson hauled it. 'We went on in this wise for a short while and I could have taken him far,' Mawson wrote, 'but he then refused even to be a passenger on the sledge. Evidently the jolting was giving him pain. There was nothing for it but to camp.'

Mawson cooked another meal, but afterwards Mertz simply sank back into his sleeping bag, and remained generally unresponsive throughout the day, leaving Mawson to consider how his own prospects were ebbing away. 'I think he has a fever, he does not assimilate his food. Things are in a most serious state for both of us – if he cannot go on 8 or 10 m a day, in a day or two we are doomed,' he wrote. 'I could pull through myself with the provisions at hand but I cannot leave him. His heart seems to have gone. It is very hard for me – to be within 100 m of the Hut and in such a position is awful . . . If only I could get on. But I must stop with Xavier, and he does not appear to be improving – both our chances are going now.'

That night Mawson convinced Mertz to keep those failing chances alive by being hauled on the sledge the following day. But before they could leave the next morning, he discovered 'Xavier in a terrible state having fouled his pants . . . I have a long job cleaning him up, then put him into the bag to warm up.' Mawson, too, returned to his sleeping bag to rest and get warm, but upon rising again found Mertz 'in a kind of a fit & wrap him up in the bag ... obviously we can't go on today, and it is a good day ... This is terrible. I don't mind for myself, but it is for Paquita and for all others connected with the expedition that I feel so deeply.' Despite taking some thick cocoa later in the day, Mertz improved only briefly. Then he had a series of fits, 'fills his trousers again and I clean out for him ... becomes more & more delirious ... Continues to rave ... for hours. I hold him down, then he becomes more peaceful & I put him quietly in the bag. He dies peacefully at about 2 a.m. on morning of 8th.'

And so Mawson was alone. For hours, he lay in his sleeping bag – inches from the body of his friend – contemplating his situation: the distance he had still to go, the food he had left, his physical condition. Outside, the wind picked up, the sky darkened, and the drift and snow began to close off everything more than a few feet from his tent. Within that makeshift shelter, he felt a wreck: 'For many days now ... Xavier's condition has prevented us going on and now I am afraid it has cooked my chances altogether ... lying in the damp bag for a week on extremely low rations has reduced my condition seriously,' he wrote. He thought he might, in fact, collapse at any instant; the pains in his stomach prevented him from holding himself in certain positions; his blackened toes were festering near the tips and the nails were coming loose; and the skin on much of his lower body had pealed off, leaving large, raw areas that refused to heal.

It would, in many senses, have been easier just to give up, to turn over, go to sleep, and consign himself to – had he known it – the same fate as Scott and *his* companions. But somehow, from somewhere, despite the apparent hopelessness of his situation, Mawson found strength. Was it because he wanted, even if he could not reach Winter Quarters, to leave his diaries and geographical and scientific notebooks where they might be found? Was it because he felt he owed it to Paquita or to the supporters and others members of the expedition? Or was it because, as he later wrote, he thought of the lines by Robert Service: 'Buck up, do your damnedest and fight. It's the plugging away that will win you the day'?

Regardless, Mawson decided that he would reach Cape Denison, or die trying. 'If Providence can give me 20 days weather ... and heal my feet quickly surely I can reach succour.' So, dragging himself out of the tent, he spent the day reorganising his equipment for a final attempt. His first step was the hardest physically. Using a small knife as a saw, he cut the sledge in half, retaining the mast and spars and making alterations so that it could carry his sleeping bag, tent, food, and the barest of other necessities. He attached the sledge-meter, and cut up Mertz's Burberry jacket and sewed it to a canvas clothes-bag to make a sail that could be quickly set or furled when the wind changed. To strengthen himself during his work, he made two boil-ups, allowing himself more food than usual.

That evening, according to his expedition account, Mawson followed these tasks with a duty equally difficult from an emotional perspective: burying Mertz. First, he toggled up his friend in his sleeping bag, then he pulled him outside the tent, and after that he piled snow blocks around and over him, mounting above the icy grave a cross fashioned from the abandoned half of the sledge. Inside the tomb he left a waterproof case holding the last camera films and a note stating what had happened. Or did he?

A couple of years later, while touring the United States, Mawson was quoted as giving a distinctly different story about the forty-eight hours after Mertz's death. 'I thought for two days about eating Mertz,' the *New York Evening Globe* reported him saying. 'I was awfully short of food ... [but] I decided that if I did get back to civilisation it would always leave a bad taste in my mouth, so I buried him and went on.' The next day, apparently picking the story up from the New York papers, the *Bridgeport Standard* from neighbouring Connecticut reported that Mawson had said, 'After remaining with the body for two days, thinking what to do, I finally buried Dr. Mertz under an ice hummock.'

Both of these reports – and similar ones – were soon refuted by Mawson. Under the headline 'Mawson Had No Idea of Turning Cannibalistic: Sir Douglas Calls Story That He Had Design on Dead Comrade Fiction,' *The Toronto Daily Star* stated: 'Regarding the despatch from New York a few days ago to the effect that Sir Douglas had considered eating Dr. Mertz . . . Sir Douglas said the report was outrageous, the invention of the New York reporter.'

Nevertheless, the question of whether he engaged in cannibalism – as had occurred in dire circumstances in the Arctic – is one that has persisted. Mawson was supremely pragmatic, and it has been argued that he would therefore have done anything necessary to stay alive. However, his diary entries clearly indicate multiple reasons why he would not have gone to that extreme. First, they show that he was willing to stay with Mertz to the very end, even if it meant sacrificing his own life. He wrote only a little more than a day before his friend died that he could reach Winter Quarters on the provisions they had, but that he would not abandon him. Mawson would not let the threat of death override his ethical and moral code, and this would have encompassed the care of Mertz's body as well. Phillip Law, the former director of the Australian National Antarctic Research Expeditions (ANARE) and a man who knew Mawson for many years, dismissed any possibility of cannibalism under the circumstances. 'He was a man of very solid, conservative morals,' Law told Philip Ayres. 'It would have been impossible for him to have considered it.'

Second, Mawson's diaries also indicate the obvious: that

when Mertz died, Mawson's rations were effectively doubled, giving him – by the standards he had been counting on – ample to reach Cape Denison. Thus, there would have been little need to eat of the dead. In addition, Mawson indicated in his diary the location of Mertz's grave, which he marked so that a relief party – with or without him – could find the body and photographs. This he certainly would not have done had Mertz's body been disturbed. There was also another reason that would have been considered by someone so eminently practical: as he did not know *why* Mertz had died, consuming 'diseased meat' would have been exceedingly risky.

In summary, the question of whether he engaged in cannibalism should be answered with a firm 'no.' Even his diary entries and reasons of the moment aside, every aspect of Mawson's behaviour, writings, and verbal statements throughout his life make the suggestion totally unfeasible. Anyone who actually knew Mawson has agreed that such behaviour was simply inconceivable.

Mawson knew that any grief for Mertz should not delay his attempt to reach Winter Quarters, which would be precarious enough without further setbacks. Unfortunately, on the morning of 9 January, the wind was howling at 50 miles per hour, and he dared not take down the tent in case he lacked the strength to set it up again. Forced to remain there, he continued with other tasks, including tearing out the blank pages from Mertz's sledging diary to eliminate extra weight and, during a lull in the gale, reading the Burial Service over his friend's grave. He also increased his food intake in the hope of boosting his strength.

The next day was more of the same, as wind and drift again prevented him from breaking camp. Instead he mended his clothing, lashed the shovel again, and cooked the rest of the dog meat, in order not to have to haul the kerosene. Late in the day, the sun came out, the wind dropped off, and it turned beautiful. He decided to leave first thing in the morning, when it would be a bit warmer for his fragile constitution. And then it would be just him versus Nature in a struggle for life – or death.

9

ALONE

A BEAUTIFUL, CALM MORNING with a bright sun but a temperature cool enough to ensure a good surface greeted Mawson on 11 January, giving him hope that he might knock out at least ten miles. So, after paying his final respects to Mertz, he headed off slowly down a slight slope. He did not go far, however, before his feet developed an 'awkwardly lumpy feeling,' and within two miles they became so painful that he was forced to sit on the sledge and take off his finnesko to inspect them. Confronting him was a gruesome spectacle: 'the thickened skin of the soles had separated in each case as a complete layer, and abundant watery fluid had escaped into the socks. The new skin underneath was very much abraded and raw.'

Steeling himself to the pain, Mawson smeared the underlying, delicate skin – already covered with burst blisters – with lanolin and bound his detached soles back in place over the raw surfaces with bandages. Outside these he put on six pairs of thick wool socks, finnesko, and crampon over-shoes. 'Then I removed most of my clothing and bathed in the glorious heat of the sun. A tingling sensation seemed to spread throughout my whole body, and I felt stronger.' After a while, he continued on, although unable to sustain a great pace. However, with the help of a liberal allowance of chocolate and an occasional drink of water – he had filled the cooker with snow and placed it atop his sledge, where it would melt in the warm sun – he managed more than six miles before having to stop at 5.30 p.m., 'so worn that, had not been delightful evening, could not have found strength to erect tent.'

The next morning was decidedly different, and 45 mph winds and blasting drift made it an easy decision to give his feet a further rest. In fact, it was not just Mawson's feet that needed medical attention. Like Mertz, he had lost the skin over much of his body, particularly his legs and private parts. '[W]herever the skin breaks it refused to heal, the nose and lips break open also,' he wrote. 'My scrotum, like Xavier's, is also getting in a painfully raw condition due to reduced condition, dampness and friction in walking. It is well nigh impossible to treat.' His symptoms were frighteningly similar to those suffered by Mertz – which Mawson had put down to exposure and starvation – and they must have caused him great alarm. But had he known their true sinister nature, he might have been even more worried.

The now generally accepted cause for his condition was not proposed for more than half a century after the first medical specialist to receive a detailed account – Archibald McLean, the expedition's chief surgeon – suggested colitis as the reason for both Mertz's death and Mawson's suffering. But in 1969, a study by Sir John Cleland and R.V. Southcott indicated that, when taken as a whole, the set of symptoms reported about both men – severe desquamation (shedding of skin in large sections), weight loss, depression, muscular weakness, evidence of central-nervous-system damage, gastro-intestinal pain, dysentery, persistent skin infections, and major hair loss – were consistent with hypervitaminosis A, the excessive intake of vitamin A. Prior toxicological data had shown that the livers of Greenland dogs and other Arctic carnivores were excessively high in vitamin A, leading the authors to the conclusion that the dog livers were responsible for poisoning Mawson and Mertz. Subsequent studies by clinical medical researchers have agreed with these conclusions and demonstrated that the level of vitamin A in a dog liver can be toxic to a human. Although it is impossible to establish proof definitively, and this theory has had its sceptics – including Phillip Law of ANARE and a recent article in *The Medical Journal of Australia* – most experts feel that the data provide 'very strong, if not almost irrefutable, evidence that their main illness was vitamin A hypervitaminosis, a toxicity from eating dog livers.'

Such insidious medical trouble meant that Mawson would not fully revive in a brief period, even though he rested while the blizzard blew throughout the day and he tried to increase his strength with larger meals. The next morning the wind died down, and he set out again, although hampered by his chronometer watch having stopped during the night, which prevented him from being able to determine his precise location. Most of the five-plus miles he covered were down-hill, as he was entering the valley of the Mertz Glacier, but even so, crossing the hard ice slopes caused great pain, and 'on camping find feet worse than ever,' he wrote. 'Things look bad but I shall perservere.'

A view of Aurora Peak in the distance helped encourage him during the following days, but when he reached the glacier itself, he was confronted with a soft, melting surface that made progress difficult. Poor visibility also made it hard to locate crevasses on the treacherous, undulating plain. On the 15th, he noted nervously that his party was due back at base to meet the ship, but the threat of stumbling into a crevasse in the bad light nevertheless forced him to camp after a march of only one hour.

Early the next morning, Mawson threw caution to the wind and entered an area of deep, soft snow, which, combined with bad light, made the passage across several long sérac ridges little more than a gamble. He had just come over the top of a long slope and 'the sledge was running easily when I noticed that the surface beneath my feet fell away steeply in front. I suddenly realized that I was on the brink of a great blue hole like a quarry,' he wrote. 'The sledge . . . was rapidly gaining speed, so I turned and, exerting every effort, was just able to hold it back . . . from the abyss. I should think that there must have been an interval of quite a minute during which I held my ground without being able to make it budge. Then it slowly came my way.' He had won the battle, but was so exhausted by the effort that he treated himself to an extra supper of 'dog jelly soup.'

The weather was again overcast on 17 January, but Mawson felt that he could no longer endure another delay, since it would necessitate a reduction in his already minuscule food allotment. So he was off by 8 a.m., despite light so terrible that several times he saw vast, open crevasses only after he had passed nearby. He blundered blindly up a hill and broke through the lid of a crevasse, just catching himself as his thighs went into the snow. But still he continued, until he suddenly dropped into mid-air, jerked to a halt by his harness fourteen feet below the surface. Initially he expected the cut-down sledge to crash down the crevasse on top of him, but when it halted his first thought was that Providence had given him another chance – admittedly a very small chance. 'In my weak condition I did not believe it possible that I would be able to climb out of that crevasse hand over hand,' Mawson later told an audience. 'A great regret swept over me that I'd left some of that dog meat on the sledge. I wished then that I had eaten it when I had the chance.'

Mawson then made his remarkable climb up the rope to the surface, only to have the snow lid burst into pieces under his weight and propel him back down again. 'Exhausted, weak, and chilled . . . I hung with the firm conviction that all was over except the passing,' he wrote. 'Below was a black chasm; it would be but the work of a moment to slip from the harness, then all the pain and toil would be over.' His hands involuntarily went towards his harness, but, he

A studio portrait of Douglas Mawson, prepared in July 1911 as part of the effort to raise funds and gain other backing for the Australasian Antarctic Expedition.

On 16 January 1909, the British Antarctic Expedition's three-man party of (*from left*) Alistair Mackay, T.W. Edgeworth David, and Mawson reached the vicinity of the South Magnetic Pole, at 72°15'S, 155°16'E. As part of the process of claiming the region for the British Empire, Mackay and David hoisted the Union Jack, while Mawson set up a camera that could be triggered by a string, which can be seen in David's hand.

Although he noted her speed left something to be desired, John King Davis was impressed with *Aurora* during his first voyage in command of her, noting: 'I find her an excellent sea-boat, and easily handled, which are both most important points that one can only judge after a passage.' Not long thereafter, he added that 'she is a splendid sea-boat in a big sea.' By the end of his association with her, Davis considered *Aurora* the best Antarctic vessel ever.

On 8 January 1912, Mawson (*holding the pick*) led a party that made the first landing at Cape Denison, where Mawson determined the Main Base would be established. The unusual calm of the period in which they landed belied the fact that the location was the windiest place on Earth.

The main hut at Cape Denison in an advanced stage of construction. Work on clearing the ground for the hut began on 20 January, the roof was in place five days later, and on 30 January the men had their first sit-down dinner in their new home.

Xavier Mertz shown exiting the main hut through a door in the roof. At other times the men had to leave via tunnels under the snow.

B.E.S. Ninnis taking a rest from shovelling out the catacombs beneath the snow. The extensive network of passages provided both storage and an exit from the hut at Cape Denison.

On a calm day, virtually all the men at Main Base would turn out to help with the complicated process of erecting the wireless masts.

Mertz comes out of the entry tunnel to Aladdin's Cave and into a bright day that appears to hold the promise of good sledging. Behind Mertz are the fully loaded sledge and, closer, a piece of canvas that served as a covering to prevent snow from filling the entrance to the cave.

Aladdin's Cave, here occupied by Bob Bage and Frank Hurley, was a peaceful retreat away from the constant and brutal winds of the Antarctic Plateau. Mawson was forced to remain in or near the cave for a week towards the end of his remarkable solo journey back to Winter Quarters.

Washing up after dinner in the kitchen at Winter Quarters. Volunteering to help the messman clean the stacks of greasy pots, dishes, and utensils was a much-appreciated demonstration of friendship. Here John Hunter and Bob Bage dry the items while Alfred Hodgeman engages in the most unpleasant job – actually washing up – which indicates that he was likely that night's messman.

One of Hurley's most famous – and evocative – pictures was taken
of these two expedition members trying to quarry ice in the midst of the
blizzard, with the huts at Cape Denison in the background.

Mawson rests against a sledge on the incredibly steep ascent to Aladdin's Cave on the first day of the Far Eastern journey. The figure at the rear is most likely Ninnis, as the photo is attributed to Mertz.

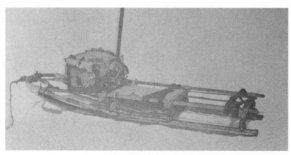

The sledge that Mawson sawed in half with a pocket tool after the death of Mertz and subsequently hauled back on his return from the Far Eastern journey.

The members of the Main Base who left Cape Denison on *Aurora* in February 1913. (*Front, from left*) Frank Stillwell, John Hunter, Percy Correll, Herbert Dyce Murphy, (*back, from left*) Leslie Whetter, Frank Hurley, Eric Webb, Walter Hannam, Charles Laseron, and John Close.

Expedition members – including the Macquarie Island party – aboard *Aurora* on the way home in 1914. (*From left*) Frank Bickerton, Alfred Hodgeman, John Hunter, George Ainsworth, Cecil Madigan, Frank Hurley (*kneeling*), Bob Bage, Leslie Blake (*behind Mawson*), Douglas Mawson, Archibald McLean (*next to Blake*), Charles Sandell, Percy Correll, and Harold Hamilton (*sitting*).

The wedding party at the marriage of Mawson and Paquita on 31 March 1914. (*From left*) Hester Berry (bridesmaid), John King Davis (best man), William Mawson (groom's brother), Douglas Mawson, G.D. Delprat (bride's father), Paquita Delprat, Henrietta Delprat (bride's mother), Carmen Delprat (bride's sister), T.W. Edgeworth David, and Willy Delprat (bride's brother).

Three cheers are given for King George V at Proclamation Island in Enderby Land on 13 January 1930. At the top of the island's 850-foot summit, Mawson read the document asserting the King's sovereignty over Enderby Land, Kemp Land, and Mac. Robertson Land.

admitted, 'I couldn't see the bottom of the crevasse and was afraid I'd simply fall on some ledge below me and linger in misery with broken bones.'

Just when all seemed lost, he thought about how Providence had protected him in the past and had overseen his marvellous escapes. 'So I summoned all my nerve ... and forced myself upward in a struggle of four and a half hours.' His strength fast ebbing and his chilled hands losing all feeling, he still somehow came closer and closer to the surface. Finally he was there, and this time he pushed himself out feet first, extended at full length, onto the solid ground. 'Then I did a thing that you may think here sounds foolish in view of my distance from help,' he told the audience. 'I cooked and ate dog meat enough to give me a regular orgy.'

'The accident of yesterday, and its bearing on my progress now, so played up on me that I could not sleep,' Mawson wrote the next day. 'Spent a rotten time.' Of course, some of the reason could also have been the glut of meat on his overtaxed system. Regardless, during that restless spell, a plan leapt into Mawson's mind: he could construct a rope-ladder, 'one end of which was to be secured to the bow of the sledge and the other carried over my left shoulder and loosely attached to the sledge harness. Thus, if I fell into a crevasse again, it would be easy for me, even though weakened by starvation, to scramble out again by the ladder, provided the sledge was not also engulphed [sic].'

He immediately assembled the ladder, and it did not take long to pay dividends. Soon after, as he wallowed through deep snow, twice within minutes he broke through into open space, but the sledge held and the ladder 'proved trumps.' But the maze of crevasses and sérac ice kept progress terribly slow in the following days, and the constant danger led Mawson to ponder if he should have tried the coastal route. He was also severely disappointed that his condition, which had initially seemed to improve, now appeared to be regressing. However, hope returned with the sun on 21 January, and although the day was one of the hardest he had ever faced – tackling 'a very steep slope . . . steeper than anything from Winter Quarters to Aladdin's Cave, then several more' – he knew that at last he had left behind the terrible glacier. That night he lightened his load by throwing away his crampons, rope ladder, rope, and 'crevasse stick.'

Although not yet to the Plateau, it was now within close range, and on 22 January Mawson totalled more than five miles up a sequence of steep terraces, pulling through soft, shifting snow. That day's combination of success and exhaustion led him to reassess his rations, which he had reduced in response to the agonising progress over the glacier. Soon after he cut into them, he was afflicted by a general lethargy and a set of painful boils developed, so he now decided to increase his intake significantly, but only so long as he maintained five miles per day. 'So had a grand pem last night – taking out meat pem and adding lot dogmeat,' he wrote, 'then this morning had real fine pem, good half tin dry, a whole biscuit and decent tea and butter. I felt very full after but a most pleasant feeling.'

Mawson had expected to increase his pace once he reached the Plateau, but crossing it proved no easier than the glaciers, and the wind became an even greater problem. On the afternoon of the 24th – with Mawson nine days late for his return to Winter Quarters – it gusted so strongly that he was forced to stop and pitch the tent, because he feared he would be unable to do so if the wind increased. 'Erecting the tent single-handed in the high wind was a task which required much patience and some skill,' he wrote. Even with three people it had been a challenge, now it was so difficult that he had to follow a very specific procedure to have any chance of success, and it frequently took him more than two hours. This in turn influenced his decisions on whether to travel each day and how far to go if the wind were picking up. In fact, blizzard-force winds

kept him pinned in his tent on 25 January, and then again
two days later.

Certainly the rest periods had their benefits, as he produced
eight- and nine-mile efforts on the following days, but
Mawson's overall health continued to degenerate. 'Both my
hands have shed the skin in large sheets, very tender and it
is a great nuisance,' he wrote, followed the next day by
'Freezing feet as too little food, new skin and no action,'
and soon thereafter: 'For the last 2 days my hair has been
falling out in handfuls and rivals the reindeer hair from the
moulting bag for nuisance in all food preparations. My beard
on one side has come out in patches.' All of these are symp-
tomatic of hypervitaminosis A, but this was not the only
problem Mawson faced. He suffered from exposure, dehydration, and a calorific intake insufficient for his level of
activity. He was also constantly stressed mentally: 'I cannot
sleep, and keep thinking of all manner of things – how to
improve the cooker, etc,' he wrote during one of the gales.
'The end is always food, how to save oil . . . have to wear
burberries in bag. The tent is closing in by weight of snow
and is about coffin size now. It makes me shudder.'

But despite all, he would not give up. He continued
throughout to write up his meteorological and navigational
field notes. And he somehow remained positive: 'I am full
of hope and reliance in the great Providence, which has
pulled me through so far.' But it was not only such conviction
that drove him on. Just as powerful was his devotion for,
and desire to return to, Paquita, to whom he later wrote:
'My love for you and duty to you was the real insentive [sic]
which finally availed in my reaching the hut.' In turn, her
own efforts would give a highly significant emotional boost
to Mawson on his final endeavours to reach safety.

The blizzard moderated early on the morning of 28 January,
and, knowing he was now almost two weeks late, Mawson
fell out first thing to release the tent and sledge – buried

two and a half feet deep – from their icy hold. It took an hour and a half and was not pleasant, as all of his gear was either sodden or frozen stiff. But then he was off, and, to his delight, within a mile the sky cleared, the sun beamed down, and he was able to hold the course he wanted. '[O]n I trudged,' he wrote, 'now for the first time feeling that there was a really good chance of my getting through to Aladdin's Cave.' The highlight, however, came late in the day, when Madigan Nunatak came into view. 'All things seen today considered,' he wrote, 'it looks as if distance to Aladdin's Cave should not be more than 31 miles.'

Despite his proximity to Cape Denison, Mawson knew that his safe return was not certain. He was down to two pounds of food, and any delay could conclude his magnificent efforts with failure. So the next morning, despite 45 mph winds blowing low drift, he set out. He struggled for five hard miles, before, suddenly, something dark loomed to his right. Wondering what on Earth it could be, he made towards it – and found a cairn wrapped at the top with black cloth. Scarcely able to contain himself, he dug into the top tier, to be rewarded with a food bag and a note in a tin. It was from McLean, Hurley, and Hodgeman, who had left it only six hours before, desperately hoping that somehow, in all that land of waste, it might be found and prove of use to their friends. It was, of course, of greater value than they had ever imagined.

'Situation 21 Miles S60E of Aladdins Cave,' the note read. 'Two ice mounds one 14 M S60E of Aladdin's Cave the other 5 miles SE of Aladdins – the first has biscuits chocolate etc. Please find biscuits pemmican, ground biscuits tea etc. Aurora arrived Jan 13th. Wireless messages received. All parties safe.' Mawson was overjoyed that his men were safe, but perhaps just as much so to realise that he was about five miles closer to Aladdin's Cave – to final safety – than he had figured. But there was more; he read that Amundsen had reached the Pole, Scott's support party had left him on the Plateau itself, and that the parties under Bage, Bickerton, and Madigan had all successfully concluded their sledging operations.

Beyond all of this, however – as Mawson clutched the bag that guaranteed him enough food to see him through to base – were facets of the situation transcending all others. Nothing could have given him more joy, more hope, than the red calico bag itself – a 'Paquita bag' sewn with love thousands of miles away and many long months before. And if she were his angel waiting at home, once again there seemed to be another sitting on his shoulder, watching over him. 'I might have approached Aladdin's Cave from anywhere through a wide arc,' he wrote, 'but Providence had guided me to that very spot.'

Mawson needed no further encouragement, and he was soon off again. Confused by McLean's bearings, however, he several times readjusted his course, and by the end of the day, having sat on the sledge and run along with a powerful wind, he had made such leeway that he found himself well to the east of Aladdin's Cave. Later on, he tried to move directly west, but was hampered by extremely icy conditions and the wind now blowing from the side. Since he had discarded his crampons to lighten the load a week before – planning to pick up steel ones at Aladdin's Cave for the descent to Winter Quarters – he fell time and again and was finally forced to camp at a point he figured to be about thirteen miles from Aladdin's Cave.

With the wind gusting strongly the next morning, and the icy surface preventing safe advancement, Mawson decided to make his own crampons. Cutting two boards from the mahogany case of the theodolite, he attached to them as many screws, nails, and tacks as he could and tied them to his finnesko with lamp-wick. He then again steered west, an eventual sighting of the Mackellar Islets providing directional guidance. By the time he had tripped and skidded five and a half miles, both new crampons were seriously damaged, and shortly thereafter the sledge became wedged in a narrow crevasse. It proved an enormous struggle to pull it to safety, and so tired him out that Mawson decided to stop for the night. 'I had to camp on first bit of half snow I could find,' he wrote. 'For about 1 mile before this I had seen ahead a beacon on a rise with snow valley to S – very like Aladdin's Cave – about W from me, but it seemed hardly likely that it could be so far as stated by McLean in note at cairn.'

It remained tantalisingly close and yet unattainable the next day, as a new blizzard stubbornly refused to let him advance. Instead, Mawson again provided himself with crampons, appropriating screws and nails from every available source, including the theodolite box, sledge-meter, and cooker box. When the wind finally subsided on the afternoon of 1 February, he headed off, two and a half miles later finding that his crampons had again virtually disintegrated but that he stood at the entrance of Aladdin's Cave. Mad with delight – 'Great joy and thanksgiving,' he wrote – Mawson descended into the refuge to find oranges, a pineapple, and other stores. But no crampons. Feeling secure for the first time in months, he rested a bit and prepared a meal to see him through the final stage. However, coming out to go the last miles to Winter Quarters, he found the wind had taken a sudden turn for the worse, and that drift was flying helter-skelter. With inadequate crampons and a badly strained right leg, suffered in a fall two days earlier, he knew that continuing was risking all at the final stage, so he decided to wait a day for better weather.

It did not come that following day, nor the next . . . nor the next. Instead, the blizzard increased in fury, forcing Mawson to prepare new crampons from benzine cases, food bags, an old dog harness, and every nail he could find. He finished one, but could not locate enough materials to complete the other, so remained holed up, unwilling to depart under such terrible conditions. Finally, he 'found several boards on hill slope with nails in them, so practically completed the crampon I was not able to finish earlier on account of want of materials.' But still the ferocious wind did not drop, and despite spending hours at a time sitting outside the cave waiting for a lull in the wind, he would not trust his home-made crampons to the dangers of the steep, slick ice down to Cape Denison – so he continued to hesitate. Yet his anxiety about catching *Aurora* before she departed was equalled by his concern over his medical condition. 'It almost appears as if scurvy or something of the kind were upon me – joints very sore,' he wrote. 'Blood keeps coming from right nostril in thin watery description, also from outbursts on the fingers. Am quite sure some of the food here is stale and I may be getting harm from it.'

But finally it was done. After a week of waiting, on 8 February the wind began to fall rapidly. Mawson waited tentatively to make sure it was not just a lull, and then by 1 p.m. he was on his way downhill. His crampons worked like a charm, but he had to redouble the rope under the runners of his sledge to offset the steepness of the grade. 'After the 2 mile [post] I was very expectant of what was to be my fate,' he wrote. '(1) Had the ship gone? (2) If so, had they left a party at the Hut? (3) Or had they abandoned us altogether?'

Even as he nervously wondered, the incredible panorama of Commonwealth Bay opened before his eyes. And there 'as I gazed about seeking for a clue, a speck on the north-west horizon caught my eye and my hopes went down,' he wrote. 'It looked like a distant ship; it might well have been the *Aurora*.'

It must have been a soul-destroying sight, but there was nothing to do but slowly continue to pick his way down the slope. After another seemingly interminable period, the familiar areas of Cape Denison burst into view, and suddenly he could see three men working next to the boat harbour. 'I waved for about 30 seconds and then got an answering wave,' he wrote, 'they evidently keeping anxious watch.' The men dashed towards him, quickly disappearing behind the crest of a hill. Mawson tried to rush to them in turn, but found that he could only continue slowly down the steep grade, which also prevented the others from reaching him for several minutes. At about fifty yards distant, he was able to recognise the first human being he had seen in weeks. 'Bickerton it was for certain,' he wrote. 'Very soon 5 had arrived – Bickerton, Bage, Madigan, McLean, Hodgeman – and I learnt that the ship had left finally only a few hours before and they, with a new wireless man, comprised the party left by Capt Davis to search for us.'

Almost overcome by being reunited with his men, Mawson told the story of the disaster and the two tragic losses, bringing tears to the eyes of those around him. Then they took the sledge that seemed so light to the rest of them and guided him gently to the hut. 'What a grand relief!' Mawson wrote. 'To have reached civilization after what appeared utterly impossible. What a feeling of gratitude to Providence for such a deliverance.'

Arriving at Winter Quarters after so many weeks of almost hopeless struggle, Mawson was a jumble of emotions, thoughts, and questions. Very quickly he was shown that the hut had been made tighter and stronger and that it had been stocked with stores, fuel, and all else needed for the search party for another year. More importantly, however, he saw that a new wireless mast and antenna had been raised. Sidney Jeffryes, a wireless operator, had been left by the ship, but Hannam, now aboard, was scheduled to listen each evening on *Aurora*'s newly installed receiving set for any communications from Cape Denison. 'Accordingly,' Mawson wrote confidently that night, 'at 8 pm the ship was called up and acquainted with the fact of my return and asked to return and pick us up.'

In hours, he thought, he would be beginning the final trip home to Australia. How wrong he was.

10

ABANDONED

WHEN MAWSON SENT the message to Davis, asking
him to return to Cape Denison and pick up the small
party still there, he was not the only one desperately looking
forward to leaving the windiest place on Earth. Five men
with whom he had spent the previous year had agreed to
stay behind and search for the members of the Far Eastern
Party, but they had not all been willing volunteers. The
organisation of the party was the result of a complicated,
nerve-racking, and at points bitter and unhappy month,
during which the crew and shore party alike were intensely
anxious, and Davis was almost overwhelmed by his
conflicting responsibilities to Mawson, the other men at
Winter Quarters, and Frank Wild's party, waiting more than
1,500 miles away on an ice shelf.

Aurora had originally begun the journey back to Commonwealth Bay on Boxing Day of 1912, crammed with 521 tons
of coal, thirty-five sheep – taken in case they needed to
provision another wintering – and twenty-one sledge dogs, a
gift from Roald Amundsen, who had sailed to Hobart after
his successful assault on the South Pole. Also aboard were
expedition secretary Conrad Eitel and several other super-
numeraries, including Sidney Jeffryes. A wireless operator originally from Toowoomba, Queensland, Jeffryes had impressed

Mawson to such an extent when he unsuccessfully applied for a position a year and a half before that Mawson wrote he wished Jeffryes had applied before Sawyer, the Macquarie Island operator. Now he was brought aboard by Eitel to establish wireless communication on the ship, which he did within several days, although the equipment allowed them only to receive, not to transmit.

The journey down was so hellacious it caused one old whaler aboard to comment that he had never seen such a fortnight's rotten weather in all his thirty-five years at sea. But once in Antarctic waters, the ice pack was considerably lighter than the previous year, and they easily steamed through areas in which it had stopped them the year before.

Early on 13 January, Davis dropped anchor in Commonwealth Bay with a sigh of relief. But many of his problems were just beginning. Having been on the bridge for forty-eight hours, Davis retired, only to be woken three hours later when a violent squall caused the protective lashings on the cutting tackle to part. This released the anchor chain, and, according to seaman Bertram Lincoln, 'before anyone could get to the brake the whole lot of cable disappeared . . . one anchor and 125 fathoms of new heavy navy-cable.'

With his best anchor gone and his hopes of sleep ruined, Davis went ashore, where the nine men at Winter Quarters were unaware of the ship's arrival. When he presented them with mail and fresh provisions, 'the delight of these lonely men, who had lived so long completely severed from their families and from the world, may be better imagined than described,' he wrote. 'To us they had the appearance almost of strangers, a band of wild, hairy veterans whose looks bore little resemblance to the hopeful young men we had landed here a year ago.'

Meanwhile, to his dismay, Davis discovered that three parties due back by 15 January were still unaccounted for, and that he was to take command in Mawson's absence. So began a period in which his uneasiness for the parties still in the field was matched only by his restlessness to get away in order to rescue Wild's group, which did not have enough supplies to last another year.

Then, on the afternoon of 16 January, the East Coast Party – Madigan, McLean, and Correll – arrived home. The next day, Davis called a private meeting with Madigan and Bage – 'both splendid men,' he thought – and the three decided that, as a precaution, preparations should begin on readying the base to be occupied for a second winter. Work commenced immediately on making the hut more wind- and snow-proof, several of the crew began re-erecting the main wireless mast, and the dogs were brought ashore. Then, early on the morning of the 18th, Bickerton's Western Party – minus the air-tractor – marched in, rousing their sleeping friends at 1.30 by shouting in unison, 'Rise and shine!' It was now only the Far Eastern Party that was missing.

Over the following days anxiety continued to build, and on 22 January – after Davis again met with Madigan and Bage – the arrangements determined behind closed doors were made public. On 25 January a party was to set out in search of Mawson, Mertz, and Ninnis. This group was to return by the 30th, following which *Aurora* would depart with most of the shore party to relieve Wild. The men remaining for another winter – Bage, Bickerton, Hodgeman, McLean, and Jeffryes, under the command of Madigan – would then instigate a more thorough search for Mawson and his companions.

In the interim, however, everyone tried to do as much as possible to prepare for the eventuality they hoped would not arise. A new 'umbrella aerial' was erected to try to improve reception. Then Hodgeman, Stillwell, and Correll made a dash to Aladdin's Cave, but could find no trace of the Far Eastern Party. On 24 January, supplies and fuel were landed. And the day after that, Hodgeman, Hurley, and McLean headed back to the Plateau for the final search before the ship was due to leave. Marching straight into the teeth of a

gale that lasted more than three days, they were severely
hampered in attempts to go inland, and, although they set
up three food depots, they were not able to reach a point
more than, they figured, twenty-one miles from Aladdin's
Cave, where they wrapped the top of an eleven-feet mound
in black bunting. Finally, fearing they might not arrive at
Cape Denison in time to catch the ship, they turned back,
little suspecting that Mawson was no more than five miles
away.

Things had not gone any more smoothly for Davis.
Anchored close to shore so that coal and other supplies could
be offloaded, *Aurora* had twice within forty-eight hours been
hit by gusts of staggering ferocity. Each time the ship left
an anchor on the bottom of the bay. With only a small kedge
anchor left, Davis was forced to steam back and forth farther
out, where the winds were not as strong. Then suddenly, on
the 29th, the weather cleared. He could stand by idly no
longer and steamed east to search the coast for Mawson's
party. But three days later, despite going as far as the tip
of the Mertz Glacier Tongue, there had still been no sign of
the missing men.

Frustrated and depressed, Davis turned back to Winter
Quarters to collect the men who were returning home. But
upon arrival there, the winds proved so violent that he could
not even do that, as 'the velocity of the squalls exceeded
eighty miles an hour and, though I endeavoured to keep the
ship in position under the cliffs, she was blown seaward in
spite of all the engines could do under a full head of steam.'
Then the temperature dropped to 19°F (−7°C), turning the sea
spray into ice, so that she 'resembled the decoration-piece of
a gigantic wedding cake.'

For more than a week the gale winds continued,
hammering *Aurora* mercilessly and keeping the men on shore
penned in the hut – and simultaneously trapping Mawson
inside Aladdin's Cave. Although Davis held out hope that
his friend – now more than three weeks late – would still

show up, he knew that the more time passed, the less likely it was he would be able to navigate the long, iceberg-studded coastline to reach Wild. And should he fail in that, it would condemn Wild and his seven men to certain death. So when the winds finally dropped on 8 February, those who were returning to Australia were quickly embarked and, shortly before noon, Davis saluted the men remaining and sailed *Aurora* west, out of Commonwealth Bay.

It is almost surprising that Walter Hannam knew what he was hearing a little after eight that evening. Hired to oversee the entire wireless operation of the AAE, as well as to be the operator at Main Base, he nevertheless had not received a single message for a year. But as he sat almost aimlessly listening at the wireless unit he had agreed to monitor on *Aurora*, out poured what he said was the biggest shock of his life. 'Arrived safely at hut,' the message read. 'Mertz and Ninnis dead. Return and pick up all hands. Mawson.'

Hannam raced to give the message to Davis, and within minutes everyone aboard knew the fate of their comrades. To a man they were stunned by the strangest mixture of tragic yet wonderful news they had ever heard. More than anything, it brought relief from the terrible doubt with which each had been plagued. Davis could hardly help but celebrate a little at the news that at least his close friend was alive.

Within minutes he had turned the ship, and they were steaming back towards Commonwealth Bay. But as they neared Cape Denison the next morning, they were greeted with the shrill screams that they knew presaged a raging gale. Anchoring was impossible, and once again the ship could only stand off throughout the afternoon, beating up and down across the bay, hoping the cruel wind would abate. Percy Gray, the second mate, signalled again and again to the shore party, but received no response. Those ashore, meanwhile, packed the records, instruments, and personal gear they considered essential, and waited anxiously, ready to race to the harbour the second the one boat they needed was launched.

But the object of their hope never materialised. Davis knew that the conditions made it impossible to lower the motor-launch to the surface, and even if it could have been put in the water, it would have been destroyed by the smashing waves. Yet there was one last hope: the whaleboat – a more vigorous vessel – was prepared, and a set of volunteers got ready to try their luck with the oars. 'If the Capt had allowed us to put a boat in the water, we wd have had a good go at it if the whole boat-load had been capsized,' Eric Webb, the magnetician, wrote. In his enthusiasm, he had struck on just the problem: it was a suicidal venture, and a man with Davis' experience and conservatism would never allow such a risk to be taken. So he and everyone else just had wait for the wind to fall – if only it would.

But hour after hour the blizzard roared on, with no sign of relenting. Finally, at 6.30 p.m., with the barometer still plummeting, Davis, now little more than a heap of nerves, could stand it no more. He called the officers, the shore party, and as many of the crew as could be spared to the wardroom. There, he told them his perspective on the situation. On the one hand, the men at Winter Quarters were safe inside a hut built on firm ground, one that had just been restocked with enough provisions and supplies for them to live safely through another year. It would be easy to pick them up if the wind stopped, but, as they had just seen, gales in that region could last a week or more. On the other hand, Wild's party had not been left with enough coal, food, or supplies for a second year, and, being on an ice shelf, their home could disappear at any point. Moreover, the distance to Western Base and the ferocious conditions of the seas around it meant that any delay might jeopardise success in reaching the eight men on that floating barrier. And it was now three weeks later than when they had left Common-wealth Bay the year before, after which they had struggled to escape the ice near the Shackleton Ice Shelf, the very ice that, a decade before, had caught the German ship *Gauss* and held her in a remorseless grip for a year. Being trapped like that would be fatal for *Aurora* and her crew, as they did not have the supplies to survive for a winter.

Thus, Davis told the assembled party, he no longer felt justified in remaining at Cape Denison and risking losing the second party, and perhaps the ship. As the weather was not improving, they would leave forthwith. He felt sorry for Mawson and the others who would be left behind, but he had no doubt that going to Wild's aid was the proper thing to do. 'I invited them to suggest any alternative measures,' Davis wrote, 'but none were forthcoming.' In fact, the shore party agreed to a man – perhaps reluctantly – that it was the correct choice. Conversely, not all of the sailors were in complete agreement with the decision. 'He made no attempt to put off in the boat which could very easily have been done as all of us were ready to go in the boat at any time and would have risked anything to get those men aboard,' wrote Cedric Hackworth, an AB. 'It is a disgrace to the Expedition to turn away like this and leave a man in such bad health in this awful hole. All hands aboard ship have turned away from Adele Land [*sic*] very unwillingly and disappointedly – in fact, very angry at the idea of it all and would be very glad to turn back again as the wind is now dropping.' Davis, however, was satisfied with his decision, and he wasted no time in having Gray hoist the ensign and dip it, as a signal of farewell. For now, he was headed west; Mawson, he would see in a year.

When the seven men at Winter Quarters looked out across the bay on the morning of 10 February, no ship was to be seen. Late in the afternoon the previous day, before conditions had degenerated even further, Hodgeman had made his way to the western ridge of Cape Denison and had spotted *Aurora* still waiting. The intense disappointment to find she had now departed must only have increased when, according to Mawson, 'The wind calmed off in the afternoon, so that we could have got off if ship here.'

Davis' decision had doomed the men to another year in the same horrid place, in the same company, doing many of the same tasks – and without the thrill of discovery and new experiences. As a result, in the following weeks there was a general lethargy among the men, a tendency to simply mark time, and a disbelief in their circumstances, manifested in a continuing notion that *Aurora* would return after picking up Wild's party.

In fact, with what must have seemed at times to be the winds of hell behind him, Davis drove his ship along at a dangerous pace, and on 23 February they arrived at the Western Base. Before the day was out, the men, dogs, scientific equipment and samples, personal gear, and everything else they were taking had been loaded, and Davis turned the ship towards Hobart, which they reached safely on 15 March. By that time, the men at Cape Denison knew that destiny had played a vile trick upon them, and that they were likely going to be there into 1914.

For Mawson, it was probably a boon – he later told Phillip Law that if had he gone on the ship, he doubted he would have survived the journey; being forced to stay at Cape Denison had likely saved his life. Certainly, after he struggled down that final slope he was in such dire physical condition – from starvation, exposure, stress, overwork, and vitamin-A poisoning – that he was able to do little other than eat, sleep, and suffer. He was in agony from the many sores that had developed all over his body, his hair and skin continued to slough off, his lower extremities were painfully swollen, and he had continuing problems with his digestive system. His saving grace was the attentiveness of the other men, particularly McLean, who, according to Paquita, 'nursed him back to health, letting him rest or talk as he wished. All told me that for the first few weeks he would follow them round, not so much to talk to them as just to be with them.'

Madigan, on the other hand, fearing another year in the Antarctic would cause the forfeiture of his Rhodes Scholarship, could see the situation as nothing but ruinous to his hopes and future – a vicious joke played upon him by some evil fate. What could be more soul-destroying than the series of near misses that had propelled them into this situation: Mawson missing the search party by only hours; Mawson throwing away his crampons, so he could not descend immediately from Aladdin's Cave; the blizzard, both before Mawson's appearance and upon *Aurora*'s return; and Davis' refusal to launch a boat Madigan was convinced could take them off?

He had not wanted to stay behind in the first place – as he told his fiancée in a letter written the day McLean, Hurley, and Hodgeman had left on the last search – but felt it was an unshirkable duty. 'The best must be done, and the best is considered by Capt Davis, Bage and Bickerton (the latter two being the next most reliable & capable men here) to be that I stay in charge of the relief party,' he wrote, continuing:

> I am the most efficient sledger . . . I know the coast line for 300 m East, where the Doctor went . . . I was the last man with him, I know his plans and his ideas, and I have all along been considered as the second man at this base. I said at once that I could not volunteer to stay . . . and I gave my reasons to Captain Davis . . . I think I lose more by staying than anyone here. But there seemed nothing else for it – Captain Davis felt obliged to ask me to stay – and I could not go without a point blank refusal – I should have felt a coward and a deserter for the rest of my life, a miserable selfish being, if I had done so – I am in this expedition, and I will see it through.

It was, in a sense, a punishment for being one of the most accomplished men at Winter Quarters. Bage and Bickerton – each of whom had also led a sledging party – were likewise selected to remain because they were highly skilled, capable, hard-working, and would have been Mawson's choices. But Bickerton was no keener on a second year in the Antarctic than was Madigan. He acceded to Davis' request because, like Madigan, he personified that age's sense of duty, and because he was particularly close to Ninnis and Mertz. But that did not mean he was happy about the situation. 'Mawson went out sledging & has seen fit for reasons best known to himself to stop out longer than was expected,' he wrote to his sister. 'So the only thing to do is to leave a party in this breezy hole for another year. It is a rotten game & a rotten place but nevertheless has to be done by someone.'

Intriguingly, with the mental arm-twisting that had obviously gone on, there had been other men who were not *allowed* to stay. According to Gray, the second mate, and Hannam, each asked Davis to be allowed to remain – and both were turned down. The other three men who were in the second wintering party were, like Madigan, Bage, and Bickerton, logical rather than emotional choices. There was no doubt that a doctor and a wireless operator were needed, so McLean and Jeffryes were natural selections. And Hodgeman gave the immeasurable advantage of being the most capable if the hut required attention, and had also been among the most vociferous in volunteering.

This then, was the 'new' party that now settled down for another stay at the windiest place on the planet.

As if to add insult to the injury of having to remain at Winter Quarters, the weather deteriorated a full month before it had the previous year. By the middle of February, summer was long gone and autumn already passing. Conditions turned bad so quickly that, concerned they would not be able to feed the twenty-one dogs Amundsen had donated and the three pups from the last litter at base, Mawson ordered Madigan and Bickerton to shoot eleven of them. The remainder were placed in Madigan's charge.

The party now settled once again into a regular pattern,

with each serving as cook and nightwatchman once per week in addition to his specific duties. The workhorses of the scientific programme were Madigan, who continued to collect meteorological data, and Bage, to whose previous work was added the magnetic observations that had been carried out by Webb. In the meantime, McLean maintained a biological log and Mawson carried out geological and biological investigations. But with a year of data already in place, it is not surprising that the men had little interest in continuing these jobs.

Of the more mundane tasks, Bage served as storeman, McLean collected the ice and coal – each performing their duties better than their predecessors, Murphy and Whetter – Bickerton took care of the power-plant, masts, and aerial for the wireless, and Hodgeman was in charge of the numerous changes around the hut, including building an annex, constructing new shelves, and reducing the size of the dining table. Mawson spent a great deal of time working up the early stages of some of the expedition reports, which in turn necessitated receiving both written and verbal accounts of the other sledging journeys.

The group that man-hauled the farthest was the Southern Party – Bage, Hurley, and Webb – in their attempt to reach the South Magnetic Pole. Letting the support party turn back on 21 November, they marched on for another month with a wind constantly in their faces, until they reached 301 miles from Winter Quarters. Unfortunately, magnetic observations showed they were still undetermined miles from the Pole. 'We searched the horizon with our glasses but could see nothing but snow, undulating and sastrugi-covered,' wrote Bage. 'To the SE our horizon was limited by our old enemy "the next ridge" only some 2 miles away. We wondered what could be beyond although we knew it was only the same endless repetition.' So, short of food and with fears of missing the ship, they reluctantly turned homeward. On the way back, they missed their last food depot and were forced to make a desperate dash to Aladdin's Cave to save themselves.

Madigan's East Coast Party also had a near miss. Crossing the Mertz and Ninnis Glacier Tongues, they ultimately halted 270 miles from base, just short of Cape Freshfield. A short way from there, they visited what they named Dreadnought Bluff, a huge vertical face of rock in the form of a breathtaking series of giant hexagonal, red, organ pipes. 'It was wonderful to think that these majestic heights had gazed out across the wastes of snow and ice for countless ages,' Madigan wrote, 'and never before had the voices of human beings echoed in the great stillness, nor human eyes surveyed the wondrous scene.' On the way back, they, too, ran out of food, and Madigan had to go ahead to the next depot and bring supplies back to McLean and Correll.

Stillwell also led several short ventures to the east, but the other major journey was by the Western Party. When the air-tractor broke down only ten miles from Winter Quarters, Bickerton, Hodgeman, and Whetter man-hauled across the Plateau, finally reaching a point 158 miles out. Despite becoming hopelessly lost on their way back, they somehow stumbled onto Aladdin's Cave, from where, reoriented, they descended to Cape Denison.

As a newcomer, Jeffryes had not, of course, been involved in any of the sledging, and Mawson had adjudged him too small for that role when they had first met anyway. But in his early days at the base, Jeffryes proved incredibly valuable in a different way: running the wireless, which finally became what Mawson had envisioned. On 15 February, the weather report from Macquarie Island was picked up. Five days later contact was at last established between the bases, and the next night Jeffryes sent out the first message for Macquarie to pass onto the outside world. Addressed to Lord Denman, the Governor-General of Australia, it asked for royal permission to give the name 'King George V Land' to the newly explored area to the east, a request that was granted. Soon thereafter, messages also went out to Professor David and the families of Ninnis and Mertz, and the first news of the outside world was received: 'Scott reached the Pole – died and 4 others.'

Winter Quarters and Macquarie Island began to 'talk' regularly, although it was not possible during daylight conditions, and auroral displays could interfere with signals at night. Now that Mawson was to remain in the Antarctic for another year, it became urgent to keep Macquarie manned as well. He was eventually able to ensure this by sending messages asking each man individually to remain until December as a personal favour.

Throughout this period, Jeffryes was a model of reliability, diligently sitting at the wireless from 8 p.m. until 1 a.m., headset on, listening for signals through the countless kinds of background distractions. His thoroughness impressed everyone, and led McLean to note: 'Jeffryes – we call him Jeff – is very anxious for the mast's safety, and takes spy-glasses out with him to see that everything is shipshape. We chaff him about his conscientious scruples. Of course the real event of the day consists in the wireless intelligence and by 10.30 we are all agog.'

Sometimes it seemed that the wireless simply hummed with communications, and one night Jeffryes recorded messages from the King, Professor David, and Ainsworth, the leader at Macquarie, among others. Personal notes also flashed through, including happy-birthday wishes to Bage, the official permission from Oxford for Madigan to postpone his Rhodes scholarship another year, and good wishes to Mawson from Kathleen Scott: 'Love and sympathy come back safe.'

Mawson replied to Kathleen the next day, as it was, in a sense, a business communication, but he avoided sending too many personal messages because, he wrote to Paquita, 'Until the business messages were got off, it was diplomatic of me to send few private messages for the others here were clamouring to send some to their loved ones.' One early one he *did* send expressed his belief to Paquita that it was unfair to hold her to her marriage commitment for an additional year: 'Deeply regret delay only just managed reach hut effects now gone but lost my hair you are free to consider your contract.' To his everlasting relief, he heard back: 'Deeply thankful you are safe warmest welcome awaiting your hairless return regarding contract same as ever only more so.'

As well as providing much-needed contact with people and events in the world at large, the wireless also played into the great frustration felt at times at Winter Quarters. Initially this was because there were periods when little seemed to get through the traffic in the ether. But in late May, Mawson put up a notice stating that all wireless messages would have to be paid for by the sender, could not be sent without his own approval, and would only go out 'as opportunity offers ... unless specially urgent.' Madigan – and perhaps others – felt this to be unjust and that the men who had stayed behind should receive the benefit of a few messages at expedition expense. Madigan's was a reasonable position, and, despite Mawson applying the same conditions to his own messages, it was an ill-considered move, although somewhat understandable when one considers his concerns about being faced with the huge, unexpected costs of *Aurora* needing to come south a third time. As it turned out, only ten days later it became a moot issue. Early on the morning of 8 June, a series of terrific gusts destroyed the top section of the main wireless mast and damaged the section below it, once again cutting them off from the outside world.

Being so isolated did not improve the quality of life at Cape Denison – no one confused it with moving to the open countryside. Madigan, in particular, sank into periods of depression and bitterness, much of which focused on Mawson, whom he saw as the cause of his enforced stay.

Bickerton, too, found the existence boring, monotonous, and dreary. But it was not just that 'the wind was unvarying as ever, the food we knew too well in every possible combination, and we felt badly the need of occasional entertainment with people not subject to our routine or monotonous climate.' Bickerton had been special friends with Ninnis and Mertz, and Madigan could hear him at times sobbing for them under his blankets in the now empty-seeming Hyde Park Corner.

Not all of the others were so gloomy and dismal, however. McLean, for example, found a project to help keep him busy and content: the *Adelie Blizzard*. Since early in the nineteenth century, British polar expeditions had produced newspapers, a tradition that Scott followed, and that Shackleton tried to improve upon with the first book written, printed, and bound in Antarctica. Mawson was strongly encouraged to follow the tradition by the fact that *South Polar Times* from Scott's first expedition had received a significant advance from a publisher in London. Mawson had hoped all of the men would participate in the first year, but the intensive preparations for sledging prevented the work from coming to fruition. Now, however, with no major sledging plans, McLean took the project forward. In six months he elicited the copy, edited and typed it, and produced five issues totalling 217 pages, with illustrations by Bickerton and Hodgeman. Its style covered the range from 'light doggerel to heavy blank verse . . . and original articles, letters to the Editor, plays, reviews of books and serial stories were accepted,' while the contributions could be about anything except the wind.

Needless to say, it was not easy to ignore the wind, which on 18 May reached a record average for twenty-four hours of 93.7 miles per hour. Two months later, the monthly record was also beaten, with an average of 63.6 miles per hour. That figure included the most intense sustained velocity of the expedition, when on 6 July it measured 116 mph for a full hour, and thereafter continued at such a rate that the eight-hour average was 107 mph. The battering of the hut was so strong that even its veteran inhabitants worried that the roof might be destroyed. They did not fret about it too long, however, as that very day their concentration and apprehension were transferred to another fearful situation in the making, one that threatened to strike them even *within* the supposedly safe confines of their hut.

11

THE LONG WAIT

THROUGHOUT THE AUTUMN, each of the six men
who had spent the previous year at Winter Quarters at
times felt envious of Jeffryes. To them, so many things were
dreary, disappointing repetitions of what had gone on before.
But, they assumed, to Jeffryes all was as fresh and novel as
life in the ferocious conditions at Cape Denison had been
to them twelve months before. Little did they know that
something in that lonesome, inhospitable setting – or deep
within the wireless operator – was affecting him in a sad
and terrible way.

It first came to light on a day otherwise notable for the
most violent continuous winds of the expedition. But it was
the environment within the hut, not outside, that caused
things to be abruptly blown apart. 'Last night Jeffryes at the
table suddenly asked Madigan to go into the next room (to
fight) as he believed that something had been said against
him – nothing whatever had,' wrote Mawson. 'Madigan had
mentioned the name of a novel he had read that day *The
Hound of the Baskervilles* and Jeffryes appears to have taken
it to be a reference to him.' Madigan, whose periods of
bitterness and melancholia kept him on edge much of the
time himself, responded heatedly, and Mawson stepped in
to calm things down, although he nervously heard that

Jeffryes had earlier tried to engage in combat with McLean over things he thought were being said about him in the *Adelie Blizzard*.

The next morning, 7 July, Madigan went to the entrance veranda to fill a lamp with kerosene. Suddenly, there was Jeffryes, challenging him to fight again and dancing around him in a rage. Madigan thought himself ready for anything Jeffryes could bring on, but the wireless operator hit the larger man in the mouth so quickly that Madigan fell backwards. In the ensuing scuffle, Madigan grabbed him by the throat, and it was not until Hodgeman saw them and called to the others that Mawson put an end to it. 'McLean thinks [Jeffryes] is a bit off his head,' Mawson wrote. 'I think that his touchy temperament is being very hard tested with bad weather and indoor life. A case of polar depression. I trust it will go now.' Never was Mawson more wrong in his predictions.

In the following days, Jeffryes' behaviour became increasingly peculiar. He stopped washing and began to keep a collection of urine on his shelf. He ominously asked Bickerton to be his second. And he approached Mawson after breakfast one morning 'and confides in me that he "went the pace" when he was younger and it left him with a venereal trouble . . . Asks me to get McLean to give him a poison. This makes me think he surely must be going off his base.' After speaking to Jeffryes that night, McLean told Mawson that the story about venereal disease was a hallucination, but one of several signs that Jeffryes was suffering from 'delusive insanity.'

The diagnosis caught the other men off guard, as did Jeffryes' ongoing episodes. On 12 July he stated that the others were sitting in judgement over him and that any problem had been brought about by McLean analysing his urine (which had not happened). The next day he wrote a series of letters asserting his sanity, including one to his sister, to whom he maintained, 'I am to be done to death by a jury of six murderers who are trying to prove me insane.' He told Madigan that he would take one good night's sleep and Madigan could shoot him in the morning. And at his birthday celebration, he 'made a speech in which he spoke clearly and well, but the matter foolish cant like his letters.'

As none of the others had any experience with or understanding of mental illness, Jeffryes' bizarre conduct varyingly produced irritation, anxiety, or fear. Bage and Hodgeman found it difficult to sleep because Jeffryes put curtains of clothes around his bunk so no one could tell if he were awake until he leered out from between them. Concerned that Jeffryes might turn violent, Mawson set out a schedule so that someone would always to be around to watch him, including at night. Being nightwatchman with Jeffryes as part of the duty brought distinct problems. At breakfast one day, Jeffryes claimed that during the night Bickerton had loaded a gun to kill him. Bickerton – according to a friend to whom he later told the story – had been advised by McLean 'to argue with him as though he were sane and try and prove calmly that he had not made any attempt to kill him.' But even after Bickerton did so, 'the madman asked "Would you swear on the Bible that you did not and will not try to kill me". [Bickerton] of course said yes bring me a bible. "Would you swear on your mother's bible". Yes if I had it. "Swear by all you ever held truest and dearest". "Certainly I would". "Well even if you did all that I wouldn't believe you".'

Sadly, since psychiatry and psychology were so primitive as practical disciplines, even McLean had no idea how to help the hapless Jeffryes. Each man tried to reassure him, ignore him, or act as if nothing unusual had happened, but none of these tactics gave any indication of benefiting him. Then, late in July, Jeffryes handed Mawson a letter that stated, 'I am now reluctantly obliged to tender my resignation as a member of this expedition as I am unable to carry on owing to the bellicose attitude shown toward me by other members.' Mawson tried to deal with Jeffryes' proposal to move out of the hut by addressing the impossibility of it at dinner, using a combination of logic and threat. Initially the move seemed to work, as Jeffryes apologised, stated he was ill, and expressed the hope that he would be forgiven. But it was not long before his mood and behavioural fluctuations became worse than ever.

Unfortunately, Jeffryes' descent into even more erratic and intransigent conduct came at just the time when his role took on increased significance. A calm day on 5 August allowed the others to re-erect the mast and aerial, and that night contact was again established with Macquarie Island. But within days, the wireless operator had taken to going to bed well before midnight, when the best transmission results could be expected. 'What can be done with him I can't imagine,' Mawson noted with distress, 'for if I try to get him to keep up to scratch, his miserable temperament is likely to cause trouble in sending. He takes the crystal out of the setting each evening so that nobody else can use the instruments. I certainly feel like skinning him, but will wait another day and see how things go.'

But a series of talks with Jeffryes about living up to his agreements – including working satisfactory hours on the wireless, bathing regularly, and completing his duties when he was cook – made little impact, and he continued to do what he wanted, when he wanted, and little more, regardless of how it impinged on anyone else. 'It appears that when we all went out Jeffryes had a hurried bath,' wrote Mawson, 'how much of his body nobody knows, but everybody is decided that the canvas bath will now want disinfecting. Before this came off McLean and Madigan spoke to him . . . He spoke insolently to them, and spoke of using violence on Dad.'

And yet what could the other inhabitants of Winter Quarters do? Bickerton practised sending and receiving, but he was not yet proficient, and they all felt their hands were tied, so as August turned into September, and then October neared, things had not changed dramatically. Each time Jeffryes became rational, Mawson hoped he would be able to maintain his sanity, but each time he slipped back. 'Jeffryes . . . said he would have to send a message to Australia that the Hut was being made too hot for him,' Mawson recorded one night. 'Complained in a dazed sort of way of banging on the wall. Rambled on. Quite bug again.' The next night was even more shocking in its way. 'Tells me that he and I are the only two not mad,' Mawson wrote. 'Says the others are making it too hot for us. Says he is sorry he could not get the message through last night apprising the world that we are all mad. Says he will try tonight.'

Nor was Jeffryes bluffing. The next evening, after he sent a load of material at a high rate without looking at the message forms, Mawson halted him and then 'accused him and extracted the confession that he had been trying to get through a message to the effect that 5 of us were insane,' he wrote to Paquita. 'I do not know whether it got through or not. He sends far too fast for any of us amateurs to read him. He was very contrite and took an oath to the effect that he would do his best in the future to follow orders implicitly . . . What can one do with a lunatic?'

The first thing was to limit the potential damage. Mawson immediately had Bickerton contact Ainsworth: 'Censor all messages Jeffryes insane Mawson.' Then he determined that Bickerton would take over the wireless operation, because, 'It is madness to let a lunatic humbug us like this. He is not rational in ordinary talking; how can he be with the wireless?' This changeover occurred during a period of several weeks, and although Mawson more than once relented and allowed Jeffryes to man the post, each time aberrant behaviour forced Jeffryes out again. Finally, in a strange combination of delusion and insight, Jeffryes wrote to Mawson that, 'I have been continuing my duties for the past two weeks under the influence of a hypnotic spell under which you have found it incumbent upon you to place me to avert a calamity. I reluctantly ask to be relieved of my duties as operator for should the present untoward conditions continue my health will suffer & perhaps my reason.' Mawson quickly acceded to the request, and Bickerton was once and for all the wireless operator.

Throughout the winter, Jeffryes proved the dominant feature in Mawson's diary, but his mental health was not the only issue of significance. Mawson's own physical condition improved only very slowly, as he noted at the end of July: 'I appear to be suffering from a mild irritation of the bladder, felt only when feet are cold. My health is very poor. Have been suffering for some days from a large deep-seated inflammation over practically the whole of the right side of my face. The day before yesterday it began to burst as a boil ... Some teeth want attending to.'

Another problem was sheer boredom, which attacked some men more intensely than others. Mawson found relief in working on his expedition account, in drawing up initial plans of the house he hoped to build for Paquita, and in immersing himself in his beloved geology, attempting to expand Stillwell's collection. McLean not only spent much time on the *Adelie Blizzard*, he also was able to enjoy the enormous library that had been compiled for the expedition. 'Conversation often flags for want of ideas,' he wrote, 'and only for our fine collection of books, I don't know how we should get on.'

The books did not seem to help Madigan, who was plagued by depression and dissatisfaction, the latter particularly with Mawson. Madigan clearly thought himself better than the others, and his belief that he would have been the best leader for the expedition was one thing that led him to criticise Mawson – at least in his diary – harshly and on a broad front. Many of his complaints seem unfair in retrospect, but indicate that at some level there was a current of dissatisfaction within the hut. A general disenchantment was still in evidence by the beginning of November, when Mawson noted: 'Said some words all round re low ebb, trying to galvanise them.'

Nothing could have picked the men up more, however, than one item of news they finally received: *Aurora* would sail south in mid-November to relieve the party at Commonwealth Bay. This information firmed up Mawson's final plans, because it gave him time to make a last sledging trip, on which – aware of the huge costs the extra year and the additional voyage would impose upon him – he hoped to retrieve the costly instruments and the specimens abandoned by both the East Coast Party and the Southern Party in order to dash to safety after suffering food shortages.

On 19 November, *Aurora* departed from Hobart, but at Winter Quarters the sledging party of Mawson, Madigan, and Hodgeman was, as on so many previous trips, delayed first by dense drift and then high winds. Finally, on the 24th, they headed up the icy slope for their last journey to the Plateau, accompanied by the remaining dogs. Going back to the desolate interior surely must have been a test of mental and emotional fortitude for Mawson after his ordeal, but at least he felt confident that he could safely leave Jeffryes. 'He says he is helpless, that I have a spell upon him,' Mawson wrote, before adding how he turned the man's delusions to his own advantage: 'I tell him that I put a spell upon him not to play monkey tricks when I am away.'

That night the trio camped at Aladdin's Cave, and the next day they set a course towards a valley running next to Mount Outlook, where the East Coast Party had established a major cache at the beginning of the year. After several days of hard travel, they camped at Mount Outlook, and on the morning of 29 November, Madigan and Hodgeman descended to the area in which the cache had been established. But so heavy had been the accumulation of snow in the intervening months that all markers had disappeared, leaving the equipment and samples irretrievably lost.

On the last day of November, the three headed towards the point where Bage, Hurley, and Webb had similarly abandoned expensive equipment. But after two days of travel, they were confined to their tent by six days of high winds and low-blowing drift, and by the time the weather moderated they had to turn back to Winter Quarters, since Mawson had left Davis a message that he would return by 10 December – and he certainly did not want to miss him yet again. It must have been a terrible wrench for Mawson to leave behind the scientific instruments, but this search was unlikely to have been any more successful than the previous one. '[T]here is little doubt in my mind that our depot was already well buried by snow, when we returned to the vicinity nearly 7 weeks after establishing it,' Webb wrote years later, explaining why the Southern Party had been unable to find the depot of food and supplies. 'Moreover, the amount of snow drifted by the S to SE wind into the Mertz Glacier valley could readily have submerged a taller flag than our 14 footer.'

So now the three men headed back to base, their last journey giving them every nasty, unpleasant turn that Nature could provide. Forty-mile headwinds and rock-hard sastrugi that damaged their sledge were bad enough, but when they reached a point only fifteen miles from Winter Quarters they were stranded in their tent for three days by winds up to 70 miles an hour. It was enough to make Mawson question what could possibly be positive about such an experience: 'The dreary outlook, the indefinite surroundings, the never-ending seethe, rattle and ping of the drift,' he wrote. 'The flap of the tent; the . . . dwindling of food, the deterioration of tent, dogs, etc. The irksomeness, bone-wearying cramped quarters, the damp or the cold. The anxiety for the future, the disappointment for prospects.'

Becoming progressively more anxious, on 12 December they braved the continuing winds and marched towards Winter Quarters. As they made their way down the tricky slopes from Aladdin's Cave, Mawson could see a trail of steam far across Commonwealth Bay. But unlike the previous year, when *Aurora* was departing, this time she was heading towards them.

The three men reached the hut shortly after midnight, and, upon hearing the news, the others all raced out to Azimuth Hill, where, smiles on their faces, they watched the ship clear the Mackellar Islets. Owing to the previous year's problems, however, Davis was exceptionally careful in finding an anchorage, and ultimately took so long that the shore party went to bed. They were awoken around 8 a.m., when Davis and others came ashore. Near the door of the hut, Mawson greeted Davis after almost two years. 'As I shook his hand I was conscious of a sudden feeling of intense relief,' Davis wrote, 'relief that he was manifestly alive and well, relief that I had been able to do my duty. My life has given me few moments that have been more rewarding.'

For the next five days, Cape Denison was a hive of industry, as the weather remained fine and the men used the opportunity to move virtually every item of the slightest personal or financial value to the ship. The heavy equipment, such as the lathe, sewing machines, air-tractor engine, and motors and dynamos, joined cases of kerosene, scientific instruments, provisions, specimens, and personal gear in being pulled on sledges to the motor-launch and then driven out to *Aurora* to be stored. Meanwhile, Davis took the opportunity to fill Mawson in on what had happened in recent months, and the two discussed plans for the rest of the voyage. Mawson decided that *Aurora* would not head straight back to Australia, but would visit nearby islands and the Mertz Glacier Tongue, carry out dredging and sounding, and then make the long voyage to explore the Shackleton Ice Shelf, which Mawson had missed the previous year when he could not be picked up.

Mawson knew from the beginning that arranging for his rescue had been no easy task. But hearing first-hand everything involved must have confirmed beyond doubt that he could not possibly have made a better selection for his second-in-command. Following *Aurora*'s arrival in Hobart in March 1913, Davis had been sent by Professor David and the expedition committee to England to raise emergency funds for the second relief voyage. Reaching England in May, Davis – with the guidance of Hugh Robert Mill, the former librarian of the RGS and a great advocate of exploration – established the 'Mawson Relief Fund 1913,' which quickly received a donation of £1,000 from Sir Robert Lucas Tooth, an Australian living in England, and then further contributions from, among others, the Royal Society, the RGS, and Kathleen Scott. It was also arranged for Davis to meet the Chancellor of the Exchequer, David Lloyd George, who set the wheels in motion for a grant of £1,000 from the British government. Perhaps even more important, Lloyd George's generosity encouraged the government in Australia to be supportive, and within forty-eight hours of a deputation being sent to Prime Minister Joseph Cook, a grant of £5,000 had been promised by the Commonwealth.

After many repairs on *Aurora* and much preparation, the relief voyage finally left Hobart on 19 November. Surprisingly, picking up Mawson's party was not Davis' first task. On the way south, he was to carry out a programme of sounding and dredging, with John Hunter accompanying the cruise in charge of biological studies. Second, Davis was to relieve the expedition members still at Macquarie Island. This also entailed dropping off a three-man government party that would continue the meteorological and wireless operations for the next year. And only finally was he to rescue those at Cape Denison.

Aurora reached Hasselborough Bay at Macquarie Island on 28 November, and for the next week, while men and supplies were swapped over, two other members of the original Cape Denison team – Hurley and Correll – made a photographic and cinematographic record of the island. Although previously having been essentially Hurley's sidekick, Correll had, since being back in Australia, made intensive studies in colour photography. While Hurley enlarged on his impressive portfolio from Macquarie, Winter Quarters, and the stops thereafter, Correll made cutting-edge efforts with the new Paget colour process. So successful was he, that Mawson used a number of his colour images when his expedition account was published as *The Home of the Blizzard*.

After the ship was loaded and iced at Cape Denison, Mawson and the other members of the shore party – including Hunter, the two photographers, and the Macquarie Island mob – were landed to make thorough investigations at the Mackellar Islets and then Cape Hunter, rocky cliffs they had been able to see but not reach for the past two years. Finally, on 23 December, Madigan and Bickerton closed up the hut. The windows were battened down, the chimney stuffed with bagging, the veranda entrance boarded up, and a notice nailed up inviting anyone who needed them to use the hut and stores.

After almost two years, Mawson and his men were ready to depart, but before they could, the blizzard returned for one last round. For more than two days a storm of almost unequalled power battered *Aurora*, which took such punishment that the davits holding the motor-launch bent and then tore out, boat and bulwark disappearing into the raging sea. Finally, on Boxing Day, conditions ameliorated and they were able to steam away from Cape Denison. As they left, the last thing visible, on the highest point of Azimuth Hill, was a large memorial cross that had been raised by Bickerton and McLean. Eleven-feet high and with a crossbar more than seven feet long, it had been constructed by Bickerton from sections of the broken wireless mast, bolted together, and bound with brass strips. At its base was a plaque Hodgeman had produced, commemorating for eternity the 'supreme sacrifice made by Lieut B.E.S. Ninnis, R.F. and Dr X. Mertz in the cause of science.'

*   *   *

For several days the ship's party explored the coast between Commonwealth Bay and the tip of the Mertz Glacier Tongue, trawling, observing the wildlife, and examining the ice. Then, turning west, they began the long cruise towards the Shackleton Ice Shelf. For more than two weeks, conditions fluctuated between gales, fog, icebergs, and consolidated pack, the last extending well beyond the western edge of the ice shelf. When they finally reached open water – near where the German exploring ship *Gauss* had been trapped in the ice for a year more than a decade before – they turned south, then back east, navigating between the shoreline and the long line of impenetrable pack they had just passed on its far side.

By this time, Davis had been sleep-deprived for days, and now, in relatively clear water for the first time, he went to bed. His rest did not last long, however, as Mawson, hoping to start a dredging operation, inconsiderately awoke him. 'Christ Almighty, leave me alone, look after your own business,' the fiery Davis blurted, Mawson unrepentantly noting only: 'It is with great difficulty that one assumes the tactful position.' Neither yet knew it, but the spat was a brief glimpse of what they would experience in their relationship in days – and years – to come.

As they approached the west side of the Shackleton Ice Shelf, the icebergs became more congested, and while passing through a particularly heavy area early on 23 January, a blizzard suddenly materialised. Within moments, 70 mph winds were blowing snow with such intensity that no one could see from one side of the ship to the other. Davis tried to bring the ship quickly to shelter but could not move ahead into the wind, even with the engines at full steam. For a full day they fought the elements, at one point losing the martingale – a chain that was one of the ship's main supports – to a blue growler that appeared at the last second. 'Quite a different storm to that of normal climates,' Mawson wrote. 'Capt Davis tired out. I get a little nervous, showing that I have never got over the dose on sledging journey.'

By 25 January, *Aurora* was still impotent in the face of
the conditions, and Davis was forced to cruise up and down
the ice shelf for protection. It was not until the morning of
the 27th that the storm blew itself out, and the party could
try to reach the Western Base so that Mawson and the others
could examine the conditions under which their colleagues
had lived. Halted well short of it, however, by giant fields
of fast ice, they instead steamed slowly north, mapping,
dredging, and sounding as near the edge of the ice shelf as
they could come. But even a period of good weather could
not overcome the strain and stress that the gale had caused.
Both Mawson and Davis became increasingly demanding
and found it more and more difficult to get along together
or with others.

The low point came on 2 February, after they reached the
northwest corner of the Shackleton Ice Shelf. Davis – unchar-
acteristically bold – started steaming east, straight down the
northern edge of the ice shelf, but Mawson was worried
about being caught between it and the pack, and asked him
to go back the way they had come. Grudgingly, Davis turned
the ship, but then, spying a lead near the corner of the ice
shelf, he headed north, rounded a large floe and again moved
east. 'I express my anxiety and state that this course is entirely
adverse to that which I had expect [*sic*] him to take,' wrote
Mawson. 'As usual nowadays he is very irritable, can scarcely
speak civilly at all. (The strain, I believe, has severely played
up with his nerves.)' Davis eventually acceded to Mawson's
request to retreat again, but the tension between the two
men came close to causing a serious rupture. 'This work is
very trying on Capt Davis as he has to be on the alert so
much,' Mawson wrote in acknowledging their difficulties. 'I
hope the strain won't tell any more on him. For myself –
my nerves, damaged by the sledging adventure, are beginning
to play up again. The anxiety is considerable.'

The only way to relieve such anxiety was to go home, but
even that took days, as they slowly followed the inside edge

of the pack that separated them from the sea to the north. Finally, after forty-eight hours forcing their way through the ice – during which Davis rarely left the bridge – they reached open water. 'I am glad to be out of the ice,' Davis wrote. 'It is a heavy strain on one man all the time, and I am afraid I have been feeling pretty grousey for some days past ... ever since we left [Winter Quarters], I have been in doubt as to what was really our programme.'

Fortunately, there was no longer any doubt as to their agenda: make for Adelaide. They added sails to the engines, and every day brought them closer to home, all – except perhaps Jeffryes, who remained in a cabin under the care of McLean – looking forward to the end of the mission. On 21 February, they were overtaken by *Archibald Russell*, a four-masted barque that was the first sign of civilisation Mawson had seen for more than two years.

And then they were there. On the afternoon of 26 February, outside Port Adelaide, they were met by a launch containing, amongst others, Professor David and Professor Masson, two men whose influence had meant so much for the expedition. A short while later, while Davis guided *Aurora* into the wharf to the cheers of an assembled crowd, Mawson dashed away in a special tender. As soon as he landed, he went directly to the South Australian Hotel. There, in a reserved room, were Paquita and her mother. 'It is hard to describe the feelings one has when meeting someone whose image has lived only in one's thoughts for so long,' Paquita wrote. 'When he entered the room, I just had time to think: "Yes, of course, that's what he is like!" Douglas said: "You have had a long time to wait," and then everything was all right.'

12

A Hero at War and Peace

IF, WHILE *AURORA* made her slow way north, Mawson
had any illusions about being able either to rest and recover
after his homecoming or to spend some quiet time with
Paquita, he was disabused of them upon his arrival in
Adelaide. He found himself a hero on a much larger scale
than after his return from Shackleton's expedition, and with
that celebrity status went a relentless procession of receptions,
fetes, and interviews. Throw in the preparations for his
wedding, which was scheduled for the last day of March,
and efforts to dig the expedition out of more than £8,000
of debt, and his life was, to say the least, hectic.

The initial taste of what was to come was given in two
public receptions the week after the expedition's return. The
first, at the University of Adelaide, was attended by Lord
Denman, the Governor-General, and included a message of
congratulations from the King. The following day, the Lord
Mayor hosted another packed event at the town hall. Typical
of the eulogy-loving speakers at these events was one who
stated:

Douglas Mawson has returned from a journey that was
absolutely unparalleled in the history of exploration – one
of the greatest illustrations of how the sternest affairs of

Nature were overcome by the superb courage, power and
resolve of man. It would have been easy to have died in such
circumstances ... to have given in to the difficulties; but it
was quite a different thing to go on and on, *alone* as Dr
Mawson did for thirty solid days. That was the finest thing
that had ever been done on such an expedition.

With such praise being heaped upon him – and not just in
Adelaide – there were potentially great advantages in travelling to Britain for the famed London 'season.' There
Mawson would have professional, social, financial, and
publishing opportunities that could never be equalled in
Australia. Understanding this, the administration at the
university once again generously granted him leave and hired
former Winter Quarters geologist Frank Stillwell as his
temporary replacement. With this in place, Mawson booked
passage to Marseilles for 1 April, the morning after his
wedding. Even from the start, theirs was not to be a normal
honeymoon. Mawson and Paquita were to be joined by Davis
and McLean, the latter serving as amanuensis to help
complete what would become *The Home of the Blizzard*
while the 'Mawson-mania' lingered and potential sales of
the book were at their height.

In the intervening month, Mawson threw himself into
scientific and governmental meetings, social receptions, and
fund-raising efforts around the country. None of these financial campaigns was hugely successful, and most of the money
raised came from selling *Aurora* to Shackleton three weeks
after the expedition's return. Despite still feeling betrayed
by the way Shackleton had simply assimilated the £10,000
Gerald Lysaght had given for the AAE in 1910, the £3,200
Shackleton now offered was too great a temptation for
Mawson to turn down. On his Imperial Trans-Antarctic
Expedition, Shackleton planned to use *Aurora* to transport
a party to Ross Island, from where supply depots would be
laid to assist his own crossing of the continent from the

Weddell Sea. At the same time, Shackleton tried to bring aboard *Aurora*'s master as well – to captain *Endurance*, the ship due to take him to the base of the Weddell Sea – but Davis turned him down.

Meanwhile, the other members of the expedition scattered. Madigan left to take up his Rhodes Scholarship in Oxford, and Bickerton also went home to England. Hurley showed interest in Shackleton's expedition but then took off to the outback to film adventurer Francis Birtles. Bage returned to duty with the Royal Australian Engineers. And Jeffryes departed even before the festivities in Adelaide, boarding a train for his home in Queensland. Unfortunately, he got off in Ararat, Victoria, instead, and his subsequent bizarre behaviour led to him being committed to a local asylum; other than brief periods in other mental hospitals, he spent the rest of his life in Ararat's asylum. Mawson's insensitive handling of Jeffryes at the end of the expedition, and his unsympathetic correspondence with the ill man's family, were not amongst his most impressive accomplishments.

On 31 March 1914, at Holy Trinity Church in Balaclava, Melbourne, the patience of Mawson and Paquita was finally rewarded. They were married in a ceremony throughout which – according to his new wife – Mawson grinned like a Cheshire cat, while Davis, the best man, was the one with a bad case of nerves, passing the ring from one hand to the other behind his back while some in the audience became more absorbed with whether he would drop it than with the couple's vows. The next morning, the three of them and McLean embarked ship for Europe. A little over a month later, Mawson already having received honours at intermediate stops in Naples, Toulon, and Paris, they arrived in Britain. On the quay at Dover, Mawson made an error that, if it occurred today, would feature in the tabloid press. Having gone ahead temporarily, he returned and, according to Paquita, 'slipped his arm into that of a woman walking just in front of me, thinking, so he said, it was I. She looked so surprised that he was quite embarrassed.' Davis and McLean both had great fun at Mawson's expense on the way to London.

A reprise of Mawson's frenzied schedule in Australia now occurred, with lectures, interviews, scientific meetings, and fund-raising efforts squeezed around his busy social agenda and – under the watchful eye of publisher William Heinemann – daily work on *The Home of the Blizzard*. McLean was a godsend; he heavily edited or rewrote the reports of Wild, Ainsworth, and the leaders of the sledging parties, as well as much of Mawson's own material, and helped make the literary quality much higher than that of most expedition accounts. Meanwhile, Hodgeman also travelled to England, where he produced the diagrams and illustrations for the two-volume work. The photographic elements were not so simple; Hurley, gallivanting off for his new projects, did not supply everything requested – including numerous auto-chrome plates and the dozen negatives Mawson considered the very best – so Mawson turned instead to Correll for a set of colour photos, which were ultimately used to excellent effect.

One of the first things the Mawsons did in England was visit Ninnis' family, unsuccessfully trying to help them find solace. Strangely, the Great War, so soon to follow, helped Mrs Ninnis in this regard, as Paquita later discovered. Ninnis' regiment, the Royal Fusiliers, 'had early been cut to pieces in France,' Paquita wrote. 'Somehow death in an icy crevasse seemed more fitting to his youth than slaughter in the mud of Flanders, however sacred the latter became to us all.'

Mawson also visited the family of another casualty from what Shackleton later termed 'the white warfare of the south,' and the effort produced a financial boon to the expedition. On 21 May, over dinner, Kathleen Scott offered Mawson £1,000 from the proceeds of the book *Scott's Last Expedition*. 'I do not like using the sum derived from the book for private purposes, my husband would not have done so,' she wrote the next day in renewing her offer. 'I had always meditated helping your venture a little if you would let me.' The only condition was that Mawson not let it be known that Kathleen was the generous source, a request with which he complied.

Although it would be unrealistic to say that Mawson was the 'lion of the London season,' as in many senses Shackleton had been, he was definitely a man in whom many had an interest, so he had interactions with far more than just those related to the polar community. At the British Empire Club, he dined with such luminaries as Lord Curzon, Lord Chelmsford, and Lord Tennyson. He was received at Buckingham Palace by King George V and at Marlborough House by the Queen Mother and the Dowager Empress of Russia. Then on 29 June, three weeks after his much-anticipated lecture to the RGS, he was knighted by the King.

Mawson's hectic schedule meant that on many evenings the newlyweds went to separate events, and even at those that Paquita attended, they were not always seated together. But once again Davis proved an able second. 'Captain Davis came with us to most of the functions and was a great comfort and support to me,' Paquita wrote about the man who gave her the compliments that normally come from a husband. 'Poor Douglas was always so engrossed in his book and the many speeches he had to make that there was no time to *see* what I wore . . . I've often told Captain Davis that I could never have got through my honeymoon without him . . . As long as I wore a hat when everyone else did, and was there on time, everything was fine to Douglas.'

In July the couple left the exhilaration of London to journey home, stopping on the way in Basle to visit the Mertz family. Aboard ship near Aden, they heard that war had been declared. It would not be long before Mawson found out how negatively that would impact his goal of resolving the AAE's financial woes.

One of Mawson's greatest hopes had been that profits from showing Hurley's film would not only pay off the remaining expedition debts, but would finance the publication of the series of Scientific Reports. However, the film company contracted to exploit its economic opportunities delayed its release due to competition from Herbert Ponting's motion picture of the Scott expedition, and then lost part of the original film. After much legal posturing, Mawson made an agreement with a new company, but while the contract was waiting to be signed, the war broke out, leading that company to renege. Finally Mawson found yet another potential distributor, but, due to financial difficulties caused by the war, it went into liquidation soon thereafter.

An equally frustrating situation was the postponement of the publication of *The Home of the Blizzard*. Even after Mawson's return to Australia, McLean remained in London working on it with proofreading help from Hugh Robert Mill, the famed former librarian of the RGS and noted historian of polar exploration. '[W]hen the book is finished it should approach perfection in accuracy and grammatical correctness which I think is a necessity before style,' McLean boasted to Mawson. But such issues proved irrelevant after the outbreak of hostilities. 'If we are still in the heat of battle, no one will take the slightest interest in your book,' publisher William Heinemann wrote upon delaying the book's appearance. 'That does not, of course, mean that there will never be again an interest in your work – but it will take some time; and it would be courting failure to press upon an unwilling public . . . anything but what they are immediately interested in . . . War and the combatants.'

Instead, to replace the lucrative speaking tour of Britain and the Continent, which the war had scuttled, Heinemann encouraged Mawson to make a lecture tour of the United States. This was scheduled to coincide with Lippincott's American publication of the book in January 1915. In the interim, Mawson briefly returned to lecturing at the university after three years away. In October, at the end of term, he gave a presentation in New Zealand, where he saw Eric Webb for the first time since saying farewell at Aladdin's Cave at the start of the sledging journeys. To the former chief magnetician, the changes wrought in Mawson during the previous two years were fully apparent. '[H]e was the same tough, self-reliant character . . . still purposeful, but he was a noticeably chastened man – quieter, humble, and I think very much closer to his God,' Webb wrote, adding, 'he told me that there was some other power he had borrowed on that journey which was superior to the willpower that pulled him through. His faith steeled him; he drew his personal strength from this faith. Yet I saw he had aged, was worn, had lost much of his hair, and I fear he was never again the same iron man who started on that fateful journey.'

But as Shackleton, Amundsen, and others before him had found, Mawson needed a strength almost equal – if totally different – to that he had shown in the Antarctic for the daunting task ahead. Sailing to New York at the beginning of 1915, he began a gruelling, repetitive, soul-destroying series of speaking engagements that forced him to travel all over the eastern half of the United States and much of Canada. Night after night he had to relate the horrors of his friends' deaths and his interminable, lonely journey in such a way as to please audiences seeking a delicious thrill rather than a painful tragedy. And although he did have the chance to meet any number of prominent figures, such as former President Theodore Roosevelt, Arctic explorers Adolphus W. Greely and Robert E. Peary, and noted American geologist W.H. Hobbs, the venture was not a triumphal, or even easy, procession. 'The rail travelling you would have hated,' he wrote to Paquita, who was in Australia, where, in April 1915, their first daughter, Patricia, was born. 'I dislike it, whereas in Australia I don't mind. These Pullman cars are bad – it is usual for me to travel each night after the lecture arriving about 7 a.m. at next place.'

Towards the end of his planned schedule, Mawson was swayed by a significant financial offer to extend his programme until the end of March, lecturing twice a day at a theatre in New York. Unfortunately, not only did he detest the experience, it also did little to promote his book. Although Heinemann relented and published *The Home of the Blizzard* in Britain and the Empire later in the year, only 3,500 copies were printed for the entire world, which drastically limited its potential. And any hopes for future press runs were crushed when 'the printing works was burnt down late in the War and the type destroyed.' The moment Mawson finished his lecturing extension, he headed for Adelaide, where he found university work a blessing by comparison.

As had been shown by his many symbolic gestures in the Antarctic, Mawson was a true patriot and a believer in the British Empire. Therefore, it was not long after his return to Australia that he began to feel keenly the need to contribute to the war effort against Germany, an entity he described as 'a criminal on a large scale run amok.' His negative feelings about the Central Powers could only have been strengthened when Bob Bage – one of the men he had most respected from the AAE and a captain in the Royal Australian Engineers – was killed on the Lone Pine Plateau of Gallipoli.

Following the lead of Professor David – who was president of the New South Wales branch of the pro-conscription Universal Service League – Mawson became one of the principal organisers of the South Australia pro-conscription campaign. At the same time, he offered his service to the Commonwealth's Department of Defence in any capacity they wished. Remarkably, his attempts to find a position through the Australian government were rejected, so he decided to go to England, where he believed his scientific knowledge could make a valuable contribution. Leaving Paquita and Patricia with the Delprats, he again took academic leave and in March 1916 sailed for San Francisco, from where he crossed the United States and took a ship to England.

Initially, Mawson's efforts in London bore little more fruit than they had in Australia. Instead, he was quickly co-opted to serve on the Admiralty's Shackleton Relief Committee, which had been formed to oversee the relief of Shackleton's party stranded at Elephant Island after the loss of his ship *Endurance* in the Weddell Sea. When Shackleton managed this himself without the assistance of the Admiralty, the committee's focus shifted to the members of his Ross Sea party marooned on Ross Island. Eventually, with the backing and financing of the British, Australian, and New Zealand governments, John King Davis was appointed commander of the relief expedition and captain of *Aurora*, in which he rescued the forlorn men.

Meanwhile, it took two months before Mawson finally was able to begin a job with the Commission Internationale de Ravitaillement (CIR), the organisation coordinating Allied supplies, for which he oversaw the loading aboard ship in Liverpool of high explosives and poison gas destined for Britain's allies in Russia. However, although it brought with it the rank of temporary captain, this was a dead-end position that any automaton could carry out, and it quickly became tedious. Its lack of intellectual stimulation was emphasised when compared to Mawson's regular scholarly and social contacts with the likes of Nobel Prize winners Sir Ernest Rutherford and William H. Bragg; Sir J.J. Thomson, President of the Royal Society; Charles Parsons, the inventor of the steam turbine; and, of course, Kathleen Scott and her young son Peter.

Despite being joined by Paquita in November 1916 – after she had left Patricia with relatives for what turned out to be the duration of the war – Mawson remained so frustrated by the lack of a challenge that he wrote to University Registrar Charles Hodge that he intended to return to Adelaide. But before they were able to leave, an appropriate, and for Mawson stimulating, position was found for him as the Ministry of Munitions' liaison with the Russian Military Commission. Mawson was assigned to prepare a series of reports relating to the manufacture of explosives and gas in munitions factories around Britain so that the Russians could start up their own similar establishments. This allowed him not only to examine the methods for making such diverse weapons components as phosgene gas, nitro-glycerine, nitric acid, sulphuric acid, and liquid chlorine, but to make comparative analyses of the strengths and weaknesses of the differing chemical methods, quality of the end products, and cost-efficiency of the processes. Mawson was scheduled to visit Russia to discuss his reports when the Bolshevik seizure of power occurred in October 1917. Instead of meeting with the military leaders of the new regime, he remained in Britain, where in that same period his second daughter, Jessica, was born during an air raid.

At the beginning of 1918, Mawson was named commanding officer of the High Explosives, Chemical Warfare and Petroleum Section of the CIR, and within a few months he was promoted to temporary major. He held this position and rank for the remainder of the war. However, in spite of the intense war-related work schedule Mawson had followed throughout this stay in Britain, his mind was never far from the Antarctic and he regularly continued his Antarctic-related efforts. None of these weighed more upon him than resolving the financial shortfalls of the expedition. Chief amongst the remaining debts was the £955 that had never been paid to Vickers for the aeroplane, and that Mawson had discovered was still outstanding only after he returned from the Antarctic. In November 1916 he mentioned this deficit to Sir Trevor Dawson, director of Vickers. With his company buoyed by numerous wartime contracts, Dawson could afford to be generous, and at a stroke half of the AAE's remaining debt was removed, Dawson noting simply that, 'I have consulted my Firm, who readily agree to allow the payment for the Monoplane to lapse.'

Mawson's other financial efforts were not as successful. Around the same time that he was the beneficiary of Vickers' generosity, he wrote to Australian Prime Minister Billy Hughes, seeking a grant of £970 as final settlement of the expedition's accounts, but with the war in progress, this was, not surprisingly, turned down. Mawson's hopes for a publishing coup also never materialised. Throughout the war he pushed Heinemann to produce a one-volume 'popular' edition of *The Home of the Blizzard*, but this proposal drew little interest, and such an edition did not finally appear until 1930. Similarly, both Mawson and McLean believed fervently that a published version of the *Adelie Blizzard* would bring in funds, but no one of influence was persuaded by their arguments, and even nine decades later this product of so many months' labour during that long, trying second Antarctic year remains unpublished.

March and April 1919 found the Mawson family returning to Australia aboard the troopcarrier *Euripides*, along with Professor (then Lieutenant-Colonel) David and his wife and daughter. During the passage of a month and a half, the two men entertained those aboard with lectures about the Antarctic. Mawson also found time to catch up on a huge backlog of correspondence, and even sent one letter to Prime Minister Hughes, urging him to encourage the other leaders of the Empire to adopt the metric system so that Britain would come into line with most of the rest of the world sooner rather than later. 'At present South America, which deals in the metric system, is almost a closed country for our manufactured tools, machinery, etc,' Mawson wrote, 'because they want metric sizes – Germany, of course, supplies these with the greatest of readiness.'

The voyage ended in Melbourne, where they were reunited with Patricia and where Paquita and the children remained with her family while Mawson continued to Adelaide to begin his university work and to engage in the lengthy task of finding a family home. But Mawson was still a famous man, and even before he left Melbourne he was hunted down by the press about Antarctica. He left no doubt that he believed Australia should claim the entire region from the Ross Sea to Gaussberg – his old Australian Quadrant – not only for the obvious economic benefits that might accrue but as a means of introducing wildlife conservation, a concept in which he had come to believe after seeing first-hand the slaughter of seals and penguins at Macquarie Island.

Within weeks of returning to the university, another Antarctic issue even closer to Mawson's heart was raised: the Scientific Reports. Ever since his return from Cape Denison these had been a major focus of his personal and financial efforts. 'I am en route to London to see what I can do to assist in the war,' he had written to Sydney Jones – who had served as the medical officer at Wild's Western Base on the AAE – while crossing the United States in 1916. 'However, affairs of the Expedition are always foremost with me ... the publication of our "Scientific Results" is in no wise to be hampered by my temporary absence. The printing has begun and will go ahead steadily.'

Mawson's prediction about the 'Scientific Results' was, unfortunately, as inaccurate as those that said the Great War would be over by Christmas. Although the first two reports – *Fishes* and *Mollusca* – appeared in 1916, and seventeen reports had been produced by the government of South Australia by 1919, shortly after his arrival back in Adelaide their publication was discontinued due to increasing costs. Mawson quickly turned instead to the government of New South Wales, which agreed to publish the reports by 1925 to the value of £5,000. But governments tend not to do such things out of pure goodness of heart, and in return they demanded that he send to Sydney all of his AAE equipment, samples and collections, photographs, diaries, geographical and sledging reports, administrative and financial documents, ship's logs and papers, and scientific logs, records, and papers. Mawson agreed, and publication resumed – for the time being.

Meanwhile, Mawson's search for a home concentrated on the seaside town of Brighton on the outskirts of Adelaide, and he soon found what he considered the perfect 1¼-acre plot for a house. The property was, in fact, owned by Paquita's father, and it was not long before he made the couple a gift of it. In the next year, Mawson oversaw the building there of 'Jerbii,' the house that he had carefully planned and designed while in the Antarctic.

In the short term, Mawson's return to university life was not as positive as these other developments. His return to Adelaide had not been as automatic as it might have appeared on the surface, because in late January 1919 he had effectively been offered the chair of geology at University of Manchester at a substantial pay rise. But the University of Adelaide had previously bent over backwards to assist him and give him numerous leaves of absence, so he felt a sense of duty not to abandon it. That obligation was tested, however, when he found upon his return that 74-year-old Walter Howchin had been made honorary professor of geology. It was not in one sense a surprising development, because Howchin had laid much of the foundation of the study of South Australian stratigraphy and in 1918 had published *The Geology of South Australia*, which would remain a basic student text for the next four decades.

Mawson, however, had a knighthood, a remarkable list of honours, and an international reputation that extended far beyond what the average academic could ever dream of (although it was more for his contributions to exploration and geography than for geological accomplishments). But more to the point of what bothered him – on the surface at least – he had a PhD, whereas Howchin had never earned a degree of any kind. All of this was true, but in retrospect,

Mawson had, one might think, received such massive recognition that he simply found it difficult to accept that others might be equally worthy of such positions or tributes. He expressed his displeasure to the university's Vice-Chancellor and Chancellor, hinting perhaps that a similar appointment for him would be appropriate, but he received little in return other than soothing words. It was not until 1921, after Howchin retired, that he was finally appointed professor of geology and mineralogy.

In the following years, Mawson's reputation as a geologist – while not equalling his status as an Antarctic explorer – continued to increase. He developed an effective teaching and research department, both parts of which were helped enormously by Cecil Madigan joining the faculty in 1922. Mawson's own research concentrated on the 'Adelaide System' of Precambrian rocks, which he investigated in the Flinders Ranges, following previous work by both Howchin and David. He also studied Precambrian glaciation, algal remains in Precambrian rocks, and the geochemistry of igneous and metamorphic rocks. He was appointed an executive member of the Australian National Research Council, was a key figure in the Australasian Association for the Advancement of Science, and, in 1923, received one of the highest honours possible for a scientist by being elected a Fellow of the Royal Society.

None of this seemed to help, however, in his efforts to succeed Professor David as the chair of the Geology Department at the University of Sydney – the most prestigious geological position in Australia. The most surprising aspect of the complex and devious behind-the-scenes struggle surrounding the appointment to the post was that the man giving the strongest support for Mawson's main opponent was Professor David!

David had long planned on retiring at the end of 1924, and he had taken steps within the appointments committee (on which he sat) to ensure that Leo Cotton would be named his successor. Cotton, who had accompanied *Nimrod* to the Antarctic, had long been a member of the department and had served as acting professor whenever David had been on leave, including during the war. However, in July 1924 the whole, carefully orchestrated situation was thrown into disarray when Mawson indicated his interest in the position. Even more problematical was that Mawson refused officially to apply for the position. In the academic world, it was widely expected that a scholar of his calibre should be sought out and invited to take up a position rather than be expected to submit an application, particularly if there was any chance he might be beaten for the job by an inferior, but internal, candidate.

In terms of reputation and research, it was widely conceded that Mawson was a much sounder candidate than Cotton or any of the other individuals who were interested in the post. Moreover, Cotton's strong-suit – that he had already served as the department's administrator for a number of years – was somewhat offset in some people's minds by the fact that he had been able to do so only because he was a conscientious objector during the war. While Mawson or other candidates had done what at the time was considered their patriotic duty, Cotton had been ensconced in his office in Sydney.

Despite his apparent stronger claim for the chair, in November, believing the situation was scandalously 'fixed,' Mawson cabled the University Registrar that he was withdrawing his name from contention. Surprisingly, David now wrote asking Mawson to reconsider, noting that 'I state frankly that I like you much better than I like Cotton.' With this prompting, Mawson once again threw his hat in the ring, although he did so with the specific proviso that he would not take the position up until the end of 1925, a condition that – implicitly stating *he* was dictating the terms – would not have endeared him to some members of the University Senate, who would make the final determination.

Finally, on 22 December, the Senate met. In Mawson's corner was the recommendation of the powerful 'Home Committee,' which was made up of highly respected scholars in England. Also on his side was W.H. Hobbs, a renowned geologist from the University of Michigan, who, at the request of David, had initially written a strong letter of support for Cotton, but had then let it be known that if Mawson was in the field, *he* was the man Hobbs would unquestionably favour. On Cotton's side, however, was the master power-broker of the situation: David. Despite apparently feeling Mawson was a better candidate in every measurable way, the Prof ultimately still believed Cotton deserved the position for his many years of running the department during David's absences. And such was David's sway that when the matter came to a vote, Cotton won ten to eight and was awarded the chair.

There not surprisingly followed a period of coolness from Mawson towards David. But a series of anguished letters from the Prof to the man whose age-old friendship he feared he had lost ultimately overcame any residual feelings of betrayal or hostility that Mawson held. By March of 1925, Mawson had more or less forgiven his mentor, and re-engaged in contact with him.

There was, however, one last twist in the tale at the University of Sydney. Mungo McCallum, Sydney's Vice-Chancellor, had been so impressed with Mawson that he wrote to him, stating that he would be recommending Mawson for the Vice-Chancellorship when he retired in 1926. The University Appointments Committee eventually supported McCallum's decision, and then early in 1926 Mawson was informed that Britain's powerful Imperial Inter-Universities Board had drawn up a list of possible men for the position, and that his name held pride of place. He was now the 'internal' candidate, and such a turnabout must have given Mawson great pleasure, but, to the surprise of all involved, he withdrew from consideration before he could officially be offered the post.

Mawson's actions must have been a complete mystery to McCallum and the others involved in this process. But in retrospect, his reasoning is clear. An era of imperial and Commonwealth political ambitions in the far south was even then burgeoning, and it seemed likely that – with the encouragement of Mawson, Davis, and others – it would only be a matter of time before Australia was once again actively involved with the frozen frontiers. The Vice-Chancellor of the Commonwealth's most respected university could certainly not abandon his position, even temporarily, for an expedition to the far south, whereas a simple professor at Adelaide could. And that is just what Mawson intended to do.

III
DISCOVERY

13

Colouring Antarctica Red

For virtually all its known history, the Antarctic has been exploited by the whaling industry. The year after James Cook first crossed the Antarctic Circle, whalers from New England visited the Falkland Islands, and two years later an Act of Parliament extended the bounty system from the north to encourage the development of a southern whale fishery. Although much of this whaling trade was actually located in the sub-Antarctic, the early decades of the nineteenth century saw the Enderby family of shipowners send out numerous expeditions to the farthest reaches of the Antarctic for sealing, whaling, and geographical discovery. One, under John Balleny, had preceded Dumont d'Urville, Wilkes, and Ross through coastal regions not again investigated until the AAE.

In the 1890s, with whale stocks in many northern regions being depleted, expeditions were sent from Scotland and Norway in search of new fisheries. These efforts were not immediately commercially successful, but in 1904 Carl A. Larsen, who had captained two of them, used knowledge he had gained to establish a whaling shore station on South Georgia. A key innovation was a small, steam-powered whale-catcher that Larsen brought south to chase rorquals – such as blue, fin, and sei whales – in so doing starting the modern era of Antarctic whaling. Within a few years, six whaling stations had been established on South Georgia, and the industry had spread throughout the region.

By 1908, whaling – conducted primarily by Norwegians – had become so pervasive that Britain established the Falkland Islands Dependencies to license whalers, regulate the industry, protect females and calves – and secure large 'catch' fees for doing so. Nevertheless, the industry continued to grow, and the 1915–16 season saw no fewer than fifty-seven catchers, eleven floating factories, and seven shore stations process the staggering figure of 11,792 whales for 558,806 barrels of oil. Then, in early 1923, Larsen and his business partner Magnus Konow received a licence to conduct operations in the Ross Sea. There were seemingly unlimited numbers of rorquals in this untapped region, but with the licence approved for twenty-one years and allowing the company two factory ships and ten catchers, it was clear that it would not be too many seasons before the Norwegian operation began to impact on the Ross Sea's natural balance. Within months, probably prompted by Larsen's expanding operations, the British government named a large section of the Antarctic – from 160°E to 150°W – the Ross Dependency and placed its control and administration under the government of New Zealand.

The industry's continuing expansion made it evident that whaling might soon extend for the full distance between the Weddell and Ross seas, and Mawson, amongst other Australians, advocated the assertion of British sovereignty over the parts of this region that he had long called the Australian Quadrant (90° to 160°E). Having witnessed the unrestrained slaughter on Macquarie Island, he believed that the living resources of the sub-Antarctic islands and Antarctic seas required controlled and scientific management – penguins, seals, and flying birds as well as whales. Without a British claim, there could be no proper regulation and no long-term financial benefits.

There were other reasons why Mawson pushed for official British action regarding these southern regions. First, he believed that officially bringing the Australian Quadrant into the British sphere would be the initial step in continuing the scientific work of the AAE. In this, he was backed by John King Davis, who in 1920 had been named Commonwealth Director of Navigation, and by the famed, Australian-born geologist Frank Debenham, the first director of the Scott Polar Research Institute in Cambridge, who stressed that as the unexplored territory of Antarctica grew smaller, the fields of scientific exploration would increase. Second, during the war Mawson had pressed the British and Australian governments to follow up on his own claims made during the AAE by asserting British sovereignty, but to no avail. Now he – like many others – was concerned that increasing Norwegian whaling would logically be followed by annexations of those same lands. This potential seemed particularly acute because many Norwegians were known to be incensed by the extension of British jurisdiction over some territories discovered by Norwegian seamen, and by the heavy licence fees that had to be paid for whaling despite it occurring outside British or New Zealand territorial waters.

Meanwhile, unbeknownst to Mawson and the general public, by 1920, the British government had secretly decided to establish control over the entire Antarctic continent anyway – in part for conservation reasons, and in part due to a growing appreciation of its strategic importance – and the Australian and New Zealand governments were confidentially informed. However, the British government favoured an only gradual extension of control. Therefore, not a great deal had been accomplished by 1924 when the French, also worried about the Norwegians, declared sovereignty over the sub-Antarctic archipelago of Iles Kerguelen as well as Terre Adélie, the thin slice of land originally spotted by Dumont d'Urville. Mawson, Professor David, Professor Masson, and other key members of the Australian National Research Council

(ANRC) met with Prime Minister Stanley Melbourne Bruce to push for an Australian challenge to the French claim. But although Bruce promised the government would pursue the issue, the matter effectively went no further, and the British and Australian governments acceded to the French claim.

Serious movement on the issue finally began at the Imperial Conference in 1926, when it was recommended that formal title should be declared over seven Antarctic regions that were appropriate for such a claim by virtue of British discovery: the outlying part of Coats Land, Enderby Land, Kemp Land, Queen Mary Land (which had been explored from Wild's Western Base), the area Mawson had named Wilkes Land, King George V Land, and Oates Land. When the report was submitted to the Australian government, its officials conferred with Davis, who suggested that the ANRC be consulted, and that body thereafter formed an advisory Antarctic Committee (which included Mawson, Davis, and Masson). In 1927, the Antarctic Committee, via the ANRC, recommended to the Australian government that an expedition be sent to the Antarctic to raise the flag and conduct scientific studies at the seven locations. Two summer seasons might well be needed for this ship-borne operation, for which the 'only existing vessel suitably constructed for this purpose' was Scott's old ship *Discovery*. The logical person to lead such an important effort, the committee reported, was Sir Douglas Mawson.

Leading an expedition for the purposes of political claims and scientific research in the Antarctic was just what Mawson had been hoping and angling for – 'all else with me takes a second place,' he had written to Masson. However, he understood the tricky and dubious nature of getting such a venture off the ground well enough that he had not concentrated on it solely, but had also pursued several other business and professional options since the fiasco of the Sydney chair.

One of Mawson's ongoing financial efforts was the

company South Australian Hardwoods, of which he was founder and chairman. Soon after returning from the war, he had bought a farm near the Kuitpo Forest, south of Adelaide. In the ensuing years he purchased more nearby properties, where he planted a variety of trees, following which, with a number of neighbours, he re-developed a local mill and began selling hardwood products to, amongst others, the South Australian government and Broken Hill Proprietary, the company for which Paquita's father had so long been a key managerial figure. In early 1926 – before withdrawing from the consideration for the Vice-Chancellorship of Sydney and before the Imperial Conference – he visited New Zealand to study the forestry industry there. He would maintain his interests in the company, hardwood trees, and forestry throughout the rest of his life.

Later that year, leaving their two daughters with his brother Will's family, Mawson and Paquita travelled to South Africa, England, and then on to the United States. Beginning in New York in February 1927, he gave a series of talks about his adventures and his scientific work in the Antarctic. These were not just for enjoyment – Mawson was hoping to make a significant amount of money, because he was extremely concerned that, once again, the publication of the Scientific Reports would soon cease. The Committee on Printing of Records of the AAE had been tasked by the New South Wales Ministry of Education with obtaining and distributing to the appropriate museums and libraries the AAE materials that Mawson had contractually promised to New South Wales. For years, various members of the Printing Committee had been demanding, begging, wheedling, and threatening in order to get hold of the artefacts and papers. Each time, Mawson had drip-fed them a small supply of materials, while explaining that he needed most of the items for the preparation and editing of the different reports. This was certainly true of some of the equipment and papers, but much less so of others. Slowly but surely New South Wales built an impressive AAE collection, but Mawson continued to sit on a vastly greater one. Meanwhile, approximately thirty-five reports had been published, but far more than that were at different stages of preparation. What Mawson could not know was when the Printing Committee might finally live up to its threats and simply pull the plug. For the time being, however, his delaying tactics continued while he tried to gain the funding that would mean he did not have to part with any more of his precious materials.

Concurrently with Mawson's return to Australia from the United States, the Antarctic Committee gave the government its whole-hearted recommendation for an Antarctic expedition. Mawson was overjoyed by the work that had been carried out in his absence, and differed only with the Antarctic Committee's opinion in that he did not believe Gaussberg should be claimed. '[T]he Germans landed upon Gauss Berg and raised their flag long before we did,' he wrote to Masson. 'Their claim for Gauss Berg is ever so much stronger than France's claim for Adelie Land.'

The hopes of Mawson, Davis, and the rest of the Antarctic Committee rose to new heights, only subsequently to wilt on the vine as, for the next year, the British and Australian governments made little obvious progress. In fact, both were hesitant to finance an expensive – and transparently political – expedition, and each hoped that the other would do so. Finally, in January 1928, frustrated by the long inaction, Mawson made a statement in Hobart about the necessity of annexing Antarctic territories, which was picked up by the press and given significant coverage throughout Australia. Coincidentally, the next day the Norwegians informed London that they had annexed the sub-Antarctic island of Bouvetøya, to which the British had a previous claim. The juxtaposition of these two events aroused great interest throughout Australia, and led David Rivett of the Antarctic Committee to write to the Prime Minister's secretary that Mawson's remarks 'appeared to indicate that the

Commonwealth Government was doing nothing at all.' Prime Minister Bruce responded hotly, indicating that the government had just adopted a policy that could be carried through quickly and that would, hopefully, produce successful results.

But once again, nothing happened, and in March Mawson again left for England, hoping, it was later written, to secure *Discovery*, 'an action which might obviously embarrass the Australian Government, for, if Mawson did secure the vessel, it might have to disclose its underlying objection to the venture – the fear of heavy costs.' Whether or not gaining *Discovery* were truly Mawson's goal, he was unsuccessful in that effort, but that might well be because he spent much of his time on a totally different project. He had previously been approached by a group of New Zealand businessmen to help promote a hydro-electric scheme that would use the waters of Lake Manapouri in the New Zealand Sounds region of the South Island to produce electricity, which would in turn bring a raft of new industries to the region. By the time he reached England, he had effectively become the point man for the proposition, and he spent large amounts of time not only meeting with potential investors, but preparing the costings and details of both the main operation itself and the proposed new industries. And yet it proved all for nought, as the scheme eventually collapsed, at least in part due to the early stages of the international Depression.

Mawson's lack of success abroad must have been disappointing, but his spirits would have been buoyed by being told confidentially not long after his return to Australia in late September that the Australian government had decided to back the expedition. Then, in November, after lengthy negotiations, the British agreed to waive any claim to Bouvetøya in return for a Norwegian promise not to occupy any of the territories mentioned by the Imperial Conference. This compromise did not provide a total safeguard for British or Australian hopes in the Antarctic, however, as the coastlines between 60° and 86°E had not been specifically mentioned and therefore lay open to a Norwegian advance. So when it became known that whaling entrepreneur and Norwegian consul Lars Christensen – who had been behind the annexation of Bouvetøya – was planning another commercial and exploratory voyage to the region, which could well turn into further territorial expansion, it made both the British and Australian governments extremely nervous. This was enough finally to overcome any immediate financial concerns from either government, and in early 1929 general agreement on the expedition was reached and Mawson officially was offered the leadership.

Mawson now faced many of the same difficulties he had experienced almost two decades before during the organisation of the AAE. Although the Australian government was officially supporting and partially funding the expedition, it was clearly limiting its financial contribution, so it still expected him to find much of the funding. The same was true of the British and New Zealand governments. Nevertheless, all of the governments insisted on input on the organising committees and, at times, in having a say about the most annoyingly small details.

One of the lengthiest debates revolved around the use of *Discovery*. The ship both Mawson and Davis actually wanted was *Aurora*, but unfortunately she was resting at the bottom of the sea. Following Davis' rescue of the Ross Sea party, she had been purchased as a coal transport vessel. Then in April 1917, after departing from Newcastle, New South Wales, heading to Chile, she vanished. In December that year, a lifebuoy reading 'SY Aurora' was found, but whether she foundered due to being overloaded or struck a mine laid by a German raider known to have been in the vicinity remains a mystery.

Discovery, meanwhile, had been in regular service, in recent years being nominally the property of the Falkland Islands Dependencies. She had been used for two years for oceanographic and hydrographical surveys of the South Georgia and South Shetland Islands whaling grounds. But the British government eventually agreed to lend her to the new expedition free of charge, while making it known that this was to be Britain's full financial contribution to the expedition and the other financing would come from Australia and New Zealand.

However, although the Commonwealth and New Zealand governments agreed to this funding arrangement, once away from the table with the British, they seemed to back off what Mawson believed he had been promised, leaving him to find an even higher percentage of the finances. Eventually two key contributors came forward. The first was Macpherson Robertson, the self-made and philanthropic confectioner who had introduced chewing gum and candyfloss to Australia, launched the exclusive 'Old Gold' line of chocolates, and pioneered the Australian production of glucose. He initially donated £10,000 and later added thousands more, at least matching the figure contributed by the Commonwealth government. The other major backer was William Randolph Hearst, the publishing millionaire, who bought the American press rights to the first voyage for $40,000 (then £8,200). By contrast, the expedition received only £1,070 from *The Times* for the British rights and £556 from the Australian United Press.

When Mawson was officially invited to lead the expedition, he was already on his way to England, where he immediately set about ordering equipment and provisions. He also quickly signed up Davis, then in Melbourne, as master of *Discovery* and second-in-command of the expedition. On the surface, a better appointment could not have been made; the two were old friends, and Davis knew how to handle a ship in icy waters as well as any man in the world. But the move also ignored the conflicts that had surfaced when the two strong-willed, arrogant, and at times petulant men had been forced into extended contact at the end of the AAE. On an even longer cruise, or pair of cruises, there was no reason to assume that two such inflexible men with ultimately differing goals – Davis' prime concern was the safety of the ship; Mawson's the success of the expedition – would be able amicably to resolve all disagreements and avoid clashing.

Indeed, the very terms of the command structure virtually *guaranteed* conflict. In a bizarre situation, Davis, although master of the ship, was in command of it only when Mawson was not aboard. 'The expedition was purely a ship expedition,' Mawson later wrote in explanation. 'Therefore Captain Davis was not in command of the ship when I was on board ... I would not have sailed if things had been otherwise.' This meant that Davis was not even ultimately responsible for the navigation of his own ship, and since Davis would not accept this, the Australian government's new advisory Antarctic Committee allowed that, 'if it is your [Davis'] opinion that to carry out an order from Mawson would involve unjustifiable danger to the ship, the ultimate responsibility is yours as Master of the ship, and your orders must prevail.' So all Davis had to do was rule that Mawson's decision was unjustifiably dangerous, and he regained his power. It was a set-up designed in such a way as to antagonise *both* men.

Not that being together was necessary for them to disagree. Shortly after Davis was appointed, he recommended to the Antarctic Committee that the expedition should start from Hobart. Taking advantage of the easterly winds and currents, *Discovery* could follow the track of his AAE voyages, heading west from Oates Land and arriving at some of the most ice-encased regions, such as Enderby Land, at the end of the summer, when conditions would most likely allow landings. The cruise would eventually end at Cape Town. The committee, agreeing that it was appropriate an Australian expedition start from Australia, concurred with Davis. Unfortunately, Mawson did not. Not believing the Norwegian guarantee against claiming Enderby Land, Mawson felt that *Discovery* needed to reach it *before* the competition. And since she was an exceptionally slow ship, following Davis' route might mean not reaching Enderby Land at all during the first season. Therefore, Mawson argued, a start from Cape Town and a reversal of Davis' schedule were required, and in this debate he ultimately prevailed.

The official plan of the expedition now became clear. Reaching Cape Town in early October, *Discovery* would depart immediately thereafter, sailing south to Iles Kerguelen to re-coal, and then arriving at the Antarctic coast near Gaussberg, west of the Shackleton Ice Shelf. From there the expedition would head west, reaching Enderby Land and continuing along its coast to 45 ° E, or even 40 ° E if possible, before reversing direction and sailing back east as far as the season would allow.

The major problem with this was that when Davis arrived in London in May to oversee the work on *Discovery* – at roughly the same time Mawson returned to Australia – he found a significantly flawed ship for such an extended operation. Moreover, since the schedule dictated leaving London at the beginning of August in order to reach Cape Town in time, he was faced with an unreasonably tight deadline to prepare her. Built for Scott's expedition almost three decades before, *Discovery* was not as manoeuvrable as *Aurora*, had less powerful engines, and was considerably less comfortable because of the way she rolled. Certainly she was incredibly strong, but her reinforced planking meant she had less space both for the men aboard and, more importantly, for coal. Davis estimated that she could take only 300 tons of coal, severely limiting her range, particularly since her fuel consumption was unusually high. Davis eventually found a way to increase her maximum capacity, but only by leaving sixty tons of coal on deck and twenty more on each side of the engine room.

But coal was only one of the problems Davis faced. Equally vexing were those brought about by his differences with

Mawson. Both men were extremely particular, and as each wanted to arrange things in his own way, disagreements and annoyance arose over issues both great and small. For example, there was 'considerable confusion,' wrote Davis, 'owing to the fact that you are duplicating work ... with the equipment of the crew which would be far better left to me.' Conversely, Mawson erupted over Davis reducing his lists of certain supplies, which thereby changed his 'elaborately-thought-out scheme' of numbering the packing cases.

Such disagreements continued throughout, but even more problematic were their differences over such basic issues as how many men would sail south. Mawson wanted thirteen scientists, whereas Davis insisted there was room for only nine. Eventually there were eleven, one of the applicants *not* making the cut being a young Cambridge geologist named Vivian Fuchs, who would later become the director of the British Antarctic Survey and lead the first crossing of Antarctica on the Commonwealth Trans-Antarctic Expedition. This manpower dispute rolled over into the selection of the crew, which Davis insisted was his prerogative. He and Mawson butted heads when the Royal Navy offered the services of a petty officer to serve as operator of both the wireless and the new echo-sounding system installed on *Discovery*. Mawson immediately advocated his acceptance because a petty officer would be housed with the crew, allowing space in the wardroom for another scientist, but Davis rejected him in favour of a merchant serviceman, who would be considered a ward-room officer and would therefore eliminate the extra scientist.

The bickering between the two men carried on about things considerably less significant than personnel. Few things, for example, upset Mawson more than Davis using stationery that was headed 'The British, Australian, New Zealand Antarctic Research Expedition of 1929–30.' That title for the expedition 'has never been agreed to either by myself or the Committee,' wrote Mawson. He wanted all such stationery scrapped and replaced with some reading 'British Australasian Antarctic Expedition,' which would leave out, he noted, 'the word "Research" and leaving out any date. As this Expedition is to [run] for two summers the date you have put on the paper is not correct. The long winded title on your paper is, in my opinion, absolutely ridiculous.' As was their foolish squabbling. However, to Mawson's disgust, the longer name became accepted, its only saving grace being the acronym BANZARE.

Despite all these difficulties, somehow Davis had the ship ready to sail on time, on 1 August 1929. When he arrived at the East India Docks that morning, he must have felt a sense of relief – as he had when *Aurora* departed London eighteen years before – to be leaving behind the preparations and getting back to where a sailor wanted to be: at sea. But before he even had a chance to take a breath, as *Discovery* pulled away from the wharf, a sudden squall blew her back into the dock wall. 'No damage was done to the vessel,' Davis wrote, 'but some slight damage is reported to have been done to the quay.' He might well have been proud of her obvious strength, but he also must have wondered, as any superstitious sailor would, if it had been some kind of omen.

14

SCIENCE OR POLITICS?

AT I A.M. ON 5 OCTOBER 1929, after a relatively uneventful cruise from Britain, *Discovery* dropped anchor in Table Bay. The passage of fifty-five days had been three quicker than she had made on her maiden voyage almost three decades before, but had still given Davis plenty of time to consider the ship and her crew. He was relatively happy with the progress made by his officers, none of whom had any previous experience with sailing ships, although he remained hesitant about leaving the bridge under the control of chief officer Kenneth MacKenzie in any but the calmest of conditions. He was less content with *Discovery* herself, noting that she was wet and uncomfortable and that a more unsuitable ship for oceanographic work could hardly have been built.

Mawson and most of the scientists arrived in Durban three days later to find the South African and British press whipping up a frenzy with a series of sensational jingoistic articles. The distinguished Norwegian pilot Finn Lützow-Holm had recently headed south from Cape Town to join the aeroplane-equipped *Norvegia* – commanded by Roald Amundsen's former number-two, Hjalmar Riiser-Larsen. The local accounts suggested that the Norwegians would be annexing sites in Enderby Land and other 'British regions' by dropping spiked flags from the aeroplanes. 'New Race to the Antarctic Starting?' blared the headline of the *Cape Argus*, beneath which it compared the situation with 'the epic race for the South Pole between the same two nations.'

Mawson made ill-considered, and widely reported, comments about the Norwegians, which indicated how stressed he was by the situation. His anxiety did not improve when he joined *Discovery* on 13 October, amidst the last of Davis' mad rush to convert the configuration of the sails and make as many other repairs and alterations as time allowed. In the middle of all this helter-skelter sat Mawson's treasured De Havilland Gipsy Moth aeroplane, which he had purchased for reconnaissance and charting work. He had cabled Davis to make sure that it was adequately housed and protected, but *Discovery*'s size had prevented this, and Mawson was enraged at the possibility of it being damaged before the expedition even began. He railed at Davis, who threatened to resign, forcing Mawson to back down, as there was no one else with the experience to take command of the ship. But the former best of friends had started the expedition as they would finish it – the worst of companions – and the aggressive behaviour of both did not bode well for a happy and supportive environment on a ship that, with thirty-eight men aboard, would be distinctly overcrowded to start with.

On 19 October, *Discovery* departed from Cape Town to the large crowds of well-wishers with which Mawson had long since become familiar. That day he wryly recorded: 'Davis arranged four boat stations in case of misfortune to ship. Am interested to find that he has allocated me to the motor boat which, after all, is not likely to live in a fair sea as free-board is so low.' Four days later, Mawson was not so tongue in cheek, as he showed strong signs of discontent with the ship's master: 'Capt Davis,' he wrote formally about his former best man, 'is most difficult for he is a confirmed pessimist and gives neither me nor anybody else credit for any nous or knowledge. I find it very difficult to get along with him because he thinks his ways best though often obviously not so.' Such sniping between the two men – some justified, much not – was to be a central feature of the voyage.

Most of the other men aboard – scientists and crew – could see strengths and weaknesses in both leaders. Ritchie Simmers, the meteorologist, recorded after a discussion about met observations that Davis was 'jolly decent, quite different from the gruff, surly, taciturn detached piece of granite that he can be . . . [but] Never for a minute does he let anything interfere with his task of "Master" and I would sooner have him on the bridge in bad weather than anyone else. One sleeps better for his presence.' Two days later, he showed equal insight into Mawson. 'Sir Douglas's conversation is always interesting and in it he lets drop continually little items of interest, which indicate in what wide fields he is interested, and being interested has a thorough knowledge of the facts and problems,' he wrote. 'But he's not absolutely the best organiser – beforehand, yes, as, for instance, in the minute detail in which we have been equipped – but in carrying out things, oh no.' More important than their individual qualities was that it was simply not healthy to have the two men in charge 'as far apart as the stars.'

Rough weather marked the first two weeks of the voyage, and on 2 November all were relieved to reach Possession Island in the group known as Iles Crozet. But when a party went ashore to start a broad scientific survey, they were horrified to find 'great numbers Sea-elephants along the shore, all being slaughtered.' Sealers from the ship *Kilfinora* were wreaking havoc according to the chief biologist, Harvey Johnston, 'shooting the animals at very close range (bulls and cows) and knocking all the seal pups on the head with a sledge-hammer.' Not a single animal was left in some of the wallows, and when Johnston approached the sealers, he was informed that 'the men would be there for another two days to clean the place up. I assumed that they meant to dispose of the carcases of the slaughtered animals, but they meant to take every seal there . . . wiping out the entire herds that congregate there to breed.'

After several days of collecting biological, botanical, and geological samples, the expedition was on its way again, reaching Iles Kerguelen on 12 November. Coal had been left for them at Port Jeanne d'Arc, a deserted whaling station, and Davis was able to moor *Discovery* to an old jetty. For twelve days the scientists ranged over the main island and some of the nearby smaller ones, while the crew hauled coal to the ship and filled the lockers. To speed the operation, the scientists and officers spent several evenings contributing to the coaling as well, much to Mawson's disgruntlement. '[C]oaled ship from 6.15 to 8.45 pm, putting on board 20 tons which went into starboard bunker and sheep pen,' he wrote. 'We had further to carry it and stacked more than the crew. Per man-ton handled more than twice crew's effort, notwithstanding that we all had been working all day.'

When, with an extra 190 tons of coal aboard, a course was finally set for Heard Island on 24 November, Mawson was still grumbling, disappointed that his party had not been able to conduct a full oceanographic programme, and laying the cause at 'constant friction with Davis.' He was also distressed to have found that the seal population had been virtually exterminated, and that the native flora and fauna of the main island had been devastated by rabbits and dogs, the ancestors of which had been left by early sealers.

Mawson's instructions from the Prime Minister and his commission from the Crown had both made it crystal clear that the chief objective of the voyage was the claiming and acquisition of the territories to be brought under the aegis of the British Empire – science was officially an afterthought. Despite this, and prevalent fears of being forestalled by the Norwegians, Mawson continued carrying out time-consuming scientific investigations and measurements, and making extensive collections, even though Heard Island was not on the expedition's official agenda. It was a sign that although he would put his name publicly to any aims or goals in order to launch an expedition, when it came down to it, science was, to him, the be-all and end-all.

For seven days after landing a shore party, high winds and terrible sea conditions threatened the ship, prevented Davis from even entering the cove where the scientists were based, and forced him to use valuable coal to maintain constant power against the elements. Finally, on 2 December, realising conditions might not improve, Mawson and three others made a wild ride in the launch out to the ship, where he asked Davis to pick up the remaining five members of the shore party. A hot debate ensued, but eventually Davis refused point blank, stating that the dangerous swell might have gone down by morning and patience was the wisest course. 'It is impossible to make a man who is not a seaman, realize that ships have to be handled with prudence,' he wrote. 'To take the Discovery into Atlas Cove today would have been quite possible to save life, but to do so in order to pick up some people who can easily wait until tomorrow, would have been the act of a fool.'

By the next morning, however, the conditions were still not ideal, and at 7.30, wittingly or not, Davis stoked the fire of antagonism. A steward delivered Mawson a message stating: 'With the Captain's compliments – he says the men can come off now, and if you are not taking the launch ashore he proposes send off an officer with it.' Rather than assuming this simply gave him an option, Mawson took it in the most negative way possible, and, 'Despite the still dangerous conditions I decide that I must try it else Capt D will make stock of it.'

Shortly thereafter, Mawson and Eric Douglas, one of the two aviators, set off in the launch in a rising wind and heavy sea. They thought they had passed the worst when suddenly the engine cut out. Douglas quickly determined that there was a problem with the fuel line, and had just undone the lead to the tank when the retaining nut fell and slipped under the lining of the boat. With the launch being steadily drawn towards a set of cliffs, upon which it would be pulverised, the two men cast out the anchor, but it did not reach the bottom. Struggling to keep calm, they attached a dredging line to the anchor rope, but before they could throw the lengthened line overboard, it tangled and they had to sort out the jumble. Finally, they managed to pass the whole lot over the side, and the anchor caught and held. Douglas pulled up the floorboards, found the nut, and, after clearing the line, reassembled everything. To their intense relief, the engine started, although they were then forced into a struggle to raise the anchor while the launch surged sickeningly up and down.

Even then the danger was not yet over. Reaching Atlas Cove, they quickly boarded the men, equipment, and samples and headed back into a still-increasing wind, which now drove snow straight into their faces. Only after several narrow escapes and a total of eighty minutes, twice as long as it should have taken to cover the distance, did everyone regain the safety of *Discovery*. 'Davis had the impudence later to ask me whether I did not realise what a fool I had been in taking such risk,' Mawson wrote that night. 'The fact is he drove me to it. I had to take undue risk in order to maintain reasonable chance of our conducting reasonably useful programme of exploration.'

The comment was unfair, as Davis had, at least on the surface, given him a choice as to whether to take the launch or not. Moreover, it had been Mawson's decision to delay the schedule by extra visits to Iles Crozet and Heard Island. Now, with the extended scientific landings completed, Mawson seemed to have remembered that there were other goals to achieve. All that stood in his way – he obviously felt – was Davis.

* * *

On 4 December *Discovery* began a track southeast from Heard Island with the intention of finding how far the Kerguelen–Heard Island submarine ridge extended towards the vicinity of Gaussberg, the extinct volcano at the western edge of Queen Mary Land. Soundings were made at regular intervals with the new Admiralty echo-sounding equipment, and a shallow region was discovered, which was later named the Banzare Rise. By the 8th, icebergs covered much of the area ahead, but plankton and hydrographic work continued. Meanwhile, both Mawson and Davis continued to gripe to their diaries about each other.

Davis was much the gentler in his entries, justifying his own actions by an overriding need for rest and treating Mawson as well-meaning but misguided. 'M regards all advice tending to regularise our operations as in some way trying to put off doing anything at all,' he wrote. 'I want to do things quietly and with due preparation, as is usual on board ship. He wishes to rush at them.' The next day he noted: 'The master of a ship like this does not get an easy time. He must be always on watch if he does his job ... I have not had my clothes off since leaving Cape Town ... M has no idea of what it means. He works hard himself and then goes to bed quite satisfied that I shall get them through somehow.'

Mawson was significantly less sympathetic, and did not approve of what he considered Davis' constant interference with the oceanographic work, inability to trust the ship's officers, and unwillingness to abide by Mawson's decisions. 'Davis' whole attitude is most deplorable,' he wrote. 'No doubt he means well but he overestimates his own abilities, underestimates others, is sulky, pigheaded, damned rude, uncouth and has no physical strength or stamina. He gets wearied and worn out and blames everybody for it.' The last statement had been shown at points to apply to Mawson as well, although he usually found one person for his whipping boy rather than everybody.

The situation did not improve when *Discovery* entered the pack ice on 12 December. Initially Mawson encouraged Davis to force a passage towards Gaussberg, but little advance was made in two days, Davis blaming *Discovery*'s lack of power, but at least some of the men believing that there was more to it. 'There is a decided feeling in the ship,' wrote seaman James Martin, 'that the Old Man is not the Pusher he used to be.'

Frustrated by the lack of movement at a high cost in coal, on 14 December Mawson decided to forgo Gaussberg, and asked Davis to concentrate on making progress to the west towards Enderby Land. But during the following week, the ship advanced only slowly to the west, changing directions virtually throughout the compass whenever confronted by heavy ice. Mawson tried unsuccessfully to enforce his will on Davis, but the latter remained resolute in his actions and held the speed to dead slow for much of the time, while shutting down movement altogether whenever he needed a rest. This course of action did not sit well with many aboard. 'We, ie. the sailors, believe the O.M. has lost his nerve,' wrote Martin. 'He seems to be afraid of getting caught in the ice for the winter. When following leads in the ice he always follows those leading to the Norrard rather than those to the southward. Also he steams round and round in circles apparently to waste time and coal rather than go south. There is no drive in him at all and everyone is disgusted and fed up.' Mawson certainly was, and actually consulted the ship's doctor about Davis' mental state.

Things seemed suddenly to take a turn for the better on Christmas Eve, when both Davis and John Child, the third officer, thought they saw an island to the southwest. Although a snowstorm eliminated any possibility of confirming the view, Davis headed in that direction, and on Boxing Day, MacKenzie, the first officer, proclaimed he could see the continent about twenty miles south. 'Great is the excitement on board,' he wrote, 'there was a wild rush for the rigging and a heavy demand on field glasses. I myself could not get down from the nest quick enough to call J.K. who is delighted and in high spirits. I feel much elated at being the first man to set eyes on what God has been pleased to hide from human eyes till now.'

They could not reach any land on which to make a claim, however, and by the next day it had disappeared from view, indicating that it was most likely a mirage induced by reflection and was much farther off than it appeared. Worse yet, the pack to the south consisted of 'peaked and hummocky ice of a striking appearance, cruel and heavy,' wrote Mawson. 'I had never imagined that floe could be so pressed up and converted to succession of pinnacles. It reminds me of a miniature model of, say, New York City.' So, to the disappointment of Davis, Mawson ordered a retreat to the northwest. Then, unexpectedly, the pack suddenly dissipated, and for the next several days *Discovery* raced along.

For more than a week, Mawson had hoped to launch the aeroplane, but engine difficulty, fog, and lack of a lead – a track of open water between sections of sea ice – from which to take off prevented it. On 31 December, having come well to the west of their Boxing Day location, conditions finally improved enough to allow aviators Stuart Campbell and Eric Douglas to take off from an ice-free pool. Soaring to 5,000 feet, they stared through a slight surface haze and saw what they thought to be hilly, ice-covered land some fifty miles off, protected by unbroken, impenetrable pack. Hoping to reach this land, Mawson suggested that they continue west along the ice edge to a point from where they could again send up the plane.

However, the next morning when he awoke, Mawson found the ship stopped in what he described as wide-open water. Anxiously awaiting an appearance by Davis, Mawson eventually became irritable about the delay and went to the Captain's cabin. The descriptions of what followed differ greatly, Davis portraying the event as a conversation between two rational souls, and Mawson recounting a set-to with a madman. 'I ask him what he is doing or waiting for. Ask him whether we cannot go west or north-west,' Mawson wrote.

> He is very ill-tempered and most rude, evidently spoiling for a row. I then spend 1½ hours with him . . . he appears hopeless – he is definitely mentally unbalanced . . . I listened to the most utter rubbish, fiction and impudent assertion, that it could well be possible to hear and not ask the perpetrator to stand down forever. But Davis is a very old friend, and am loath to break off my patience for am certain he is mentally strained. He is in some ways not unlike Jeffryes was prior to his dementia – he sits for hours in chair in his room and stares into vacancy.

This time Davis did not just sit, but exclaimed that the open water was rapidly disappearing ahead with heavy pack extending towards the north. According to Mawson, he emphatically added that, as far as he was concerned, the ship could stay put for a week, thereby allowing the wind a chance to blow away the pack. Noting the low probability of this and that the ship was burning two and a half tons of coal per day, Mawson suggested making an attempt to continue either west or northwest instead. 'He then commenced a tirade against me,' Mawson wrote, 'said I was nothing but impatience . . . the ship had been a bedlam ever since I had come on board . . . that one of the most foolish things I did was overworking everybody . . . even Shackleton, failure though he was in many respects, had the decency to thank his men . . . I had not said a good word to anybody; that even the most miserable leader would surely have done this.' And so, according to Mawson, it went on and on, with Davis eventually telling him that without his own intervention the previous expedition would have been a fiasco. 'You owe everything to me. I made you. But I get no thanks for that,' Mawson recorded him as saying, before commenting himself that 'It has been a very painful and hopeless business for me to listen to him in this tirade based on utterly false statements. The man is quite unsound mentally.'

Davis' account was decidedly different. 'I considered what the best course should be, and decided the only thing to do would be to come out North again, if we could, before endeavouring to go West,' he wrote. 'I spoke to Mawson about it. He was doubtful whether we could not get West where we are at.'

Regardless of how vigorous the discussion was, Davis did make to the west, and after being stopped by huge floes, took *Discovery* north around the solid ice. By the 3rd, they were back in relatively open water and again steaming south-west. But all along, Davis – 'the world's super pessimist' according to Mawson – was projecting solid ice just ahead. Then at lunch, a dispute broke out in front of the other men when Davis 'argued strongly that the Norwegians had every right to try and anticipate us at Enderby Land,' wrote Mawson. 'He said we had been most disgracefully secret about our plans. He went on in this disloyal way, trying to find fault with our expedition where there was no fault, forgiving the faults of others.' When Mawson tried to justify the Australian position with the notion that it was a scientific expedition, Davis exclaimed: 'that was all eyewash, we were out to grab land. If we were really scientific we would certainly not leave Australia where there was a much better field for scientific work . . . He had everybody at the table laughing to themselves, and Dr Ingram went over to the gramophone and turned it on to drown Davis' twaddle.'

For the men whose main goal was to conduct scientific studies, the situation was becoming progressively more unbearable. Morton Moyes, the expedition cartographer who had been the meteorologist at Western Base on the AAE, summed it up by commenting that 'all are heartily tired of the bickering which goes on over courses to be steered, speed & such matters. It makes things very unpleasant.'

*   *   *

'Land was sighted during the morning watch,' Davis wrote matter-of-factly on 4 January. 'Two volcanic peaks showing bare rocky faces.' But even if *he* could contain his excitement, most of the men could not: after all, it was the first time this land had ever been seen by human eyes. True to his scientific background, Mawson oversaw a dredging operation while preparations were made for the aeroplane to go up the following morning and Frank Hurley – once again serving under Mawson as expedition photographer and cinematographer – spent hours viewing the shifting scenes from the crow's nest. By evening they could all easily make out a rising ice plateau, with many high, rocky peaks extending from it.

The next day Campbell took to the air with Mawson in the front seat of the Gipsy Moth. They estimated that the Plateau rose to 3,000 feet, and the mountains pushing through it to at least 500 more. Unfortunately, the camera did not work and in trying to fix it Mawson accidentally pulled the cover off, exposing the film. After an hour, they returned to the ship, but they had investigated the location enough to give it a name: Mac. Robertson Land.

Early the next morning, the snow began to fall and the wind picked up, and within a few hours winds of hurricane force were buffeting the ship, 'cursing us,' wrote Child, 'for seeing these sights and seeing the land here, which it has hitherto kept from man or beast.' The conditions continued into the next day, when icicles accumulating on the rigging began to crash to the deck below. As Campbell watched from the bridge, the ice darts suddenly started descending onto the aeroplane, and 'in about a minute, gaping tears began to appear all over the mainplanes and tail . . . [including] One long sliver about six feet long' that drove 'straight through both upper and lower port mainplanes.' Within minutes, sixty tears had been produced in the plane's fabric, and ten ribs damaged. For the time being, the aeroplane was out of action.

Worse was to come. On 8 January, Mawson wrote an official proclamation claiming Mac. Robertson Land, which he intended to read aboard the ship at noon the next day. But early on the 9th, a wireless message from the Australian government informed him that the Norwegians under Riiser-Larsen had claimed a 100-kilometre [62-mile] stretch of coast between Enderby Land and Kemp Land, 'just where we are now. This is most exasperating, for they have evidently made a direct voyage here to raise their flag, and they knew this was in our itinerary,' he complained. 'This sort of thing is not helpful to science, for it means to compete with such "explorers" an expedition should not arrange any organised programme of detailed scientific work but just rush to most likely points of coast to make landing and raise flags.'

One could feel more sympathy were it not that BANZARE had been launched for that specific reason, as Davis had pointed out the previous week. In fact, it was Mawson's dawdling with science, at the expense of what he had truly been sent south for, that had ensured the Norwegians' priority. As it turned out, it mattered little, because the Norwegian government, standing by the agreement it had made with the British, later declined to acknowledge Riiser-Larsen's claim.

Not knowing this, however, Mawson was desperate to make a landing to validate his own claim. For two days he tried to persuade Davis to coast east along the pack, looking for avenues south, but Davis considered entering the ice in that fashion far too dangerous and was having none of it. Then suddenly realising that if he waited in one place the Norwegians might pick off one location after another, Mawson decided that he could stay no longer but must press on towards the west and Enderby Land itself. This Davis was willing to do, and when the weather cleared on the afternoon of 12 January, they saw to the south a series of rocky peaks rising several thousand feet above a dome of ice. They continued along the edge of the heavy pack off the Enderby Land coast, and although unable to reach the continent, late that night they saw, far ahead, a small black island.

By the morning of the 13th, *Discovery* had reached what would be named Proclamation Island, and Mawson loaded most of the scientific staff in the launch and headed for shore. Ascending through an Adélie penguin rookery, they made a steep climb to the 850-foot summit of the island. There they erected a flagpole, to which a wooden tablet carved by Hurley was attached. At noon, Mawson finally read his proclamation, asserting the sovereignty of King George V over Enderby Land, Kemp Land, and Mac. Robertson Land. The Union Jack was raised, 'God Save the King' sung, three cheers given to the King, and Hurley photographed the historic occasion. Then, prompted by Davis' demand that they hurry back because there was no safe place to anchor, the party returned to the ship, most of them disappointed in the short amount of time they were allowed ashore, although Simmers and Alfred Howard had run magnetic tests while the others had climbed to the summit. On the way down, Mawson, an old hand at making the best of such situations, collected 'quantity of rocks, making very heavy load. Had rucksack of rocks, camera case with rocks inside, rocks in pockets and hands ... very arduous descent.'

Mawson and company might have been ecstatic over finally making a landing, but as they continued west the next evening they were brought firmly down to Earth. Suddenly ahead of them was a tiny – only 114 feet, compared to 172 for *Discovery* – double-masted ship manned by only seventeen men, but that nevertheless sported two large aeroplanes. She was *Norvegia*, and after each party dipped its flag in greeting, the Norwegians asked if Riiser-Larsen could come aboard *Discovery* to meet Mawson.

The larger-than-life figure who had once been Amundsen's right-hand man soon clambered up the ladder wearing a black flying suit and scarf, and by the end of his visit had thoroughly charmed Mawson, Davis, and the others. Mawson found that Riiser-Larsen and Lützow-Holm had first made an aerial survey of Bouvetøya. They then approached Enderby Land, but were halted far short of the coast by pack ice. Unlike Mawson's flights, which had remained in the vicinity of the ship, they had flown ninety miles to the coast, landed on water, reversed the plane onto the land ice, and then skied some five miles inland. They had claimed the region for the King and Queen of Norway, and it had only been four days before the present meeting that Riiser-Larsen had found that his government had repudiated the annexation. Now Mawson and Riiser-Larsen agreed that the Australians would continue exploration in the region to the east of 40°E and the Norwegians would head back to the west of that point. In doing so, Riiser-Larsen went on to discover and claim huge swathes of territory now known as Dronning Maud Land.

Discovery, meanwhile, continued west for another day. Then, despite not yet having reached 40°E, Mawson decided that, based on Riiser-Larsen's report, there was little that could be done in that region. Moreover, he had received a wireless message reminding him that the flag should be hoisted as often as possible, and knowing that he had done so only once, and then not on the mainland, he realised his duty lay to the east. But now, after an extended period of fine weather, when repairs had been made on the aeroplane, high winds culminating in a three-day gale stopped any hope of flying, and the scientific staff spent much of the time sorting through a series of dredges from the bottom of the sea.

Although little geographically or politically was accomplished during these days, the coal continued to dwindle, and on 19 January Davis told Mawson that it would not be possible to complete the programme Mawson had outlined for him. Davis believed it would be unsafe to depart for Kerguelen with anything less than 120 tons of coal, and with only 147 tons remaining, he said Mawson needed to compress as much work as possible into the next fine spell of weather. Mawson vehemently disagreed with Davis' figures as well as his concerns about the possibility of missing Kerguelen and having to continue to Australia. 'It is a difficult matter to reason with M on such matters, and I don't think he even now believes that I am serious,' wrote Davis. 'It is however a duty to those who are on board and their belongings, to consider and provide against unnecessary folly, and to arrive off Kerguelen with no coal in the ship, on the assumption we should meet fine weather, is not a "daring act" but a "foolish one".'

No previous issue had seemed quite so important, and this dispute now pushed each of the two men to the verge of breaking. The entire situation degenerated to one that, in the most undignified scenario imaginable, came to include not just them, but the crew and scientific staff. On 22 January Mawson claimed in his diary that he was 'informed by officers that JK had addressed himself to all and sundry on the bridge in a loud voice, saying derogatory things about me . . . A nice sort of thing for a Second-in-Command to be doing. Davis is quite impossible for an expedition.' But did it actually happen that way, or was the shoe on the other foot? The same day, seaman Martin recorded that: 'D.M. addressed the starboard watch this p.m. and said he considered the O.M. was too old for his job. That he was scared to take chances, all he would do now was to growl and curse and that our best plan was to get to Melbourne as soon as possible and find another man. Also that the O.M. was too used to a soft shore job.'

Regardless of the accuracy of these statements, tempers remained prickly, and they did not improve in the following days when twice virtually the entire ship's company – excited about the possibility of making a landing – was disappointed by Davis' refusal to go into the ice towards land. First, near Cape Biscoe, the ice that Davis had hoped would have blown out was still firmly fixed. 'Launch the plane we may, but go in there we can't,' he said decisively to Mawson. So they continued back towards Proclamation Island, hoping conditions would allow them to land at the nearby coast.

On the morning of 25 January, from the open water near Proclamation Island, several flights were made, and Hurley was able to take both still photographs and cinematic film. Then Campbell and Mawson flew several miles inland from the coast, where Campbell dropped a flag attached to a mast over the side while Mawson again read his proclamation, this time including all of the land they had seen to the west. Upon returning to the ship, Mawson advised Davis that there was a passageway through the ice to the mainland, with 'too many small pieces loose ice in water for safe aeroplane landing but quite easy for ship to come into this open water. Then we could make landing upon the mainland from motor boat.'

Davis, however, was not convinced and, after steaming around the general area for four hours, flatly refused to take the ship into the ice. Mawson was disgusted, feeling that risk was part of an expedition. But Davis – the most experienced Antarctic navigator in the world – believed that pushing into the pack when any sudden movement of it might prove fatal to all aboard could not be justified, particularly when the object was simply to plant a flag on the mainland five miles from where one had already been raised. 'It is unpleasant having to decline to meet the wishes of the leader of the expedition,' he wrote, 'but when so little sense of responsibility is manifested one must put the safety of those on board first.'

Safety was also Davis' concern the next morning when he passed Mawson a note reporting that the coal was down to 120 tons, the minimum amount required for a secure return to Australia via Kerguelen. Mawson was adamant that 80 tons would suffice, although his arguments conveniently ignored a point Davis had made almost a year before:

'Ballast: At least 50 tons of ballast would be required in the bottom of the vessel when returning from Enderby Land.' Without such protection, the ship might founder in a gale, and to Davis, that possibility far outweighed Mawson's claim that the extra week gained in the Antarctic would allow the completion of an important aerial survey and local oceanographic studies.

The two men were obviously not going to agree, but after another dredging effort and a pair of flights to film and chart the coastline, Mawson grudgingly acquiesced and *Discovery* turned north. Mawson had one last hope of remaining in the south – being coaled from the whaler *Radioleine* – but by the time the ship's owners had consented to his request two days later, the whaler was at least 200 miles away. Besides, Davis had argued that coaling at sea would be a dangerous affair, and the chief engineer had found that *Discovery*'s boilers would only last another three weeks without cleaning. And so, with great regrets for those aspects of the agenda he had failed to accomplish, Mawson watched as the Antarctic disappeared in the wake of their passage north.

The mountains of Kerguelen loomed in the distance on 7 February, and at noon the next day *Discovery* once again moored at Port Jeanne d'Arc. Now Mawson had almost a month to conduct a comprehensive programme of scientific research in the archipelago, while *Discovery*'s boilers and engines were serviced, the ship was loaded with coal, and Davis began compiling a set of information and sailing directions about Kerguelen to help future mariners.

Finally, on 2 March, a course was set to Australia, with dredging, trawling, and sounding-station measurements regularly scheduled for the duration. But Mawson and Davis had had too much of each other, and even in these final stages they could agree on almost nothing. 'I cannot conceive a more haphazard enterprise than this one,' Davis wrote soon after leaving Kerguelen. In the following days, his complaints continued: 'He messes about with everything from the food to the storage of the holds ... I have to find excuses for him and endeavour to pretend that I like the ship being reduced to a bedlam, or there would be friction,' and 'there is something about this show which is missing. It is what I would call the Shackleton touch which made the ward room a brighter spot as soon as one went into it ... There are two distinct parties, the ship and the scientists, and the two seem never to have merged into one.'

According to Mawson it was even worse for him, because Davis had ceased all attempts at civility. 'I listen to storms of abuse from him,' Mawson – who had always been bothered by profanity – wrote, continuing:

> He is really a disgusting fellow – losing his temper, absolutely and perfectly illogical, contradictory and against all established things except JKD ... he lets out abusively at me on the bridge or deck or elsewhere in hearing of everybody. Talking in his room, with officers working in adjacent chart room, he storms and abuses me. I find the only way is to let him rave on for a while; then he blows himself out ... I have had no troubles or trials on this expedition, *only Davis* ... He is really a very mean and despicable fellow – or he is merely non compos mentis. He certainly gets brainstorms and should not be entrusted with responsibility.

The last major row between the two men came when, midway through March, Mawson wrote Davis an official memo outlining the remaining oceanographic work he planned to conduct before arriving at Adelaide. Davis, who had been making for Albany in Western Australia for fresh provisions, exploded at what he considered a vast increase in both labour and the time before *Discovery* would reach port. According to Mawson, he threatened to take the ship into Albany anyway, resign on the spot, and abandon *Discovery* there.

Mawson anticipated that there would be a second cruise – although this was not yet definite – and he realised that if Davis created a scandal by doing this, the government might well send the ship directly back to England, completing the expedition a year earlier than he had hoped. By continuing to Adelaide, where he could immediately influence his political and business supporters, he would increase the probability of being granted a second year. So Mawson reduced his scientific programme, eliminated the work scheduled for the Great Australian Bight, and brought forward his arrival date for Adelaide.

These moves did the trick – outwardly at least – and the leaders managed better to control their disagreements during the final two weeks of the cruise, which concluded with a great celebratory welcome upon their arrival in Adelaide on 1 April. But once back in Australia, Mawson had much more to overcome than just Davis, as would be seen in the days ahead.

15

A FINAL VISIT

IT IS HARD TO imagine a more difficult climate for obtaining support for an Antarctic expedition than that faced by Mawson when he arrived home on April Fools' Day, 1930. Most of the Western world was reeling from the early months of the Great Depression, and it had hit Australia, with its dependence on exports of products such as wool and wheat, extremely hard. Labour's James Scullin had been sworn in as Prime Minister only the week before the collapse of the Wall Street stock market, and by mid-1930 he would subscribe to the 'Melbourne Agreement' and its solutions for the crisis: slashing government expenditure, cutting social services and public works, and reducing public servants' wages. With these changes in the pipeline, it did not look promising to gain governmental aid for something as remote from the average man's life as another voyage to the far south.

Nevertheless, refusing to be daunted by the economic situation or to allow his university duties to interfere with his efforts, Mawson promptly launched his bid for a second cruise to examine the section of Antarctic coast between his most recent discoveries and his earlier ones. One of his first moves was to ask Macpherson Robertson for further aid, and the sweets manufacturer again responded generously, offering £6,000 on the condition that the government matched it.

An even more significant ally proved to be a totally unexpected one: the Norwegian whaling industry. While Mawson was in the Antarctic, Lars Christensen's fleet had continued to enter new areas, and their success was beginning to encourage the idea of building a robust Australian counterpart. Highlighting the Norwegian achievements was the return to Australia or New Zealand in March 1930 of four of their factory ships laden heavily with whale oil. Between them, they totalled 279,000 barrels worth more than £1.3 million. Such quantities fired the imagination of the Australian press over a potentially huge new industry, and many articles appeared, arousing public – and consequently governmental – interest.

Eventually, the hopes of future whaling riches, combined with a political determination to secure those Antarctic regions over which they still had not officially asserted sovereignty, proved more alluring than the economic situation was frightening. On 22 May, the day after Mawson's report of the first BANZARE cruise was tabled in Parliament, the Prime Minister informed the House of Representatives that: 'The Government have decided that the work in the Australian Sector of the Antarctic, which is of considerable national interest and importance to the Commonwealth from economic, scientific, and other points of view, will be continued during the coming Antarctic summer season.' *Discovery*, he pointed out, would again be made available without charge, and the leader would once more be Mawson. He did not mention that the master would not be Davis.

Long before the end of the voyage, Davis had decided not to return for a second season. He mentioned this to Professor Henderson of the Antarctic Committee when *Discovery* arrived at Adelaide, but he did nothing official until he had taken the ship on to Melbourne, where she was to be refitted,

after which he submitted a formal letter of resignation.
Although the Committee had been made aware of the
problems between the leaders, Davis displayed tact and
discretion by indicating that he would not return because
he did not feel equal to the responsibility, which should be
taken on by a younger man. It therefore was a great surprise
to him – and also to the members of the Committee, who
had assumed such issues would be addressed in private –
when Mawson's report, still unseen by the Committee and
with highly inappropriate comments, was introduced in
Parliament on 21 May.

The report described the new lands and their claiming,
detailed the extensive scientific and geographical work, and
then blamed Davis for any shortcomings in the expedition.
Concerning the days of late January when the issues of coal
reached their climax, Mawson wrote:

> Captain Davis reported that our coal reserve had now been
> reduced almost to the limit of 120 tons without which
> quantity he considered it would not be reasonably possible
> to get the ship back to a coaling port. This was a great
> disappointment to me, for earlier in the voyage we had arrived
> at a verbal understanding that a limit of 80 tons would suffice
> ... On the evening of 26th January Captain Davis informed
> me that having reached the limit of 120 tons of coal he would
> carry on no longer in Antarctic waters and was about to set
> a course for Kerguelen.

This was highly unfair. Mawson had been told many months
before that Davis felt there was a need for 50 tons of coal
as ballast, and even Mawson had noted that as a safety
precaution they needed 25-plus tons over what it would take
to steam to Kerguelen, lest they had difficulty getting into
the islands; when the ballast is added to this figure, Davis'
total for what he said was needed was not excessively high.
More importantly, in the note he wrote about reaching 120

tons, Davis straightforwardly asked Mawson to furnish him with instructions. When Mawson did so, it showed that although he regretted having to leave the Antarctic, he accepted and concurred with Davis' analysis. This was a far cry from Davis unilaterally making a decision to leave.

And there was more of what was arguably misrepresentation: Mawson stated that after he arranged for a re-coaling by *Radioleine*, 'Captain Davis took a very serious view of the difficulties of coaling the *Discovery* at sea, so that the proposal had to be abandoned.' Yet although Davis expressed his concerns about the potential dangers of coaling at sea, and that the delay of meeting a ship by then 200 miles away might prevent *Discovery* reaching Kerguelen if the coaling could not be carried out due to bad weather, the final say was Mawson's. And when Mawson ultimately declined the refuelling, the manager of *Radioleine* wired back 'agree with Captain Davis.' Mawson did not make clear that there was this outside support for Davis' position.

Finally, Mawson reported that, once having filled with coal at Kerguelen: 'Captain Davis was averse to making another short visit to the Antarctic coast, en route to Australia (a call at Queen Mary Land having been in view).' Again, this was unjust to Davis, as it ignored the high potential of being caught in the ice when going to Queen Mary Land that late in the season. Also, it implied – wrongly – that Davis had at one point been supportive of such a plan.

Mawson tried to sidestep criticism over his report, stating the next day that 'I did not know that there was any intention of publishing the report, otherwise the wording might have been more carefully revised, so that no unwarranted construction could be placed upon certain paragraphs therein.' But the Committee members were incensed, correctly believing that it should have been submitted to them in the first instance, and that by his improper actions Mawson had treated them with discourtesy and Davis with injustice. Davis felt so too, but it is to his everlasting credit that after presenting his interpretation of the events to the Committee, he quietly returned to his position as Commonwealth Director of Navigation and was able to work amicably with Mawson in other contexts for almost three decades more.

Once the expedition was scheduled to go ahead, one of Mawson's first jobs was to replace those members who were not returning. The position of master and second-in-command – with the same confusing leadership roles – was assumed by MacKenzie, who was taking charge of a ship for the first time in his career. Max Stanton filled MacKenzie's former role as first officer. Several scientific posts also changed, with Morton Moyes and J.W.S. Marr being replaced by Alec Kennedy, the magnetician from Wild's Western Base during the AAE, and Lieutenant K. Oom.

Another task for Mawson had a touch of the claims made about the twenty-first-century British Labour Party: cash for honours. A condition for Robertson's major contribution for the second voyage was Mawson's efforts to help him obtain a knighthood. With the reigning Australian Labour government unwilling to make such recommendations, Mawson wrote to the previous Conservative Prime Minister, and also worked on Major Richard Casey, then the Australian government's liaison officer in London, and, through him, Sir Harry Batterbee of the Dominions Office. Mawson's efforts might or might not have been of importance, but Robertson received a knighthood in 1932.

Meanwhile, *Discovery* was refitted, her aeroplane overhauled, and the shipborne scientific, wireless, and photographic equipment modified based on assessments of it made on the previous cruise. All this material was vital to the second cruise since the official orders issued to Mawson required that as well as annexing lands whenever practical, he 'carry out to the best of your ability all scientific work and investigations . . . comprising amongst other things, meteorological and oceanographic observations and investigations . . . concerning fauna, notably whales and seals, of seas and lands visited by you, and all matters connected therewith which may assist in future economic exploration of such fauna.' Although the government's major concern, other than claiming land, was contributing to the growth of the Australian whaling industry, Mawson did not need to be told twice to make concerted efforts on the scientific front.

At the same time, the route of the expedition was settled upon. Sailing from Hobart, Mawson was ordered to proceed to Macquarie Island, which he had long campaigned to make a wildlife sanctuary. The expedition would then investigate the little-known Balleny Islands, near where *Discovery* would re-coal from *Sir James Clark Ross*, a Norwegian factory whaling ship. Mawson was then to revisit his old base at Cape Denison, and move west along the coastline. This would link the various points previously discovered in King George V Land, Adelie Land, Queen Mary Land, and Kaiser Wilhelm II Land with Mac. Robertson Land, while simultaneously investigating the mysterious areas between Adelie Land and Queen Mary Land. It was a substantial plan that in theory would be greatly assisted by the aeroplane, which Mawson proudly announced had a 200-mile cruising range – assuming he was now willing to use it out of sight of the ship.

On Saturday, 22 November 1930, *Discovery* sailed from Queen's Wharf in Hobart, almost nineteen years after Mawson had left the same location in *Aurora*. The next day the first oceanographic work was conducted, including echo sounding, dredging, and sampling of water temperatures and salinity. As they progressed south, soundings continued, Mawson trying to delineate more precisely the outlines and features of the Mill Rise, a large underwater shoal first investigated when Davis led two cruises dedicated to oceanographic studies on *Aurora* during the first year of the AAE. After several dredging efforts were found laden with barnacles and seaweed from the hull, Mawson and MacKenzie had a wooden scrubber used to try to remove such marine growth.

When this met with indifferent results, a chain was run under the keel with somewhat greater success.

On the last day of November, they passed a series of small icebergs at 53°29'S, unusually far north for such physical features, and the next day they spied a tabular berg at least seventy feet high. That afternoon Macquarie Island appeared through the mists. Mawson had not scheduled a great deal of time at Macquarie, so when the scientific party landed on the morning of 2 December, they quickly split up to secure the best results in the time available. Mawson found that although the old sealing lease on the island had been cancelled by the government of Tasmania in 1916, sealers had continued to go there until at least 1919, and the grave of Otto Bauer, who had been in charge of the sealing operation when the AAE base was established, was dated '1st May 1918.' Mawson also discovered the old wireless masts snapped off at the ground, and he was puzzled because they had both fallen towards the prevailing wind, making him wonder if they had been felled by an earthquake.

The party camped on the spit south of Wireless Hill, near the tattered remains of the AAE base. Although three strong tents were erected in comparative shelter for the other men, Mawson, chief biologist Harvey Johnston, and Alec Kennedy chose to stay in the 'magnetic tent' that Kennedy was using for his measurements. Unfortunately, it proved unsuitable in the strong winds that whipped up, and to prevent it collapsing and the pole in its centre injuring one of them, Kennedy lowered it on top of them – a rash mistake. 'A very poor night. I slept some, but others not,' Mawson wrote. 'I get up at 4 a.m. and Johnston and Kennedy follow – get fire alight in wreck of stove in ruins of digester house.' Mawson decided if he was up and about it was time for all of the party to be so, but he had 'difficulty rousing the other tents . . . [so] Kennedy and I divert a Sea-elephant and drive it to one of the tents where its roar soon brings out the occupants in alarm.'

After only three days, the party was off south again, with a quick – and almost disastrous – effort at making soundings and taking exact sightings around the tiny Bishop and Clerk Islands, just south of Macquarie. With a heavy fog blowing in, the ship's officers could not even make out the two islets until a sudden clearing proved them dangerously close and showed numerous icebergs uncomfortably near to the ship. When his sounding suddenly revealed the seabed only eighteen fathoms down, MacKenzie realised he 'was in a tight corner with no clear way out. Ice showed up ahead and the sound of breakers seemed to be all round. To get out the boats would only cause panic and in any case no launching could ever be made in those breakers. I stopped and waited and hoped that the fog might lift, but it only came in thicker.' Knowing that in those conditions any moment might be their last, he simply guessed, and took a direction he hoped would take them away from danger. Three hours later, when the fog cleared, he discovered that, mercifully, it had.

The weather left MacKenzie no time for self-congratulations, however, as a gale lasting more than two days caused *Discovery* to roll heavily and ship vast quantities of water. The conditions gave the new captain a chance to appreciate what Davis had complained about: 'It is only four days since my last entry – and yet it seems like four weeks – four long days and four longer nights. I have not had my clothes off since leaving Macquarie and my bed has been undisturbed for three nights – fitful snatches of restless sleep on my settee.'

Even when the gale blew itself out, conditions remained difficult, as *Discovery* entered pack ice much farther north than usual. For a week, they picked their way through it, making slow progress but, frustratingly, not even heading in the planned direction. Instead of being near the Balleny Islands, *Sir James Clark Ross* had steamed off in search of whales far to the east, near Scott Island on the verge of the

Ross Sea. It took an extra four days to reach the factory ship, and Mawson estimated it lost the expedition a total of ten days and sixty tons of coal.

When they did reach the whalers on 15 December, however, Mawson was highly impressed with the technology aboard the ship, the efficiency of the operation, and the welcome that the Norwegians gave their erstwhile competitors. With whale carcasses serving as fenders between the ships, the Norwegians sent a gang of men to help transport 100 tons of coal to *Discovery*; they then volunteered to trim it as well. The entire operation, including giving the expedition ship twenty-five additional tons of water, took only five hours. Meanwhile, Mawson and MacKenzie dined with the captain and were shown around the remarkable vessel, which was able to flense four whales at a time and could hold 20,000 tons of whale oil.

Once ready to steam west, Mawson discovered that Hurley, whom he had assigned to get film footage from a whale catcher, had returned but then gone back out again in company with Douglas, the pilot. For twenty-four hours *Discovery* waited, while Mawson became more and more irritable. Upon their return, MacKenzie told the miscreants in no uncertain terms that the next time they disappeared they would be left to their fates, regardless of where they were.

Difficult conditions prevailed as they continued west, and on 23 December Mawson decided to abandon further attempts to reach the Balleny Islands due to the heavy pack surrounding them, and to move slowly southwest towards King George V Land. On the 29th, a chance encounter with *Kosmos*, a Norwegian factory whaling ship slightly larger than *Sir James Clark Ross*, led to an offer of fifty tons of coal, which Mawson gratefully accepted. During the transfer, again with a whale pushed between them and made during a period of high swell, *Discovery* banged up against the giant ship, receiving damage. MacKenzie was heard to exclaim that 'he wouldn't go alongside a 20,000 tonner again in such a swell for 50 tons of gold, let alone coal.'

Soon after leaving *Kosmos*, a force-10 hurricane began to hammer *Discovery*. MacKenzie tried to guide her into a less frenzied area, but icebergs Mawson described as 'evil in intent' seemed to surround the ship and threatened to make every move her final one. Then early in the morning on 2 January, while enclosed in heavy ice, a violent smacking sound rang out three times, the last so loudly that all hands were woken. Mawson raced to the bridge in his pyjamas, fearful that the propeller had been snapped off. Anxiously awaiting the result of MacKenzie's inspection, he soon found that the propeller had been driven straight into ice at high speed, but, by a miracle, it had not been damaged.

On 4 January, Mawson's memories of earlier times were powerfully revived. It was not only the blizzard that blew in Commonwealth Bay and the sight of Winter Quarters that took him back in time, but a virtual repeat of interactions from the previous year. As *Discovery* passed into the broad coastal indentation at the base of which is Cape Denison, MacKenzie asked Mawson for any assistance his local knowledge could provide. Studying the scene, Mawson was suddenly worried and told the captain that he was 'running into some terrible place . . . nowhere near our old base.' He passionately urged MacKenzie to head back out to sea to take sightings. Having taken them the previous day, the captain was extremely annoyed, and ordered Mawson off the bridge. A short while later, Mawson returned and demanded they make a retreat. MacKenzie refused heatedly, and was soon 'rewarded by sighting the rocky patch on our port bow.' Although MacKenzie had proven right, the conflict had the very feel of 'Mawson v. Davis' about it, and it marked the beginning of a qualitative change in the two men's interactions.

For the time being, however, the expedition had reached

its first major destination, and when the wind dropped the next morning, Mawson took a large party ashore. As at Macquarie, the scientists concentrated on their own work, the most extensive being that of Kennedy, who hacked the ice out of the Magnetograph House and spent eighteen hours taking measurements, determining in the process that the South Magnetic Pole had continued to move towards Cape Denison and was now probably no more than 250 miles away.

Meanwhile, Mawson, MacKenzie, and others investigated the huts. The exposed timbers outside showed that the incessant winds had abraded more than half an inch off the wood slats. But snow and ice were packed up next to most of the outside area of the huts, meaning that the only way in was through one of the skylights. Even from there, a passage had to be forced into the spaces below, and when this was accomplished, parts of the interior were found to be filled with compacted snow. There were also some areas still relatively snow-free, and on the table Mawson found the note he had left telling others they could use the hut. Some items appeared to be just as they were left seventeen years before: food, books, clothing, cans, and implements of a wide variety. Perhaps most poignant was the half sledge that he had brought back on his long, solo trek; this was removed and taken back to the ship for return to Australia.

At noon, Mawson read a proclamation claiming the region. He had done so in 1912, of course, but this time it was with official approval, and he now claimed all of the area extending west to French Terre Adélie under the name of King George V Land. MacKenzie raised the flag, the national anthem was sung, and Hurley took photographs. That night Mawson and five others camped in tents ashore for a final time at the base he had known so well. The next evening, *Discovery* passed the Mackellar Islets and turned west.

On the day after departing from Cape Denison, Campbell and Douglas made a preliminary reconnaissance flight, and their description convinced Mawson that the high ice cliffs reported by Wilkes and d'Urville and called 'Clarie Land' had been 'an immense flat-topped ice formation, possibly a berg, grounded on shoal waters which certainly extend considerably north of the mainland.' To Mawson this meant that the sighting from *Aurora* in 1912 had been the first ever of that coastline, and reinforced his belief in his right to name the region to the west of Terre Adélie, which became Wilkes Land.

An extended gale kept the ship away from the coast and grounded the aeroplane for about a week, but on 15 January a brief period of intensive oceanographic data-collection and aerial survey began. That day Campbell and Oom ascended to 8,000 feet, as did Douglas and Oom the following afternoon. From this vantage point they could see the coast some 100 miles away, a previously undiscovered region that Mawson named Banzare Land. Two days later, in an area first claimed to have been seen in 1839 by John Balleny – who called it Sabrina Land – Campbell and Mawson went aloft. 'In the south-south-west,' wrote Mawson, 'near the limit of vision, was a definite change in the view, and there is there either a great jam of icebergs or what appears to be ice-covered low land. Should the latter prove to be the case on further investigation, we propose that the term Sabrina Land be applied to it to commemorate Balleny's effort.'

For most of the next week MacKenzie allowed *Discovery* to drift slowly near the edge of the ice pack, conserving coal while waiting for better weather to launch the plane. Finally, on 27 January, Mawson could wait no longer for his examination of this section of coast, and despite rough sea conditions he and Douglas took off. 'What appeared to be undulating ice-covered land showed up to the south,' wrote Douglas, 'but as we could not be certain that it was in fact part of the Antarctic continent, Sir Douglas recorded the sighting as probable land in the vicinity of Wilkes's Knox Land.' Douglas then made a difficult landing, but as the

plane was being lifted from the water towards the deck of
the ship, a violent roll damaged the fuselage while causing
the plane to dip its starboard wing into the sea. Mawson
fell towards the water but managed to grab a strut and hang
on. As Douglas left his seat to go to his assistance, the lifting
sling broke, dropping all into the frigid water. A boat was
quickly launched, and the men and damaged airplane rescued.
'We knew from repute and other incidents that Sir Douglas
always acted with great activity and determination in
emergencies, and this was no exception,' wrote Douglas, 'for
I had noticed that when he was hanging onto the strut he
had complete presence of mind, and indeed he was more
concerned with saving the plane than himself.'

The plane was out of action for ten days, which was a
disappointing period, as they were prevented from reaching
the Shackleton Ice Shelf or Queen Mary Land by heavy pack
and hundreds of icebergs, the latter possibly from the break-
up of the sixty-mile-long Termination Ice Tongue that Davis
had discovered at the northwest corner of the ice shelf.
Knowing that the coal would not last forever, Mawson
elected to wait no longer for the plane to be repaired, but
continued west towards the yet unnamed and unexplored
coast east of Mac. Robertson Land.

Unnamed, and unclaimed, it might have been, but Mawson
soon found that it was not unexplored. On 6 February, when
the Gipsy Moth was ready to be tested, *Discovery* encoun-
tered two Norwegian whalers, which were spied south of,
and nearer to the coastline than, the exploring ship. Hurley
was particularly horrified that the whaling ships had stew-
ardesses aboard – meaning that *women* had been where his
own party had failed to reach. One of the whaling captains
graciously donated twenty tons of coal to *Discovery*, and
during the transfer process he chatted to Mawson, informing
him there were at least forty Norwegian factory whaling
ships and 240 catchers operating in the Antarctic, many
charting coastlines in the process. Enough of these were in

the same region as *Discovery* to lead former seaman James
Martin, who had been promoted to boatswain, to write that
they made it 'quite like the [English] Channel.'

This time, however, Mawson had an advantage over the
Norwegians, as none of those ships were equipped with aeroplanes, and flights were made by *Discovery*'s plane on three
consecutive days. On 9 February, Campbell and Mawson
saw a great, solid pack to the south. 'Behind all this low
light-blue line on horizon suggests possibly land from ESE
to SSW at which later point it arrives behind great belt of
slack pack . . . some 20 m to W of us,' Mawson noted. With
hopes of getting nearer to the land, the ship headed southwest,
and the next day a brief flight suggested open water even
farther in that direction. On the 11th, they suddenly arrived
in a great ice-free sea, in which they steamed south and then
spent hours following the nearby coastline. In a flight of an
hour and a half, Campbell and Oom made a detailed survey,
and dropped a flag over the mainland.

These days were, in many senses, the highlight of BANZARE.
What Mawson saw on 9 February were the previously
unknown icy slopes of a new land, which MacKenzie
convinced him to name Princess Elizabeth Land in honour of
the young daughter of Prince Albert, the Duke of York – 'our
popular little Scottish princess' MacKenzie called the girl who
later became Queen. On the 11th, from both the land and
the ship, the shores of the eastern regions of Mac. Robertson
Land were seen for the first time, as was Princess Elizabeth
Land again from the air. Intriguingly, the great Amery Ice
Shelf – into which pours the Lambert Glacier, one of the
world's largest and most dynamic ice rivers – was not recognised as such by Oom, who mistook it for ice covering land.

MacKenzie now continued west through a large bay later
named for him, and on 13 February *Discovery* reached a
series of monoliths, the first a striking mass of black rock
rising a thousand feet straight out of the sea. A party under
Mawson approached the shore around what became known

as Murray Monolith, but with a bad swell, no shelter, and the sea breaking, Stanton, the first officer, refused to come close enough to allow anyone to disembark. 'We touch rock with oar then throw cylinder with proclamation on amongst boulders above beach – after reading,' wrote Mawson, 'then throw wood plate with copper inscription – it strikes rocks and tumbles into sea. Matheson throws flag on pole – it strikes rock & falls into sea.' After a photograph they returned to the ship and proceeded to another of the massive features, a crescent-shaped, 2,000-footer that Mawson named for Prime Minister Scullin. Not to be denied this time, Campbell jumped ashore holding a line to the boat, followed by Mawson, Hurley, ornithologist Robert Falla, and John Child, the third officer. While the others waited in the launch, the five erected a flag, listened to Mawson again take possession, and gathered a number of biological and geological specimens, which made getting back into the boat dangerous and difficult. There was no doubt that it had been worth it, however, Simmers commenting in his diary that the actions of the five had 'saved the name of the expedition as we have landed and raised the flag at last.'

For the next several days, they took advantage of a lack of ice by steaming much closer to land than the previous year, allowing the men to map new coastal features, observe new mountain ranges, and improve charting done previously from a distance. On 18 February, with the coal officially down to 100 tons, MacKenzie decided it was time to return to Australia, but agreed to make a final effort for a landing that day. Having been allowed only two hours, a large party under Mawson made for shore at Cape Bruce – named for the former Prime Minister who had supported BANZARE – and reached a beach that led into a little valley between two steep, rocky bluffs.

'Dux [Mawson] jumped ashore and ran up the valley waving a flag and looking as pleased as punch – and so he was,' wrote Simmers, 'because at last we were in a position to make a legal, complete and entire observance of claiming land.' In a number of other instances, various parts of the official procedure had not been fulfilled, but 'this time things have been done properly – mainland, cairn, board, proclamation, several people, lusty singing – lusty because in the confined space of the valley our voices seemed very loud and cheerful compared with previous efforts which have been on the tops of hills where the voices seem thin & are easily lost in space.' Hurley again took photographs, and then he and the scientists headed up the hills for a final grab-bag of specimens, but only after 'the pouring of a little champagne over the cairn – only a little as we wanted to (and did) drink the rest.'

Having taken an extra hour, the party returned to a 'hopping mad captain,' who, after telling them off, promptly turned the ship north.

Throughout the early stages of the second cruise, Mawson and most of the scientific staff had preferred MacKenzie's style to that of Davis. By the return voyage, however, that goodwill had evaporated. After departing from Cape Bruce, MacKenzie brought the ship into the lee of a large iceberg and spent a day having *Discovery*'s yards rigged. Several scientists complained that they could see landing places on the coast where they could have done valuable research while work proceeded on the ship, but, despite it being a perfect day, MacKenzie would not consider it. Hurley, whose chances for cinematography had been limited, was annoyed by this stop as well, but *his* dissatisfaction had existed for much of the voyage. He perceived MacKenzie as churlish and 'sadly lacking in determined ice navigation & only open water with bright sunshine might be regarded as good water.' His contempt reached new heights when the captain asked him to produce a disclaimer indemnifying the ship in case of accident while Hurley was clambering on the rigging. 'Nothing could be more childish or unseamanlike than this request,' wrote Hurley. 'If I am not game to take some trifling risk in doing my work then I have no right to be on an expedition.' He wrote out the requested letter, however, which made the matter 'a popular joke on board.'

Mawson's problems with MacKenzie also increased as time went on, partly based on one of the same issues as with Davis: coal. Mawson became suspicious about MacKenzie's claims for the amount on board, and on 12 March conducted an inventory himself, arriving at the figure of seventy-six tons, more than twice what the captain claimed. Not letting him know the discrepancy, Mawson asked if they might proceed to Melbourne instead of Hobart. 'He agreed that Melbourne was only 60 miles further than Hobart but held that with the ship as it is (light) there is a danger trying to make Melbourne.' This angered Mawson, in part because he figured there were 150 tons of materials serving as ballast. The situation was not made better by MacKenzie telling Mawson 'that as this is his first command his whole future depends on his getting the ship back to port safely . . . I see that it is not a good thing to have a beginner as master of an exploring vessel. He is nervous and over cautious, considering everything in the light of its effect on his own future career . . . This is all rather disgusting.'

But that was not the end of their quarrels. About a week later, MacKenzie blamed Mawson and the scientists for holding up the ship's progress with a sounding operation. 'This is parallel with several other cases earlier in the voyage,' wrote Mawson, 'when without any warrant whatever MacKenzie launched out in accusing the scientific staff of being entirely selfish and not helping the ship in critical time. Such talk is, and always has been, balderdash arising from his own hot head and limited viewpoint.' In response, Mawson 'flared and said, "It is all damned rubbish you are talking" and I turned on my heel and went below . . . No matter what sacrifice we make these merchant Captains do not appreciate it. Perhaps their habit of using a telescope has made them one-eyed.'

The day after this last entry, *Discovery* reached Hobart, MacKenzie undoubtedly feeling he had triumphed by not taking her to Melbourne. But the true victors from the BANZARE voyages were the international scientific community – the knowledge of the far south increasing impressively due to the scientific data compiled – and the Commonwealth of Australia. In February 1933, a British Order in Council affirmed the sovereign rights of King George V and the British Crown over the Antarctic regions south of 60°S and between 45° and 160°E, with the exception of Terre Adélie. That same year, the Australian Antarctic Territory Acceptance Act – transferring those lands to the authority of the Common-wealth of Australia – was passed, and in 1936 it came into force, establishing the Australian Antarctic Territory. Thus was made official the Australian possession of the vast space that way back in 1909 Mawson had been one of the first to think about.

ANTARCTICA FROM AUSTRALIA

MAWSON NEVER AGAIN experienced the hardships, marvels, or accomplishments that came from being in Antarctica. But he remained active in many roles related to the great white south for the rest of his life.

One of Mawson's great hopes when BANZARE returned was that Hurley's film of the expedition would help pay for the series of Scientific Reports that would come from the voyages. But just as such profits never materialised from the film of the AAE, they did not appear following BANZARE, either. The year before, after the first voyage, Hurley released *Southward Ho! with Mawson*, but it bombed, in part because it was a silent film just when talkies were becoming the rage. More importantly, its lack of success sabotaged the market for the main film, *Siege of the South*, which covered the entire expedition. This second production included sound, and Hurley went to great lengths to add audio bites to the parts of the first film that he incorporated into it. He also filmed fake scenes in Australia for those parts of the storyline he had not been able to film in the Antarctic.

Sadly, all was for nought. Despite drawing significant crowds in Adelaide and Brisbane, *Siege of the South* did not capture the national or international acclaim that had been lavished on Herbert Ponting's film about Scott's expedition.

When the final accounts were produced late in 1932, they showed Hurley's film in the red.

A far longer-lasting frustration to Mawson – one that continued throughout his life – was the publication of the Scientific Reports, both from the AAE and BANZARE. Mawson saw these not only presenting the scientific data gained from his expeditions, but justifying their costs. For years, the government of New South Wales lived up to its agreement with Mawson and continued to publish the Scientific Reports, despite him doling out his promised AAE materials only slowly. The government actually went well beyond what would have been expected, since Mawson did not reply to many official enquiries about the materials and treated the Printing Committee shabbily in other instances, as when they expressed concern about receiving any more material due to Mawson's approaching departure on the first BANZARE cruise. Indicating he would be gone only five or six months, he rather rudely advised them 'not to get rattled.'

It would have been Mawson who was shaken up about the Scientific Reports, however, following his return from the second BANZARE voyage. In mid-1931, the Department of Education of New South Wales announced that, due to the depressed economy, they were halting publication of the series. There is no doubt that the Great Depression was the prime culprit in this decision, but other factors undoubtedly included the Printing Committee's unhappiness at not receiving the items contractually agreed upon, that the costs of the publications had already exceeded the promised £5,000, and that a surprising number of the reports were still outstanding, having never been received by the Government Printer.

Non-submission of manuscripts was even more aggravating to Mawson than to the government. A number of the scientists who had agreed to write the reports proved unreliable, and over a period of years some reports had to be reassigned, several of them multiple times. This dragged on and on, and a few key biological reports, including *Birds*, *Penguins*, and *Seals and Whales* were never published at all. Fortunately for Mawson and for scientific knowledge, however, in 1937, having overcome the worst of the Depression and despite Mawson's continuing reticence to turn over his effects, the government of New South Wales again began publication. This new effort continued until 1947, by which time ninety-six individual Scientific Reports in twenty-two volumes had appeared.

The BANZARE Scientific Reports did not cause Mawson the same sort of grief, as they were financed by a trust fund established by the Commonwealth Treasury, and the authors proved more reliable. Nevertheless, they took even longer to complete, and Mawson's daughter Patricia eventually took over his role as editor. By 1975, more than sixty reports had been published in nine volumes.

In the decades after BANZARE, Mawson not only finished a variety of follow-up work for his own past expeditions, but continued to be interested in the changes in and the future of the Antarctic. He served in an assortment of capacities, including as adviser for the Australian government and various scientific organisations. One of his great political triumphs occurred in 1933, when, after years of advocating protection for the flora and fauna of Macquarie Island, the island was officially declared a wildlife sanctuary. The importance Mawson attributed to Macquarie was further recognised in 1997, when it was added to the World Heritage List.

Even in his thirties, Mawson was clearly one of the world's foremost Antarctic scientists. Following the deaths of Shackleton and Amundsen in the 1920s, he further became recognised as the unchallenged expert on Antarctic exploration. This combination of scientific and practical experience made him a figure anyone serious about mounting an expedition to the Antarctic – scientific or geographical – would turn to for advice.

One of the men seeking such guidance was Richard E. Byrd, who in 1928 sought Mawson out in advance of his first Antarctic expedition in order to get input from the man who, he later wrote, had been its inspiration, along with Scott and Shackleton. Byrd epitomised the new mechanical and technological age of polar exploration, which Mawson had helped pioneer, whereas Mawson was Byrd's link with the 'Heroic Age,' of which he always wished he could have been part. The two began a relationship that lasted until Byrd's death in 1957, and Byrd considered Mawson 'the greatest living authority on the Antarctic.'

Another explorer with whom Mawson had contact was Lincoln Ellsworth, who in 1925 had unsuccessfully attempted to fly aeroplanes to the North Pole with Amundsen. The next year, Ellsworth joined Amundsen and Umberto Nobile in crossing the Arctic Basin in the airship *Norge*. Ellsworth then wanted to make the first crossing of Antarctica, and, although it took him almost a decade, in November 1935 he took off in a specially built aeroplane to fulfil this goal. However, what he had figured as a fourteen-hour flight took twenty-two days, as refuelling and bad weather forced him and his pilot to land three times. They then ran out of fuel sixteen miles short of Byrd's 'Little America' base, to which they walked.

However, Ellsworth's radio had stopped functioning, and the outside world assumed that the two men were in need of aid. Mawson suggested that RRS *Discovery II* be sent to conduct a search-and-rescue operation, and the Australian government followed his recommendation, dispatching the ship with two aeroplanes aboard. Mawson volunteered to go, but his offer was declined due to space limitations and the operation being primarily an aerial one, lessening the value he could bring. In January 1936, the men were safely picked up from Little America.

That voyage was not Mawson's last attempt to go south. In November 1938 he wrote to Davis, asking for backing in leading an expedition. The two were long since back on solid terms, but Davis could still be as difficult as ever, and he categorically refused. Mawson had likened the proposed effort to the British Graham Land Expedition (BGLE) recently led by another South Australian, John Rymill, but Davis awkwardly countered that the BGLE was not, like Mawson's proposed work, 'in the nature of a summer vacation.' In addition, Davis made it clear that he personally had 'no intention of taking further part in any Antarctic exploration,' which, he felt, should be carried out by 'younger men.'

Undaunted by these blatant hints about his own age, Mawson came up with a new idea: establishing a permanent research station in the region of Cape Freshfield, near the limit of both his and the East Coast Party's treks in late 1912. This was quite a leap in faith, because neither party actually had reached Cape Freshfield, and neither Mawson nor Madigan was certain if there was enough ice-free land to establish such a base. But Mawson was thinking big now, and he decided this station could be manned for at least a decade, the staffing supplied by each Australian university rotating through one or two men per year. With this concept for the source of personnel, he proposed the idea at the Australian Vice-Chancellors' Conference in early 1939 and gained their support. Things soon looked even brighter when the government agreed to buy Ellsworth's ship and aeroplanes, and Mawson must have been delighted at the prospects of again sailing for the Antarctic. But in September all such plans fell apart, as Australia entered the Second World War.

Mawson did not wait long after the cessation of hostilities in 1945 before beginning a campaign for more Australian participation in the Antarctic. By now, he was in his sixties, and too old to be a field scientist, but in 1946 he was brought into a series of interdepartmental government meetings called to formulate recommendations on what Australia would do with its vast Antarctic territory. Early the next year, the Executive Committee on Exploration and Exploitation was formed, and with several proposals by Mawson amongst the starting points, the members decided that in the summer of 1947–48 an expedition would sail south to search for a potential landing site for a more extensive scientific operation, which would begin the following year.

On 9 July, the committee – renamed the Australian National Antarctic Research Expedition (ANARE) – met again under the chairmanship of Stuart Campbell, the former BANZARE chief pilot who had been designated its head. Amongst other committee members present were Mawson, Davis, and ANARE's new Senior Scientific Officer, Phillip Law. This group oversaw a remarkably speedy recruitment and organisation for the voyage south, which began on Boxing Day, 1947. Unfortunately, mechanical problems and heavy ice combined to prevent the expedition ship from reaching the Antarctic mainland, but, with the use of an old naval landing craft, meteorological stations were established at both Heard Island and Macquarie Island.

In 1948, an Antarctic Division was created within the Department of External Affairs to oversee ANARE's activities. Campbell, with whom Mawson had a long and friendly relationship, was then replaced as director of the Antarctic Division by Law. It would have been easy at this stage for a lesser man than Mawson to withdraw his backing from the much younger, comparatively inexperienced leader whose manner could be rather prickly. But 'he never showed any envy or antagonism to me,' Law told Film Australia years later. 'Here was I, a young, brash person with all the government financial support he'd never been able to muster, with an era expanding out in front of me, which embraced all the things he would have loved to have done. He was never jealous of the fact that I had these chances and he was very supportive in everything I wanted to do.'

Mawson also always maintained his support for ANARE as a whole, despite being periodically disenchanted with some of the directions in which it was taken. Based on his own experience, Mawson believed that scientific research should be independent of government and that ANARE should pay for itself without long-term government financing. Despite these differences, he proved a strong and positive influence. 'Mawson served on [the Executive Planning Committee] from 1947 right up to 1958, I think,' Law said, 'so that for ten or eleven years, I saw quite a lot of Mawson and had his support in the committee for my ideas. I found him not only a most gracious and charming person, but a vigorous exponent of Antarctic ideas, and a man who was always looking forwards, looking for new ideas, looking for new things, supporting innovative projects.'

One of these projects was the establishment of a permanent base in eastern Mac. Robertson Land. In the early 1950s, when government financial retrenchment threatened to terminate the funding needed for the new base, Mawson turned to an old governmental contact, Richard Casey, by then Minister for External Affairs, and, through convincing him of the project's efficacy and worth, helped push its approval through the Cabinet. The construction of the base – named Mawson Station – finally began in 1954.

Coincidentally, Mawson's last great Antarctic battle was about another station. In 1957–58, he strongly opposed the proposal to take over the American Wilkes station after the International Geophysical Year. Mawson believed that such a move would adversely affect the second Australian station – Davis – which was located in Princess Elizabeth Land, and which appeared to him to offer better opportunities for science. 'The Davis area is geologically unexplored and I'd be loath to close the station there,' he said. 'There's nothing geologically interesting at Wilkes.'

In April 1958, at a meeting Mawson was unable to attend, the decision was taken to back Law's position and accept the station from the Americans. When he heard the news, it seemed to Mawson that he had lost the debate, but that it would only be a matter of time before he was proven accurate. Ultimately, however, both men were shown to be correct. Davis Station was indeed forced to shut down for four years while the new base – renamed Casey Station – was rebuilt. It was later reopened, however, and since then both Davis and Casey, like Mawson, have been important research and data-collection centres.

By the time of that decision, Mawson had been afflicted by various health problems for several years, and in September 1958 he suffered a slight stroke, which affected his speech. 'Knowing that he was not remembering words properly, he made himself write them down,' wrote Paquita, 'carefully writing line after line to aid his slowly recovering memory. His mind was clear and active, and before long he was practically normal in speech.'

But about a month later, only three days after writing to a former commander at Mawson Station, he suffered a severe stroke and lost consciousness. It was the fiftieth anniversary of the day in which he – with Professor David and Alistair Mackay – had first touched the Antarctic continent, arriving at Butter Point on their marathon quest for the South Magnetic Pole. It was also forty-six years to the day from 'Black Sunday,' when the strongest winds the AAE ever experienced blasted apart the wireless mast at Cape Denison.

Sadly, Mawson would not have the chance to recall these highlights of a career as the greatest combination of scientist, explorer, and survivor in the history of Antarctica. On the following evening, 14 October 1958, having never regained consciousness, the man who, more than any other, had uncovered the mysteries of that long, unknown coastline south of Australia, passed on to an even more obscure and inscrutable place. Having outlasted Nature's most vigorous challenges in the south, he died peacefully in the house that he had so long before first made preliminary sketches of, while recovering from his desperate, epic journey during a long, cold Antarctic winter.

GLOSSARY

AB: able-bodied seaman

arête: a sharp ascending mountain ridge or spur

barranca: a shallow, icy, heavily crevassed ravine

bergy bit: a large fragment of ice (usually glacier ice) up to the size of a small house; although usually free-floating, they can also be frozen into sea ice or grounded

blue ice: old, hard glacier ice of a variety of bluish tones; when snow-free it can be glassy smooth and exceptionally difficult to walk on

brash ice: small, floating fragments of ice, the debris from the wreck of larger pieces, typically bordering tracts of pack ice

calve, calving: the breaking-off of an iceberg from a glacier or of smaller pieces of ice from a parent iceberg

crevasse: a crack, rift, or fissure in glacier or shelf ice

drift: surface snow driven by the wind

fast ice: relatively immobile sheets of sea ice attached to the shore, particularly found in coastal bays and around grounded icebergs

finnesko: fur boots worn by Laplanders. They were made from reindeer skin, worn with the fur outside, and, as they were designed for walking through soft snow, had no hard sole. The insides of the bottoms were lined with sennegrass, a plant that absorbs moisture and provides insulation.

floe: a section or piece of comparatively flat, free-floating sea ice, a transitional stage in the formation of pack ice

glacier tongue: the extension of a valley glacier into the sea as a floating formation; also called an ice tongue

growler: a piece of iceberg or other ice smaller than a bergy bit, almost submerged beneath the water's surface and therefore dangerous to ships

hoosh: a thick, soup-like concoction made by mixing pemmican with water, and adding hard biscuit. For flavouring, hoosh could contain bacon, cheese, pea flour, sugar, or oatmeal.

hummocky ice: broken, irregular ice forced by pressure into rough mounds

hypsometer: an instrument using atmospheric pressure to determine land elevations, by measuring the temperature at which distilled water boils

ice pack: see 'pack ice'

ice shelf: an extensive area of glacial ice floating on the sea but still attached to the glaciers that feed it on the land. Ice shelves rise and fall with the tide and calve tabular icebergs.

lead: a track of open water between sections of sea ice

man-haul(ing): a human pulling by walking while wearing a harness roped or attached to the object being towed (usually a sledge)

moraine: an accumulation of boulders, stones, or other debris carried and deposited by a glacier

névé: the compacted snow that is in a stage of transition between soft, loose snow and glacier ice

pack ice: large areas of relatively closely packed sea ice, often combined with ice floes from fast ice, which drift under the influence of wind and ocean currents

pannikin: a small bowl or mug

pemmican: a concentrated mixture of dried meat and fat or lard made into cakes or canned for use at base or on sledging trips. Originally prepared by the Cree Indians with a significant element of dried fruit, it was then adopted by French voyageurs and British traders in North America and later became the main sledging ration for the Royal Navy's polar expeditions.

Plasmon: a soluble milk protein added as a supplement to polar sledging rations, notably cocoa and sledging biscuits; it was a trade name of the Plasmon Manufacturing Company

Plimsoll line: a line or set of lines on the hull of a ship that indicate the depth to which it may be legally loaded under specified conditions

pressure ridge: a hummock or ridge on sea ice or shelf ice forced above the normal surface by converging areas or sections of ice

sastrugi: waves and ridges of compacted snow – from a few inches to six feet high – produced by strong wind laden with drift snow

sennegrass: the sedge *Carex vesicaria* from Scandinavia, which when dried was used in finnesko to keep the feet warm. Moisture absorbed by the fibres could be shaken out when frozen and the fibres used again.

sérac: a sharp, irregular ridge or pinnacle of ice that appears on the surface of a glacier where it rides over an unusually rough or inclined bottom. A field of such pinnacles, jammed together in broken confusion, is called sérac ice.

sledge-meter: a wheel hooked to a sledge that measures the distance travelled

snow bridge: an arch of snow spanning a crevasse or a stream; frequently highly unstable and subject to collapse

trace: a rope or strap harness by which sledge dogs are connected to a sledge

Venesta board: a forerunner to plywood, made of triple layers of chestnut or oak glued together with waterproof cement

NOTES

The following abbreviations have been used:

AAE   Australasian Antarctic Expedition
BAE   British Antarctic Expedition
BESN   Belgrave Edward Sutton Ninnis
CFL   Charles Francis Laseron
DM   Douglas Mawson
EHS   Ernest H. Shackleton
JKD   John King Davis
MAAE   Douglas Mawson's personal set 'Australasian Antarctic
       Expedition 1911–1914'
MAC   Mawson Antarctic Collection, South Australian Museum
PM   Paquita Mawson
SPRI   Scott Polar Research Institute, University of Cambridge
TWED   T.W. Edgeworth David
XM   Xavier Mertz

Prologue

Page

xx 'My whole body': DM, diary of AAE, 11 January 1913; MAC 68DM,
    Notebook 5
xx 'So this is': DM, diary of AAE, 17 January 1913; MAC 68DM,
    Notebook 5

1 Trespassers in a World of Ice

Page

4 'if there be': J.W. 'Boss' Turner, quoted in PM, *Mawson of the Antarctic*: 23

6 'charm a bird': EHS, letter to Emily Shackleton, 22 January 1908; SPRI MS 1581/1/3

7 'My idea was': DM, draft letter to Margery Fisher, undated [1956]; MAC 48DM

7 'This was rather': DM, draft letter to Margery Fisher, undated [1956]; MAC 48DM

8 'a place that': Raymond Priestley, diaries of BAE, 1–8 January 1908; SPRI MS 298/1/1

8 'an awful hole': DM, diary of BAE, 10 January 1908; MAC 68DM, Notebook 1

8 'Mawson is useless': Eric Marshall, diary of BAE, 9 January 1908; SPRI MS 1456/8

9 '[A]s daylight came': JKD, *High Latitude*: 71–73

10–11 'First about 20': TWED, in *The Daily Telegraph* (Sydney), 3 April 1908: 7

11 'had gone sound': EHS, *The Heart of the Antarctic*: vol. 1, 120

14 'After a continuous': TWED, The Ascent of Mount Erebus

15 'nearly dead': Eric Marshall, diary of BAE, 11 March 1908; SPRI MS 1456/8

16 'made a pile': EHS, *The Heart of the Antarctic*: vol. 1, 148

16 'Aroused by expostulations': Eric Marshall, diary of BAE, 3 August 1908; SPRI MS 1456/8

17 'received a good': EHS, *The Heart of the Antarctic*: vol. 1, 233

2 The Other Pole

Page

19 'To take magnetic': EHS, letter to TWED, 19 September 1908; quoted in EHS, *The Heart of the Antarctic*: vol. 2, 73–75

20 'Prof . . . comes in': DM, diary of BAE, 8 October 1908; MAC 68DM, Notebook 1

21 'what I had': DM, diary of BAE, 23 October 1908; MAC 68DM, Notebook 1

21 'Have just found': DM, diary of BAE, 29 October 1908; MAC 68DM, Notebook 1

21 'He is full': DM, diary of BAE, 29 October 1908; MAC 68DM, Notebook 1

22 'The Prof is': DM, diary of BAE, 23 November 1908; MAC 68DM, Notebook 1

22–22 'formed of jagged': TWED, Professor David's Narrative: 130

23 'I had scarcely': TWED, Professor David's Narrative: 145

23–24 'I was busy': DM, in *The Sydney Morning Herald*, 17 April 1909: 13

24 'secured some ice': TWED, Professor David's Narrative: 156

25 'We are now': DM, diary of BAE, 6 January 1909; MAC 68DM, Notebook 2

25 'the polar centre': TWED, Professor David's Narrative: 179

27 'Occasionally, in an': TWED, Professor David's Narrative: 190

27 '[The Prof] is': DM, diary of BAE, 31 January 1909; MAC 68DM, Notebook 2

28 'now certainly partially': DM, diary of BAE, 3 February 1909; MAC 68DM, Notebook 2

29 'In a second': DM, diary of BAE, 4 February 1909; MAC 68DM, Notebook 2

29 'At the sight': TWED, Professor David's Narrative: 211

29 'Mawson has fallen': TWED, Professor David's Narrative: 212

29–30 'had the weather': JKD, *High Latitude*: 107

31 'Just as Shackleton': TWED, quoted in *The Sydney Morning Herald*, 31 March 1909: 13

31 'I suddenly found': DM, *The Home of the Blizzard*: vol. 1, xiii

3 Australasian Antarctic Expedition

Page

37 'stated that it': DM, Abbreviated Log: Australasian Antarctic Expedition; MAC 54AAE

37 'stated finally that': DM, Abbreviated Log: Australasian Antarctic Expedition; MAC 54AAE

37 'I have decided': EHS, quoted in DM, Abbreviated Log: Australasian Antarctic Expedition; MAC 54AAE

37–38 'rather taken aback': DM, Abbreviated Log: Australasian Antarctic Expedition; MAC 54AAE

39 'had many get-rich-quick': DM, Abbreviated Log: Australasian Antarctic Expedition; MAC 54AAE

39 'I intend to': Shackleton's Contract and Promise, 16 May 1910; MAC 8DM

39 'I understood that': DM, Abbreviated Log: Australasian Antarctic Expedition; MAC 54AAE

40 'on purpose so': DM, letter to Robert Falcon Scott, October 1910; quoted in PM, *Mawson of the Antarctic*: 43

40 'that he could': DM, Abbreviated Log: Australasian Antarctic Expedition; MAC 54AAE

41 'make all haste': DM, Abbreviated Log: Australasian Antarctic Expedition; MAC 54AAE

42 'my problem was': JKD, *High Latitude*: 144

42 'My husband is': Nina Lysaght, letter to DM, 26 March 1911; MAC 11AAE

43 'He certainly had': DM, letter to H.R. Mill, 18 July 1922; SPRI MS 100/75/6

43 'I do wish': DM, letter to Kathleen Scott; quoted in PM, *Mawson of the Antarctic*: 45

44 'She is splendid': DM, letter to William Bragg, 'Tuesday' [April 1911]; MAC MI 35

44 'I think we': JKD, *High Latitude*: 151

45 'infinitely more stable': Kathleen Scott, letter to DM, 26 April 1911; MAC 13AAE

46 'you intend making': XM, letter to DM, 15 March 1911; MAC 13AAE

46 'smoke to their': *Daily Mail*, 11 May 1911: 8

47 'The Board of': JKD, letter to DM, 3 August 1911; MAC 142AAE

48 'I feel I': DM, quoted in PM, *Mawson of the Antarctic*: 51

49 'had to sell': DM, Abbreviated Log: Australasian Antarctic Expedition; MAC 54AAE

49 'got into a': H.E. Watkins, letter to H.F. Wood, 10 October 1911; MAC 137AAE

49 'to my surprise': Frank Wild, letter to Maggie Wild, 13 October 1911; SPRI MS 1078/3/4/3

52 'The exertion of': DM, *The Home of the Blizzard*: vol. 1, 22

52 'sledges and skis': CFL, *South with Mawson*: 20

52 'Bickerton, Kennedy, Moyes': BESN, diary, 29 November 1911; SPRI MS 1618

4 The Only Available Place

Page

54 'We had the': Frank Wild, letter to Maggie Wild, 27 January 1912; SPRI MS 1078/3/4/4

54 'It seemed as': DM, *The Home of the Blizzard*: vol. 1, 27–28

55 'the seamen threw': XM, diary of AAE, 10 November–2 December 1911; MAC MI 16

55 'an auxiliary vessel': DM, letter to Alfred Reid, 22 September 1911; MAC 141AAE

55–56 'On the main': DM, *The Home of the Blizzard*: vol. 1, 26

56 'expect fresh south westerly': H.A. Hunt, telegram to DM, 2 December 1911; Mitchell Library MS 171

57 'causing the machine': Frank Bickerton, Western Sledging Journey: 1; SPRI MS 1509

58–59 'two steel-wire carrying': DM, *The Home of the Blizzard*: vol. 1, 39–40

59 'The last few': DM, letter to Paquita Delprat, 15 December 1911; quoted in Nancy Flannery, *This Everlasting Silence*: 24

60 'Icebergs are eye-openers': Frank Stillwell, letter for private circulation, 6 January 1912; Basser Library MS 40/4/2/b

60 'in high ecstasy': Frank Hurley, *Argonauts of the South*: 24

61 'Davis says very': XM, diary of AAE, 8 August 1911; MAC MI 16

61 'knew that my': JKD, *High Latitude*: 167

62 'the Main Base': DM, *The Home of the Blizzard*: vol. 1, 62

63 'Doctor Mawson leapt': Frank Hurley, *Argonauts of the South*: 45
63 'about one mile': DM, *The Home of the Blizzard*: vol. 1, 64
64 'twenty-three tons': DM, *The Home of the Blizzard*: vol. 1, 68
64 'I could have': BESN, diary, 19 January 1911; SPRI MS 1618
65 'As we were': DM, *The Home of the Blizzard*: vol. 1, 86
66 'Round the outside': DM, *The Home of the Blizzard*: vol. 1, 84
67 'At last I': DM, *The Home of the Blizzard*: vol. 1, 88, 90
67 'I looked on': CFL, *South with Mawson*: 65
68 '[It] would have': BESN, diary, 31 March 1912; SPRI MS 1618
69 'Northward from the': DM, *The Home of the Blizzard*: vol. 1, 115

5 Hurricane Force

Page
71 'It really looks': BESN, diary, 11 April 1912; SPRI MS 1618
72 'Simple as the': BESN, diary, 25 February 1912; SPRI MS 1618
73 'To the south': DM, *The Home of the Blizzard*: vol. 1, 100
73 'From inside my': DM, *The Home of the Blizzard*: vol. 1, 101
74 'He showed nothing': CFL, letter to PM; quoted in PM, *Mawson of the Antarctic*: 66
74 'After his first': Eric Webb, letter to A.G.E. Jones, 20 May 1980; SPRI, A.G.E. Jones papers
74–75 'though sometimes as': CFL, diary of AAE, 31 January 1912; Mitchell Library MSS 385, Item 1
75 'in an outburst': BESN, diary, 1 April 1912; SPRI MS 1618
75–76 'An occupation which': DM, *The Home of the Blizzard*: vol. 1, 158
76–77 'adhered firmly to': DM, *The Home of the Blizzard*: vol. 1, 123
77 'Before discovering the': DM, diary of AAE, 22 May 1912; MAC 68DM, Notebook 3
77 'In a temperature': CFL, *South with Mawson*: 64
77–78 'No light from': DM, diary of AAE, 9 April 1912; MAC 68DM, Notebook 3
78 'skilled at seeking': Clive Wilson-Roberts, Photography in the Mawson Gallery: 2
78–79 'I had just': Frank Hurley, *Argonauts of the South*: 58–59
80 'The Dr informed': Walter Hannam, diary of AAE, 10 September 1912; Mitchell Library MSS 384
81 'of his complexion': CFL, *South with Mawson*: 21
81 'amongst those here': DM, diary of AAE, 3 May 1912; MAC 68DM, Notebook 3
82 'Hurley . . . always went': CFL, *South with Mawson*: 66
83 'so hot that': BESN, diary, 25 July 1912; SPRI MS 1618
83 'to a slight': DM, *The Home of the Blizzard*: vol. 1, 139
83 'the misfortune to': BESN, diary, 18 May 1912; SPRI MS 1618
84 'This is rot': DM, diary of AAE, 4 June 1912; MAC 68DM, Notebook 3

84 'He sleeps all': DM, diary of AAE, 11 June 1912; MAC 68DM, Notebook 3

84 'I showed him': DM, diary of AAE, 18 June 1912; MAC 68DM, Notebook 3

85 'Murphy's work appears': DM, diary of AAE, 3 May 1912; MAC 68DM, Notebook 3

85 'Murphy is an': DM, diary of AAE, 18 May 1912; MAC 68DM, Notebook 3

85 'Once again "D.I." ': BESN, diary, 1 May 1912; SPRI MS 1618

85 'Close is watchman': BESN, diary, 24, 25 April 1912; SPRI MS 1618

85–86 'The life and': John Close, Frank Hurley in the Antarctic

86 'The vista is': DM, diary of AAE, 14 May 1912; MAC 68DM, Notebook 3

6 Start the Sledging

Page

87 'Any one who': DM, *The Home of the Blizzard*: vol. 1, 176

88 'Murphy was engaged': DM, diary of AAE, 5 August 1912; MAC 68DM, Notebook 3

90 'We call it': DM, diary of AAE, 12 August 1912; MAC 68DM, Notebook 3

91 'there was plenty': BESN, diary, 15 August 1912; SPRI MS 1618

91 'We slowly moved': XM, diary of AAE, 16 August 1912; MAC MI 16

91–92 'If it depended': XM, diary of AAE, 20 August 1912; MAC MI 16

92 'I fed them': XM, diary of AAE, 21 August 1912; MAC MI 16

92 'with the sun': CFL, *South with Mawson*: 123

93 'Having a hell': quoted in George Ainsworth, A Land of Storm and Mist: 225

93 'It was literally': CFL, *South with Mawson*: 128

94 'often pushed Murphy': XM, diary of AAE, 13 September 1912; MAC MI 16

94 'yodelled with joy': XM, diary of AAE, 14 September 1912; MAC MI 16

95 'Tents similar to': DM, Australasian Antarctic Expedition: 269

95 'I was talking': BESN, diary, 28 September 1912; SPRI MS 1618

96 'I was very': DM, diary of AAE, 3 October 1912; MAC 68DM, Notebook 4

97 'a fair day's': DM, diary of AAE, 3 October 1912; MAC 68DM, Notebook 4

97 'Mawson says no': BESN, diary, 18 October 1912; SPRI MS 1618

98 'He states that': DM, diary of AAE, 21 October 1912; MAC 68DM, Notebook 4

98–99 'After trying me': Eric Webb, letter to A.G.E. Jones, 18 July 1973; SPRI, A.G.E. Jones papers

7 A Far Eastern Tragedy

Page

101 'I am writing': DM, letter to Paquita Delprat, 9, 10 November 1912; quoted in Nancy Flannery, *This Everlasting Silence*: 47

101–02 'I must close': BESN, diary, 9 November 1912; SPRI MS 1618

102 'During this expedition': BESN, diary, 7 March 1911; SPRI MS 1618

102 'The weather is': DM, letter to Paquita Delprat, 9, 10 November 1912; quoted in Nancy Flannery, *This Everlasting Silence*: 47–48

102 'At the evening': BESN, diary, 22 October 1912; SPRI MS 1618

104 'spread the three': CFL, *South with Mawson*: 118

105 'seems to have': XM, diary of AAE, 15 November 1912; MAC MI 16

105 'Other animals, including': XM, diary of AAE, 14 November 1912; MAC MI 16

105 'Blizzard had always': Cecil Madigan, Narrative of the East-Coast Party: 12; MAC, MAAE, vol. 4

106 'ate "Gadget" meat': XM, diary of AAE, 18 November 1912; MAC MI 16

106–07 'In sledging over': DM, *The Home of the Blizzard*: vol. 1, 221

107 'He thought the': BESN, diary, 6 July 1912; SPRI MS 1618

107 'at times the': BESN, diary, 21 July 1912; SPRI MS 1618

107 'At the start': BESN, diary, 26 October 1912; SPRI MS 1618

108 'Next moment I': DM, *The Home of the Blizzard*: vol. 1, 226–27

109 'Looking down into': DM, *The Home of the Blizzard*: vol. 1, 227–28

109–10 'This precaution was': DM, *The Home of the Blizzard*: vol. 1, 229

110 'Their desire to': DM, *The Home of the Blizzard*: vol. 1, 221

110 '[W]e saw the': XM, diary of AAE, 27 November 1912; MAC MI 16

111 'Dogs very done': DM, diary of AAE, 29 November 1912; MAC 68DM, Notebook 5

111 'Exerting all my': DM, *The Home of the Blizzard*: vol. 1, 233

112 'It is obvious': DM, diary of AAE, 1 December 1912; MAC 68DM, Notebook 5

112 'One day in': DM, *The Home of the Blizzard*: vol. 1, 235–36

113 'provide a guaranteed': DM, *Geographical Narrative and Cartography*: 150

114 'At 8 pm': XM, diary of AAE, 13 December 1912; MAC MI 16

115 'similar to the': XM, diary of AAE, 14 December 1912; MAC MI 16

115 'There was no': DM, *The Home of the Blizzard*: vol. 1, 239

115–16 'From the other': DM, diary of AAE, 14 December 1912; MAC 68DM, Notebook 5

116 'We heard no': XM, diary of AAE, 14 December 1912; MAC MI 16

116 'Ninnis certainly died': XM, diary of AAE, 14 December 1912; MAC MI 16

117 'We could do': XM, diary of AAE, 14 December 1912; MAC MI 16
117 'Why had the': DM, *The Home of the Blizzard*: vol. 1, 240
118 'practically all the': DM, diary of AAE, 14 December 1912; MAC 68DM, Notebook 5
118 'Mawson and I': XM, diary of AAE, 14 December 1912; MAC MI 16
118 'May God help': DM, diary of AAE, 14 December 1912; MAC 68DM, Notebook 5

8 Racing with Death

Page

119 'we were on': XM, diary of AAE, 14 December 1912; MAC MI 16
119 'a languid feeling': DM, *The Home of the Blizzard*: vol. 1, 244
121 'The meat was': DM, *The Home of the Blizzard*: vol. 1, 245
121 'We forgot to': XM, diary of AAE, 16 December 1912; MAC MI 16
122 'Great disappointment to': DM, diary of AAE, 16 December 1912; MAC 68DM, Notebook 5
122–23 'The most uncomfortable': XM, diary of AAE, 18 December 1912; MAC MI 16
124 'Outside the hungry': DM, *The Home of the Blizzard*: vol. 1, 249
124 'All the dogs': DM, *The Home of the Blizzard*: vol. 1, 247
124 'It was a': DM, *The Home of the Blizzard*, Popular edition: 167
125 'Are we at': XM, diary of AAE, 23 December 1912; MAC MI 16
125 'We found that': DM, *The Home of the Blizzard*: vol. 1, 251
126 'We cooked a': XM, diary of AAE, 24 December 1912; MAC MI 16
126 'I visited a': DM, *The Home of the Blizzard*: vol. 1, 251
126 'were eating largely': DM, *The Home of the Blizzard*: vol. 1, 253–54
126 'have a Christmas': XM, diary of AAE, 25 December 1912; MAC MI 16
126–27 'The drift is': XM, diary of AAE, 27 December 1912; MAC MI 16
127 'Had a great': DM, diary of AAE, 29 December 1912; MAC 68DM, Notebook 5
127 'Xavier off colour': DM, diary of AAE, 30 December 1912; MAC 68DM, Notebook 5
127–28 'did not complain': DM, *The Home of the Blizzard*: vol. 1, 256–57
128 'The dog meat': XM, diary of AAE, 1 January 1913; MAC MI 16
128 'Did 5 miles': DM, diary of AAE, 3 January 1913; MAC 68DM, Notebook 5
128–29 'I tried to': DM, diary of AAE, 5 January 1913; MAC 68DM, Notebook 5
129 'a rattling good': DM, diary of AAE, 5 January 1913; MAC 68DM, Notebook 5
129 'We went on': DM, *Geographical Narrative and Cartography*: 158
129 'I think he': DM, diary of AAE, 6 January 1913; MAC 68DM, Notebook 5

129–30 'Xavier in a': DM, diary of AAE, 7 January 1913; MAC 68DM, Notebook 5

130 'For many days': DM, diary of AAE, 8 January 1913; MAC 68DM, Notebook 5

131 'Buck up, do': Robert Service, quoted in DM, *The Home of the Blizzard*: vol. 1, 260

131 'If Providence can': DM, diary of AAE, 11 January 1913; MAC 68DM, Notebook 5

131–32 'I thought for': *New York Evening Globe*, 13 January 1915; MAC News Cuttings Album 257.3

132 'After remaining with': *Bridgeport* [Connecticut] *Standard*, 14 January 1915; MAC News Cuttings Album 257.3

132 'Regarding the despatch': DM, quoted in *The Toronto Daily Star*, 22 January 1915; MAC News Cuttings Album 257.3

132 'He was a': Phillip Law, quoted in Philip Ayres, *Mawson: a Life*: 78

9 Alone

Page

135 'awkwardly lumpy feeling': DM, diary of AAE, 11 January 1913; MAC 68DM, Notebook 5

135 'the thickened skin': DM, *The Home of the Blizzard*: vol. 1, 261

135 'Then I removed': DM, *The Home of the Blizzard*: vol. 1, 261

136 'so worn that': DM, diary of AAE, 11 January 1913; MAC 68DM, Notebook 5

136 '[W]herever the skin': DM, diary of AAE, 9 January 1913; MAC 68DM, Notebook 5

137 'very strong, if': Robert E. Feeney, *Polar Journeys*: 173

137 'on camping find': DM, diary of AAE, 13 January 1913; MAC 68DM, Notebook 5

137–38 'the sledge was': DM, *The Home of the Blizzard*: vol. 1, 263–64

138 'In my weak': DM, quoted in *Chicago Sunday Tribune*, 14 February 1915; MAC News Cuttings Album 257.3

138 'Exhausted, weak, and': DM, *The Home of the Blizzard*: vol. 1, 265

139 'I couldn't see': DM, quoted in *Chicago Sunday Tribune*, 14 February 1915; MAC News Cuttings Album 257.3

139 'So I summoned': DM, quoted in *Chicago Sunday Tribune*, 14 February 1915; MAC News Cuttings Album 257.3

139 'The accident of': DM, diary of AAE, 18 January 1913; MAC 68DM, Notebook 5

139 'one end of': DM, *The Home of the Blizzard*: vol. 1, 266

140 'a very steep': DM, diary of AAE, 21 January 1913; MAC 68DM, Notebook 5

140 'So had a': DM, diary of AAE, 23 January 1913; MAC 68DM, Notebook 5

140 'Erecting the tent': DM, *The Home of the Blizzard*: vol. 1, 268

141 'Both my hands': DM, diary of AAE, 24, 25, 27 January 1913; MAC 68DM, Notebook 5

141 'I cannot sleep': DM, diary of AAE, 25 January 1913; MAC 68DM, Notebook 5

141 'I am full': DM, diary of AAE, 25 January 1913; MAC 68DM, Notebook 5

141 'My love for': DM, letter to Paquita Delprat, 26 December 1913; quoted in Nancy Flannery, *This Everlasting Silence*: 122

142 '[O]n I trudged': DM, *Geographical Narrative and Cartography*: 162

142 'All things seen': DM, diary of AAE, 28 January 1913; MAC 68DM, Notebook 5

142 'Situation 21 Miles': Archibald McLean, note left with depot, 29 January 1913; MAC 48AAE

143 'I might have': DM, *Geographical Narrative and Cartography*: 162

144 'I had to': DM, diary of AAE, 30 January 1913; MAC 68DM, Notebook 5

144 'Great joy and': DM, diary of AAE, 1 February 1913; MAC 68DM, Notebook 5

144–45 'found several boards': DM, diary of AAE, 5 February 1913; MAC 68DM, Notebook 5

145 'It almost appears': DM, diary of AAE, 3 February 1913; MAC 68DM, Notebook 5

145 'After the 2': DM, diary of AAE, 8 February 1913; MAC 68DM, Notebook 5

145 'as I gazed': DM, *The Home of the Blizzard*: vol. 1, 271

145 'I waved for': DM, diary of AAE, 8 February 1913; MAC 68DM, Notebook 5

146 'Bickerton it was': DM, diary of AAE, 8 February 1913; MAC 68DM, Notebook 5

146 'What a grand': DM, diary of AAE, 8 February 1913; MAC 68DM, Notebook 5

146 'Accordingly at 8': DM, diary of AAE, 8 February 1913; MAC 68DM, Notebook 5

10 Abandoned

Page

148 'before anyone could': Bertram Lincoln, *Aurora* diary, 13 January 1913; MAC MI 179

148 'the delight of': JKD, *High Latitude*: 197

149 'both splendid men': JKD, private journal of SY *Aurora*, 22 January 1913; State Library of Victoria MS 8311, Box 3232/5

150 'the velocity of': JKD, *High Latitude*: 212

151 'Arrived safely at': JKD, *High Latitude*: 214

152 'If the Capt': Eric Webb, letter to DM, 12 October 1913; MAC 175 AAE

153 'I invited them': JKD, *With the 'Aurora' in the Antarctic*: 98–99

153 'He made no': Cedric Hackworth, diary, 9 February 1913; National Library of Australia MS 9683

154 'The wind calmed': DM, diary of AAE, 10 February 1913; MAC 68DM, Notebook 5

154 'nursed him back': PM, *Mawson of the Antarctic*: 92

155 'The best must': Cecil Madigan, letter to Wynnis Wollaston, 25 January 1913; quoted in W.N. Hoerr, *Clipped Wings*: 205–06

156 'Mawson went out': Frank Bickerton, letter to Dorothea Bussell, 31 January 1913; courtesy of Rosanna Bickerton

157 'We searched the': Robert Bage, Narrative of Southern Sledging Journey: 37; MAC, MAAE, vol. 4

158 'It was wonderful': Cecil Madigan, Narrative of the East-Coast Party: 53; MAC, MAAE, vol. 4

159 'Jeffryes – we call': Archibald McLean, typed diary of AAE, 18 March 1913; Mitchell Library MSS 382/2

159 'Love and sympathy': Kathleen Scott, wireless message to DM; MAC 28AAE

159–60 'Until the business': DM, letter to Paquita Delprat, 10 June 1913; quoted in PM, *Mawson of the Antarctic*: 94

160 'Deeply regret delay': DM, wireless message to Paquita Delprat; quoted in PM, *Mawson of the Antarctic*: 92

160 'Deeply thankful you': Paquita Delprat, wireless message to DM; quoted in PM, *Mawson of the Antarctic*: 92

160 'as opportunity offers': DM, typed and signed statement, 29 May 1913; loose page between pages 84 and 85 of MAC 92 M462.m

161 'the wind was': Frank Bickerton, Australian Antarctic Expedition 1911–14: 6; SPRI MS 1509

161 'light doggerel to': DM, *The Home of the Blizzard*: vol. 2, 140

11 The Long Wait

Page

163 'Last night Jeffryes': DM, diary of AAE, 7 July 1913; MAC 68DM, Notebook 4

164 'McLean thinks [Jeffryes] is': DM, diary of AAE, 7 July 1913; MAC 68DM, Notebook 4

164 'and confides in': DM, diary of AAE, 10 July 1913; MAC 68DM, Notebook 4

164 'I am to': Sidney Jeffryes, letter to Norma Jeffryes, 13 July 1913; MAC 177AAE

165 'made a speech': DM, diary of AAE, 21 July 1913; MAC 68DM, Notebook 4

165 'to argue with': Stella Benson, diary, 23 April 1928; Cambridge University Library MSS 6762–6803

165 'I am now': Sidney Jeffryes, letter to DM, 27 July 1913; MAC 177AAE

166 'What can be': DM, diary of AAE, 10 August 1913; MAC 68DM, Notebook 4

166 'It appears that': DM, diary of AAE, 12 August 1913; MAC 68DM, Notebook 4

167 'Jeffryes ... said he': DM, diary of AAE, 1 September 1913; MAC 68DM, Notebook 4

167 'Tells me that': DM, diary of AAE, 2 September 1913; MAC 68DM, Notebook 4

167 'accused him and': DM, letter to Paquita Delprat, 15 September 1913; quoted in Nancy Flannery, *This Everlasting Silence*: 100

167 'Censor all messages': DM, wireless message to George Ainsworth, 3 September 1913; MAC 28AAE

167 'It is madness': DM, diary of AAE, 9 September 1913; MAC 68DM, Notebook 4

167–68 'I have been': Sidney Jeffryes, letter to DM, 21 September 1913; MAC 177AAE

168 'I appear to': DM, diary of AAE, 30 July 1913; MAC 68DM, Notebook 4

168 'Conversation often flags': Archibald McLean, typed diary of AAE, 10 August 1913; Mitchell Library MSS 382/2

169 'Said some words': DM, diary of AAE, 1 November 1913; MAC 68DM, Notebook 4

169 'He says he': DM, diary of AAE, 22 November 1913; MAC 68DM, Notebook 4

170 '[T]here is little': Eric Webb, Magnetic Polar Journey 1912: 17–18; SPRI MS 705

170 'The dreary outlook': DM, diary of AAE, 11 December 1913; MAC 68DM, Notebook 6

171 'As I shook': JKD, *High Latitude*: 229

174 'Christ Almighty, leave': JKD, quoted in DM, diary of AAE, 21 January 1914; MAC 68DM, Notebook 6

174 'It is with': DM, diary of AAE, 21 January 1914; MAC 68DM, Notebook 6

174 'Quite a different': DM, diary of AAE, 24 January 1914; MAC 68DM, Notebook 6

175 'I express my anxiety': DM, diary of AAE, 2 February 1914; MAC 68DM, Notebook 6

176 'I am glad': JKD, private journal of SY *Aurora*, 7 February 1914; quoted in Louise Crossley, *Trial by Ice*: 95

176 'It is hard': PM, *Mawson of the Antarctic*: 102–03

12 A Hero at War and Peace

Page

177–78 'Douglas Mawson has': quoted in PM, *Mawson of the Antarctic*: 103

179–80 'slipped his arm': PM, *Mawson of the Antarctic*: 107

180 'had early been': PM, *Mawson of the Antarctic*: 107

180 'the white warfare': EHS, dedication to *South*
180–81 'I do not': Kathleen Scott, letter to DM, 22 May 1914; MAC 51DM
181 'Captain Davis came': PM, *Mawson of the Antarctic*: 109
182 '[W]hen the book': Archibald McLean, letter to DM, 27 August 1914; MAC 178AAE
182 'If we are': William Heinemann, letter to DM, 11 September 1914; MAC 151AAE
183 '[H]e was the:' Eric Webb, An Appreciation: 231
183 'The rail travelling': DM, letter to PM, January 1915; quoted in PM, *Mawson of the Antarctic*: 123
184 'the printing works': DM, letter to W.H. Garrison, 5 November 1934; MAC 48DM
184 'a criminal on': DM, letter to W.H. Hobbs, 23 August 1915; Hobbs Papers, University of Michigan
186–87 'I have consulted': Trevor Dawson, letter to DM, 21 November 1916; MAC 183AAE
187 'At present South': DM, letter to Prime Minister William Hughes, March 1919; quoted in PM, *Mawson of the Antarctic*: 140
188 'I am en route': DM, letter to Sydney Jones, 6 April 1916; National Library of Australia MS 9273/4/2
191 'I state frankly': TWED, letter to DM, 16 November 1924; quoted in Philip Ayres, *Mawson: a Life*: 134

13 Colouring Antarctica Red

Page
200 'only existing vessel': Foreign Office document FO 371/13359/1928/ W950/532/50; The National Archives
200 'all else with': DM, letter to David Orme Masson, 2 May 1927; MAC 34BZE
202 '[T]he Germans landed': DM, letter to David Orme Masson, 2 May 1927; MAC 34BZE
202–03 'appeared to indicate': David Rivett, letter to Prime Minister's secretary, January 1928; quoted in A. Grenfell Price, *Geographical Report*: 16
203 'an action which': A. Grenfell Price, *Geographical Report*: 16
206 'The expedition was': DM, letter to J.S. Cumpston, 24 March 1953; MAC 23DM
206 'if it is': David Orme Masson, letter to JKD, 19 September 1929; quoted in Louise Crossley, *Trial by Ice*: 122
208 'considerable confusion ... owing': JKD, letter to DM, 13 June 1929; MAC 1DM
208 'has never been': DM, letter to JKD, 27 June 1929; MAC 1DM
209 'No damage was': JKD, letter to Antarctic Committee, 7 August 1929; quoted in Louise Crossley, *Trial by Ice*: 122

14 Science or Politics?

Page

211 'New Race to': *Cape Argus*, 8 October 1929

211 'Davis arranged four': DM, diary of BANZARE, 19 October 1929;
MAC 68DM, Notebook 7

211–12 'Capt Davis is': DM, diary of BANZARE, 23 October 1929; MAC
68DM, Notebook 7

212 'jolly decent, quite': R.G. Simmers, diary of BANZARE, 6 November
1929; MAC Reports, BANZARE 919.9 S59, Part II, vol. 1, 64

212 'Sir Douglas's conversation': R.G. Simmers, diary of BANZARE,
8 November 1929; MAC Reports, BANZARE 919.9 S59, Part II,
vol. 1, 67

212 'as far apart': J.W.S. Marr, letter to the Secretary of the *Discovery*
Committee, 28 July 1930; SPRI MS 1403/3

212 'great numbers Sea-elephants': DM, diary of BANZARE, 2 November
1929; MAC 68DM, Notebook 7

212 'shooting the animals': Harvey Johnston, journal of BANZARE, 3
November 1929; MAC 15BZE

213 '[C]oaled ship from': DM, diary of BANZARE, 16 November 1929;
MAC 68DM, Notebook 7

213 'constant friction with': DM, diary of BANZARE, 24 November
1929; MAC 68DM, Notebook 7

214 'It is impossible': JKD, personal journal kept on board *Discovery*,
2 December 1929; quoted in Louise Crossley, *Trial by Ice*: 131

214 'With the Captain's': quoted in DM, diary of BANZARE, 3 December
1929; MAC 68DM, Notebook 7

215 'Davis had the': DM, diary of BANZARE, 3 December 1929; MAC
68DM, Notebook 7

216 'M regards all': JKD, personal journal kept on board *Discovery*,
8, 9 December 1929; quoted in Louise Crossley, *Trial by Ice*:
134, 135

216 'Davis' whole attitude': DM, diary of BANZARE, 9 December 1929;
MAC 68DM, Notebook 7

217 'There is a': James Martin, journal of BANZARE, 14 December
1929; SPRI MS 429/2/1

217 'We, ie. the': James Martin, journal of BANZARE, 20 December
1929; SPRI MS 429/2/1

217–18 'Great is the': K.N. MacKenzie, diary of BANZARE, 26 December 1929;
quoted in Ann Savours, *The Voyages of the Discovery*: 241–42

218 'peaked and hummocky': DM, diary of BANZARE, 26 December
1929; MAC 68DM, Notebook 7

219 'I ask him': DM, diary of BANZARE, 1 January 1930; MAC 68DM,
Notebook 7

219 'He then commenced': DM, diary of BANZARE, 1 January 1930;
MAC 68DM, Notebook 7

220 'I considered what': JKD, personal journal kept on board *Discovery*,
1 January 1930; quoted in Louise Crossley, *Trial by Ice*: 144

220 'argued strongly that': DM, diary of BANZARE, 3 January 1930; MAC 68DM, Notebook 7

220 'all are heartily': Morton Moyes, diary of BANZARE, 1 January 1930; MAC 93BZE

221 'Land was sighted': JKD, personal journal kept on board *Discovery*, 4 January 1930; quoted in Louise Crossley, *Trial by Ice*: 145

221 'cursing us for': John Child, diary of BANZARE, 6 January 1930; quoted in Ann Savours, *The Voyages of the Discovery*: 244

221 'in about a': Stuart Campbell, letter of 4 June 1962; quoted in John Grierson, *Challenge to the Poles*: 219–21

222 'just where we': DM, diary of BANZARE, 9 January 1930; MAC 68DM, Notebook 7

223 'quantity of rocks': DM, diary of BANZARE, 13 January 1930; MAC 68DM, Notebook 7

225 'It is a': JKD, personal journal kept on board *Discovery*, 20 January 1930; quoted in Louise Crossley, *Trial by Ice*: 153

225 'informed by officers': DM, diary of BANZARE, 22 January 1930; MAC 68DM, Notebook 7

225 'D.M. addressed the': James Martin, journal of BANZARE, 22 January 1930; SPRI MS 429/2/1

226 'Launch the plane': JKD, quoted in James Martin, journal of BANZARE, 25 January 1930; SPRI MS 429/2/1

226 'too many small': DM, diary of BANZARE, 25 January 1930; MAC 68DM, Notebook 7

226 'It is unpleasant': JKD, personal journal kept on board *Discovery*, 25 January 1930; quoted in Louise Crossley, *Trial by Ice*: 155

227 'Ballast: At least': JKD, letter to DM, 12 March 1929; MAC 1DM

227–28 'I cannot conceive': JKD, personal journal kept on board *Discovery*, 4, 5, 6 March 1930; quoted in Louise Crossley, *Trial by Ice*: 172

228 'I listen to': DM, diary of BANZARE, 17 March 1930; MAC 68DM, Notebook 7

15 A Final Visit

Page

231 'The Government have': *Parliamentary Debates* vol. 124, 2044

232 'Captain Davis reported': DM, British, Australian and New Zealand Antarctic Research Expedition Report

233 'Captain Davis took': DM, British, Australian and New Zealand Antarctic Research Expedition Report

233 'Captain Davis was': DM, British, Australian and New Zealand Antarctic Research Expedition Report

233 'I did not': DM, quoted in *The Register-News Pictorial* [Adelaide], 23 May 1930

234–35 'carry out to': J.J. Daly, sailing orders issued to DM, 30 October 1930; quoted in Ann Savours, *The Voyages of the Discovery*: 263

236 'A very poor': DM, diary of BANZARE, 2 December 1930; MAC 68DM, Papers A

237 'was in a': K.N. MacKenzie, diary of BANZARE, 8 December 1930; quoted in Ann Savours, *The Voyages of the Discovery*: 266

237 'It is only': K.N. MacKenzie, diary of BANZARE, 8 December 1930; quoted in Ann Savours, *The Voyages of the Discovery*: 266

239 'he wouldn't go': K.N. MacKenzie, quoted in A. Grenfell Price, *Geographical Report*: 112

239 'running into some': DM, quoted in K.N. MacKenzie, diary of BANZARE, 6 January 1931; quoted in Ann Savours, *The Voyages of the Discovery*: 274

239 'rewarded by sighting': K.N. MacKenzie, diary of BANZARE, 6 January 1931; quoted in Ann Savours, *The Voyages of the Discovery*: 274

241 'an immense flat-topped': DM, quoted in A. Grenfell Price, *Geographical Report*: 118

241 'In the south-south-west': DM, quoted in A. Grenfell Price, *Geographical Report*: 122

241 'What appeared to': Eric Douglas, quoted in A. Grenfell Price, *Geographical Report*: 128

242 'We knew from': Eric Douglas, quoted in A. Grenfell Price, *Geographical Report*: 129

243 'quite like the': James Martin, journal of BANZARE, 8 February 1931; SPRI MS 429/2/3

243 'Behind all this': DM, diary of BANZARE, 9 February 1931; MAC 68DM, Notebook 8

244 'We touch rock': DM, diary of BANZARE, 13 February 1931; MAC 68DM, Notebook 8

244 'saved the name': R.G. Simmers, diary of BANZARE, 13 February 1931; MAC Reports, BANZARE 919.9 S59, Part II, vol. 4, 45

244–45 'Dux jumped ashore': R.G. Simmers, diary of BANZARE, 18 February 1931; MAC Reports, BANZARE 919.9 S59, Part II, vol. 4, 64–65

245 'sadly lacking in': Frank Hurley, quoted in Alasdair McGregor, *Frank Hurley*: 320

245–46 'Nothing could be': Frank Hurley, quoted in Alasdair McGregor, *Frank Hurley*: 323

246 'He agreed that': DM, diary of BANZARE, 12 March 1931; MAC 68DM, Papers A

246 'This is parallel': DM, diary of BANZARE, 18 March 1931; MAC 68DM, Papers B

16 Antarctica from Australia

Page

249 'not to get': DM, response written in pencil on letter from A.J. Kent to DM, 19 March 1929; MAC 153AAE

251 'the greatest living': Richard E. Byrd, *Little America*: 13

252 'in the nature': JKD, letter to DM, undated, but in November 1938; MAC 1DM

253 'he never showed': Phillip Law, interviewed on Film Australia, *Australian Biography*

254 'Mawson served on': Phillip Law, interviewed on Film Australia, *Australian Biography*

254 'The Davis area': Minutes of ANARE Executive Planning Committee meeting, 25 November 1957; MAC 1ANR

255 'Knowing that he': PM, *Mawson of the Antarctic*: 220

BIBLIOGRAPHY

Published Sources

Books

Amundsen, Roald, and Lincoln Ellsworth. 1925. *Our Polar Flight*. New York: Dodd, Mead

Amundsen, Roald, and Lincoln Ellsworth. 1927. *The First Crossing of the Polar Sea*. New York: Doubleday, Doran & Company

Ayres, Philip. 1999. *Mawson: a Life*. Melbourne: Miegunyah Press, Melbourne University Press

Baughman, T.H. 1999. *Pilgrims on the Ice: Robert Falcon Scott's First Antarctic Expedition*. Lincoln, NE, and London: University of Nebraska Press

Bickel, Lennard. 1977. *This Accursed Land*. Melbourne: Macmillan

Branagan, David. 2005. *T.W. Edgeworth David: a Life*. Canberra: National Library of Australia

Byrd, Richard E. 1930. *Little America: Aerial Exploration in the Antarctic & the Flight to the South Pole*. New York: Putnam's

Crossley, Louise (ed.). 1997. *Trial by Ice: the Antarctic Journals of John King Davis*. Bluntisham: Bluntisham Books and Banham: Erskine Press

David, M.E. 1937. *Professor David: the Life of Sir Edgeworth David*. London: Edward Arnold

Davis, John King. 1919. *With the 'Aurora' in the Antarctic 1911–1914*. London: Andrew Melrose

Davis, John King. 1962. *High Latitude*. Melbourne: Melbourne University Press

Ellsworth, Lincoln. 1938. *Beyond Horizons*. New York: Doubleday

Feeney, Robert E. 1997. *Polar Journeys: the Role of Food and Nutrition in Early Exploration*. Fairbanks: University of Alaska Press

Fisher, Margery, and James Fisher. 1957. *Shackleton*. London: James Barrie Books

Flannery, Nancy Robinson (ed.). 2000. *This Everlasting Silence: the Love*

Letters of Paquita Delprat & Douglas Mawson 1911–1914. Melbourne: Melbourne University Press

Fletcher, Harold. 1984. *Antarctic Days with Mawson: a Personal Account of the British, Australian and New Zealand Antarctic Research Expedition of 1929–31.* Sydney: Angus & Robertson

Fogg, G.E. 1992. *A History of Antarctic Science.* Cambridge: Cambridge University Press

Grierson, John. 1964. *Challenge to the Poles: Highlights of Arctic and Antarctic Aviation.* London: Foulis

Haddelsey, Stephen. 2005. *Born Adventurer: the Life of Frank Bickerton, Antarctic Pioneer.* Stroud, Gloucestershire: Sutton Publishing

Hains, Brigid. 2002. *The Ice and the Inland: Mawson, Flynn, and the Myth of the Frontier.* Melbourne: Melbourne University Press

Hayes, J. Gordon. 1928. *Antarctica: a Treatise on the Southern Continent.* London: The Richards Press

Hoerr, W.N. 1995. *Clipped Wings, or Memories of My Childhood and Youth.* Adelaide: Privately published

Howchin, Walter. 1918. *The Geology of South Australia.* Adelaide: The South Australian Education Department

Huntford, Roland. 1985. *Shackleton.* London: Hodder & Stoughton

Hurley, J. Frank. 1925. *Argonauts of the South.* London: Putnam's Sons

Innes, Margaret, and Heather Duff. 1990. *Mawson's Papers: a Guide.* Adelaide: Mawson Institute for Antarctic Research

Jacka, Fred, and Eleanor Jacka (eds). 1988. *Mawson's Antarctic Diaries.* Sydney: Allen & Unwin

Joerg, W.L.G. (ed.). 1928. *Problems of Polar Research: a Series of Papers by Thirty-One Authors.* New York: American Geographical Society

Joyce, Ernest. 1929. *The South Polar Trail.* London: Duckworth & Company

Kennet, Lady [Kathleen Scott]. 1949. *Self-Portrait of an Artist.* London: John Murray

Laseron, Charles F. 1947. *South with Mawson.* London and Sydney: George C. Harrap & Company

Madigan, D.C. 2000. *Vixere Fortes: a Family Archive.* Kingston, Tasmania: Privately published

Martin, Stephen. 1996. *A History of Antarctica.* Sydney: State Library of New South Wales

Mawson, Douglas. 1915. *The Home of the Blizzard.* 2 vols. London: William Heinemann

Mawson, Douglas. 1930. *The Home of the Blizzard.* Popular edition. London: Hodder & Stoughton

Mawson, Douglas. 1942. *Geographical Narrative and Cartography.* In: Mawson, Douglas (ed.). *Australasian Antarctic Expedition 1911–14: Scientific Reports* (Series A. Vol. 1). Sydney: Government Printing Office

Mawson, Paquita. 1964. *Mawson of the Antarctic.* London: Longmans, Green and Co.

McGregor, Alasdair. 2004. *Frank Hurley: a Photographer's Life.* Camberwell, Victoria: Viking

Mills, Leif. 1999. *Frank Wild*. Whitby: Caedmon of Whitby Press

Nasht, Simon. 2006. *No More Beyond: the Life of Hubert Wilkins*. Edinburgh: Birlinn

Philbrick, Nathaniel. 2004. *Sea of Glory: the Epic South Seas Expedition 1838–42*. London: HarperCollins

Pound, Reginald. 1966. *Scott of the Antarctic*. London: Cassell & Company

Price, A. Grenfell. 1962. *The Winning of Australian Antarctica: Mawson's BANZARE Voyages 1929–1931*. Sydney: Angus & Robertson

Price, A. Grenfell. 1963. *Geographical Report Based on the Mawson Papers*. In: Thomas, P.M. (general ed.). *B.A.N.Z. Antarctic Research Expedition 1929–1931: Reports* (Series A. Vol. 1). Adelaide: Mawson Institute for Scientific Research

Riffenburgh. Beau. 2004. *Nimrod: Ernest Shackleton and the Extraordinary Story of the 1907–09 British Antarctic Expedition*. London: Bloomsbury

Ross, James Clark. 1847. *A Voyage of Discovery and Research in the Southern and Antarctic Regions, During the Years 1839–43*. 2 vols. London: John Murray

Savours, Ann. 1992. *The Voyages of the Discovery*. London: Virgin Books

Scott, Robert Falcon. 1905. *The Voyage of the 'Discovery'*. 2 vols. London: John Murray

Shackleton, Ernest (ed.). 1908. *Aurora Australis*. Cape Royds: British Antarctic Expedition

Shackleton, Ernest. 1909. *The Heart of the Antarctic*. 2 vols. London: William Heinemann

Shackleton, Ernest. 1919. *South*. London: William Heinemann

Suzyumov, E.M. 1960. *A Life Given to the Antarctic: the Antarctic Explorer Sir Douglas Mawson*. Moscow: Foreign Languages Publishing House

Swan, R.A. 1961. *Australia in the Antarctic*. Melbourne: Melbourne University Press

Taylor, George. 1934. *Making It Happen: the Rise of Sir Macpherson Robertson*. Melbourne: Robertson & Mullins

Taylor, Griffith. 1962. *Douglas Mawson*. Melbourne: Oxford University Press (Great Australians series)

Watson, Moira. 1997. *The Spy Who Loved Children: the Enigma of Herbert Dyce Murphy 1879–1971*. Melbourne: Melbourne University Press

Articles, Chapters, and Monographs

Ainsworth, George. 1915. Life on Macquarie Island. In: Mawson, Douglas. *The Home of the Blizzard*. 2 vols. London: William Heinemann: vol. 2, 167–94

Ainsworth, George. 1915. A Land of Storm and Mist. In: Mawson, Douglas. *The Home of the Blizzard*. 2 vols. London: William Heinemann: vol. 2, 195–236

Ainsworth, George. 1915. Through Another Year. In: Mawson, Douglas. *The Home of the Blizzard*. 2 vols. London: William Heinemann: vol. 2, 237–54

Alderman, A.R., and C.E. Tilley. 1960. Douglas Mawson 1882–1958. *Biographical memoirs of Fellows of the Royal Society* 5

Carrington-Smith, Denise. 2005. Mawson and Mertz: a re-evaluation of their ill-fated mapping journey during the 1911–14 Australasian Antarctic Expedition. *The Medical Journal of Australia* 183 (11–12): 638–41

Cleland, Sir John, and R.V. Southcott. 1969. Hypervitaminosis A in the Antarctic in the Australasian Antarctic Expedition of 1911–1914: a Possible Explanation of the Illnesses of Mertz and Mawson. *The Medical Journal of Australia* 1 (26): 1337–42

Close, John. 1919. Frank Hurley in the Antarctic. *The Sydney Morning Herald*, 19 April 1919

David, T.W. Edgeworth. 1908. The Ascent of Mount Erebus. In: Shackleton, Ernest (ed.). *Aurora Australis*. Cape Royds: British Antarctic Expedition.

David, T.W. Edgeworth. 1909. Professor David's Narrative. In: Shackleton, Ernest. *The Heart of the Antarctic*. 2 vols. London: William Heinemann: vol. 2, 73–222

Davis, John King. 1913. The Australian Antarctic Expedition. *Geographical Journal* 41 (6): 550–53

Ellsworth, Lincoln. 1936. My Flight Across Antarctica. *National Geographic Magazine* 70 (1): 1–35

Jacka, Fred. 1986. Mawson, Sir Douglas (1882–1958). *Australian Dictionary of Biography* 10: 454–57

Landy, D. 1985. Pibloktoq (Hysteria) and Inuit Nutrition: Possible Implication of Hypervitaminosis. *Social Science and Medicine* 21 (2): 173–85

Leane, Elizabeth. 2005. The *Adelie Blizzard*: the Australasian Antarctic Expedition's Neglected Newspaper. *Polar Record* 41 (216): 11–20

Mawson, Douglas. 1908. Bathybia. In: Shackleton, Ernest (ed.). *Aurora Australis*. Cape Royds: British Antarctic Expedition

Mawson, Douglas. 1911. The Australasian Antarctic Expedition. *The Geographical Journal* 40: 609–620

Mawson, Douglas. 1912. The Proposed Australasian Antarctic Expedition, 1911. *Reports of the AAAS* 13: 398–400

Mawson, Douglas. 1914. Out of the Jaws of Death: I. *The Strand Magazine* August 1914: 199–211

Mawson, Douglas. 1914. Out of the Jaws of Death: II. *The Strand Magazine* September 1914: 311–23

Mawson, Douglas. 1914. Australasian Antarctic Expedition. *Geographical Journal* 45: 257–86

Mawson, Douglas. 1915. The Australasian Antarctic Expedition, 1911–14. *Scottish Geographical Magazine* 31 (7): 337–60

Mawson, Douglas. 1930. The Antarctic Cruise of the 'Discovery', 1929–30. *Geographical Review* 20: 535–54

Mawson, Douglas. 1930. British, Australian and New Zealand Antarctic Research Expedition Report. *Commonwealth Parliamentary Papers, 1928–31* 2: 823–27

Mawson, Douglas. 1932. The BANZ Antarctic Research Expedition, 1929–31. *Geographical Journal* 80: 101–31

Quilty, Patrick G., and Peter H. Goddard. 2004. The Lower Deck on *Aurora*: H.V. Goddard's Diary, 1913–14. *Polar Record* 49 (214): 193–203

Riiser-Larsen, Hjalmar. 1930. The 'Norvegia' Antarctic Expedition of 1929–1930. *Geographical Review* 20: 555–73

Shearman, D.J.C. 1978. Vitamin A and Sir Douglas Mawson. *British Medical Journal* part 1: 283–85

Southcott, R.V., N.J. Chesterfield, and Desmond J. Lugg. 1971. The Vitamin A Content of the Livers of Huskies and Some Seals from Arctic and Subantarctic Regions. *Medical Journal of Australia* part 1: 311–13

Webb, Eric. 1977. An Appreciation. In: Bickel, Lennard. *This Accursed Land*. Melbourne: Macmillan: 227–33

Wendler, Gerd, Charles Stearns, George Weidner, Guillaume Dargaud, and Thomas Parish. 1997. On the Extraordinary Katabatic Winds of Adélie Land. *Journal of Geophysical Research* 102 (D4): 4463–74

Wilson-Roberts, Clive. 2004. Photography in the Mawson Gallery. Adelaide: MAC

Newspapers and Periodicals
Bridgeport [Connecticut] *Standard*
Cape Argus (Cape Town)
Chicago Sunday Tribune
Daily Mail (London)
The Daily Telegraph (Sydney)
New York Evening Globe
The New York Times
The Register-News Pictorial (Adelaide)
The Sydney Morning Herald
The Times (London)
The Toronto Daily Star

Unpublished Sources

The following abbreviations have been used:

AAE	Australasian Antarctic Expedition
BAE	British Antarctic Expedition
BANZARE	British, Australian, New Zealand Antarctic Research Expedition
LaT	La Trobe Library, State Library of Victoria, Melbourne
MAC	Mawson Antarctic Collection, South Australian Museum, Adelaide
MAAE	Douglas Mawson's personal set 'Australasian Antarctic Expedition 1911–1914'
ML	Mitchell Library, State Library of New South Wales, Sydney
NL	National Library of Australia, Canberra
SPRI	Scott Polar Research Institute, University of Cambridge

Diaries and Journals

Benson, Stella. Diary (Cambridge University Library)

Bickerton, Frank. Australasian Antarctic Expedition 1911–14: a Log of the Western Journey (SPRI)

Davis, John King. Private Journal of SY *Aurora* (LaT)

—Personal Journal kept on board *Discovery* (LaT)

Hackworth, Cedric. *Aurora* diary (NL)

Hannam, Walter Henry. Diary of AAE (ML)

Hunter, John. Diary of AAE (NL)

Hurley, Frank. Sledging journal of AAE (ML)

Johnston, Harvey. Journal of BANZARE (MAC)

Laseron, Charles Francis. Diaries of AAE (ML)

Lincoln, Bertram. *Aurora* diary (MAC)

Mackay, Alistair. Diary of BAE northern journey (National Museums of Scotland, Edinburgh)

—*Nimrod* diary (SPRI)

MacKenzie, K.N. Diary of BANZARE (National Maritime Museum, Greenwich)

Marshall, Eric. Diary of BAE (SPRI)

Martin, James. Journal of BANZARE (SPRI)

Mawson, Douglas. Diary of BAE (MAC)

—Abbreviated Log: Australasian Antarctic Expedition (MAC)

—Diary of AAE (MAC)

—Diary of BANZARE (MAC)

McLean, Archibald. Diaries of AAE (ML)

Mertz, Xavier. Diary of AAE (MAC)

Moyes, Morton. Diary of BANZARE (MAC)

Ninnis, B.E.S. Diary of AAE (SPRI)

Priestley, Raymond. Diaries of BAE (SPRI)

Simmers, R.G. Diary of BANZARE (MAC)

Stillwell, Frank. Diaries of AAE (Basser Library, Canberra)

Webb, Eric. Sledging diary of AAE (ML)

Correspondence and Other Manuscript Sources

AAE Papers (MAC; ML)

BANZARE Papers (MAC)

Bickerton, Frank. Correspondence (Courtesy of Rosanna Bickerton)

—Western Sledging Journey (SPRI)

David, T.W. Edgeworth. Correspondence and Papers (MAC; ML; SPRI)

Davis, John King. Correspondence and Papers (LaT; MAC)

Dawson, Trevor. Correspondence (MAC)

Dovers, George. Correspondence and Papers (MAC; ML)

Dovers, Robert. Correspondence and Papers (MAC; ML)

Heinemann, William. Correspondence (MAC)

Hunter, John. Notes and Papers (NL)

Hurley, Frank. Correspondence (MAC)

Jeffryes, Sidney. Correspondence (MAC)

Lysaght, Nina. Correspondence (MAC)
Marr, J.W.S. Correspondence (SPRI)
Masson, David Orme. Correspondence (MAC)
Mawson, Douglas. Correspondence and Papers (MAC; SPRI; ML)
McLean, Archibald. Correspondence and Papers (MAC)
Mertz, Xavier. Correspondence (MAC)
Ninnis, B.E.S. Correspondence (SPRI)
Scott, Kathleen. Correspondence (MAC)
Shackleton, E.H. Correspondence and Papers (SPRI; MAC)
Stillwell, Frank. Correspondence and Papers (MAC; Basser Library, Canberra)
Watkins, H.E. Correspondence (MAC)
Webb, Eric. Magnetic Polar Journey 1912 (SPRI)
—Correspondence and Papers (ML; MAC; SPRI)
Wild, Frank. Correspondence (SPRI)

Reports
Bage, Robert. Narrative of Southern Sledging Journey (MAC, MAAE)
Bickerton, Frank. The Western Sledge Journey from Cape Denison (MAC, MAAE)
Madigan, Cecil. Narrative of the East-Coast Party (MAC, MAAE)
Stillwell, Frank. Report of the Eastern Coast Party (MAC, MAAE)
Wild, Frank. Report on Operations of the Western Base Party (MAC, MAAE)

INDEX

A NOTE ON THE AUTHOR

Beau Riffenburgh is a historian specialising in exploration, particularly that of the Antarctic, Arctic, and Africa. Born in California, he earned his doctorate at the Scott Polar Research Institute of the University of Cambridge, where he then served for fourteen years as the editor of *Polar Record*, the world's oldest journal of polar research. He is the author of the highly regarded *Nimrod: Ernest Shackleton and the Extraordinary Story of the 1907–09 British Antarctic Expedition* and *The Myth of the Explorer*. He also edited the multi-volume *Encyclopedia of the Antarctic*, and has contributed to six other books about exploration.

A NOTE ON THE TYPE

The text of this book is set in Linotype Sabon, named after the type founder, Jacques Sabon. It was designed by Jan Tschichold and jointly developed by Linotype, Monotype and Stempel, in response to a need for a typeface to be available in identical form for mechanical hot metal composition and hand composition using foundry type.

Tschichold based his design for Sabon roman on a font engraved by Garamond, and Sabon italic on a font by Granjon. It was first used in 1966 and has proved an enduring modern classic.